TRACING LINES

*The Story of a Brazilian Girl
Who Refused to Stay Small*

CHRISTINA SIEPIELA

Copyright ©2025 Christina Siepiela

Jetlaunch Publishing

ALL RIGHTS RESERVED. This book contains material protected under International and Federal Copyright Laws and Treaties. Any unauthorized reprint or use of this material is prohibited. No part of this book may be reproduced or transmitted in any form or by any means, electronic or mechanical, including photocopying, recording, or by any information storage and retrieval system, without express written permission from the author/publisher.

ISBN: 979-8-89079-348-5 (hardcover)
ISBN: 979-8-89079-349-2 (paperback)
ISBN: 979-8-89079-350-8 (ebook)

DEDICATION

To my mother, Lígia, and my father, Rogério:

You each traced your dots across time, shaped by your pain, your triumphs, your fears, and your resilience. And somehow, I was placed along that path. The line I've walked wasn't always smooth, but it was mine to follow, born from the ones you laid before me.

Through your mistakes and wisdom, through what you gave and what you couldn't, I learned. I grew. I stumbled and found my way. And with time, empathy, and compassion, I've come to understand you. I've come to love you in full color, not as flawless parents, but as brave, complex humans who did the best you could.

Because of that, I live in peace. Because of that, I've found forgiveness. And above all, I am deeply and fiercely grateful for being chosen to be your daughter.

Yours, one and only,
Maria Christina

To Debby Duddley, my therapist:

Thank you for your extraordinary gift of guiding me toward kindness, especially the kind I needed to give myself. Through thirteen years of sessions, you helped me find the little girl inside me and instilled the courage in me to listen to her. Because of you, I can now hold her close and whisper: *Don't let the fear "inter-fear" anymore.*

A note of gratitude to Alex and Marcy:

When this story was still only inside my heart and mind, your words of support and encouragement ignited my courage to share it. It was the white paper, the dream, and me. But I had you both, your talent as guides to inspire me to find the best way to share what had made me and who I would like to become. I wrote this book, yes. But your presence in each word is very vivid, and without it, this wouldn't have turned out the way it did.

TABLE OF CONTENTS

Foreword vii
A Note to My Daughters ix
Prologue: The First Dot xi

ACT I: THE DOTS

1. CLINGING 3
2. FABIO'S LAUGH 12
3. BAIXINHA 19
4. GOD, GUILT, AND GOOD HAIR 24
5. GRAFFITI AND SHAME 33
6. INVISIBLE GIRL WITH RED RIBBONS 40
7. ONE DOT AT A TIME 48
8. THE FIRST YES 54
9. THE HOUSE ON RUA XV 62
10. THE POWER SUIT 65

ACT II: THE LINES

1. SKIRTING THE REAL ISSUES 71
2. DOCTOR PIMENTINHA ON A MISSION 74
3. FASANO'S SMILE 81
4. COCAINE AND COMPROMISE 85
5. SILENCE AND THE MIRROR 92
6. RUNNING IN HEELS 95
7. MOM'S HANDS 103
8. WHITE SHEETS AND RED STAINS 106

9. DOTS KEEP FALLING 109
10. THE SUITCASE AND FREEDOM 112
11. BAIXINHA BUT BOUNDLESS 118
12. BENDING LINES 120
13. TRACING IT BACK 125
14. DR. SPICY, REDEEMED 129
15. THE FALL OF THE FATHER 132
16. CLINGING BECOMES A SYNDROME. 136
17. ESCAPING BEFORE EXILING 142
18. INTERRUPTION AS GRACE. 147

ACT III: THE CONNECTIONS

1. THE OTHER SIDE OF FEAR 151
2. FLAVORING NEW FEELINGS 160
3. FROM DOTS TO THREADS 166
4. BRAZIL, TEXAS, AND EVERYTHING IN
   BETWEEN 181
5. LEGACY IN LIVING 183
6. LIVING, IN COURSE. 193
7. FORGIVENESS IN TRANSLATION. 200
8. LOOSENING THE GRIP 206
9. THE MARRIAGE I MISTOOK FOR FREEDOM... 214
10. DOTS CREATING FIGURES 219
11. THE SHOW MUST GO ON 228
12. THE ART OF TRACING 230
13. BREASTMILK AND MOURNING 233
14. FIGHTING FOR SOPHIA. 237
15. THE LAST SLAP. 240
16. THE DOOR HANDLE. 243
17. MOTHERING BACKWARD AND FORWARD 245
18. CRAFTING SELF 253
19. LOST IN MY DOTS 261
20. CONNECTING MY DOTS 265
21. THE LAST TIME I HELD HER. 271
22. A DAUGHTER AT THE GATE 277

FOREWORD

Curitiba, March 12, 2019.

Tininha and I had just met. Her joy and captivating smile opened a channel of communication between us. We arranged to meet. Reciprocity, harmony, a cappuccino, an hour and a half of relaxed conversation—the kind that only happens when there's an instant sense of intimacy—some shared points uncovered, and the request she made for me to create a piece of art for her yoga school. It felt as though we had known each other for years.

The title of this book takes me back to that childhood game of connecting the dots to discover the hidden image. That new line we traced changed my own design.

I don't know if I believe in destiny.

I left our meeting flooded with an energy that, soon enough, you, dear reader, will also come to discover. Straight to my studio, I sketched a beautiful woman kneeling at the base of a flourishing tree, its leaves replaced by yoga poses—an allusion to movement, diversity, and to what I sensed was her purpose: deeper layers of self-development. That's how I saw her, nurturing the tree, a symbol of life, with the feelings that had surfaced during our dialogue. *Feeding My Life* is the title of the piece. The name came before the work itself, as so often happens in my creative process.

Curitiba, June 18, 2019.

Tininha and Jô came to my studio to collect the piece. She was astonished. Tininha saw herself in it, free, deliberately folded, accepting and watering her own life, breathing and bringing every second of her existence into consciousness.

Dallas, June 6, 2024.
I witnessed the author herself reading aloud the first chapter of this book. I broke down. I then spent the last year imagining how Tininha had arrived here.

Curitiba, August 29, 2025.
Entrusted with the honorable task of writing this preface, I must confess that my curiosity was tested to its limits. Fourteen months and no further clue, until finally I received, straight from Puglia: *"Aninha, the manuscript is in your inbox."* I rushed to read it and devoured it! Between one commitment and the next, just one more paragraph, please. By the end, I felt pride and immense joy for the connection that has always been ours—since that first cappuccino—for the poetic interpretation that *Feeding My Life* expresses.

Before my words sound like self-praise, let this be my gratitude—for being at the right time, in the right place, with an open heart, drawing the line that united me with Tininha.

This time, I was the one astonished. I found myself here, in the coming pages, represented by the voice of someone who suffered and recovered, who did not quite know which way to go, but gathered strength and went anyway, who felt fear and faced it, who made mistakes and discovered the true meaning of forgiveness. Someone who walked an irreverent path, broke patterns, and came face-to-face with pain. Bravely, she recognized her masters and released the illusion of control.

No one can love what they do not know.

Dr. Pimentinha offers us a good dose of courage, restlessness, and curiosity to help us look into the mirror.

For us, the testimony of one who dares to write her own story.

Thank you, my friend,
Ana Lecticia Mansur

A Note to My Daughters

Every story is a love story, which is why mine can't be any different.

Sure, the events that make up my story differ from everyone else's on the planet, but at its core, mine is a love story. Yours is, too.

In this book, I contemplate the difficulty of loving oneself, not the love of identity or the love of ego, but the love of our authentic selves.

The challenge is that so few people are aware of themselves, their true selves. So, how can we love what we aren't aware of?

Have you ever wondered if there's more to life?

When I was a child in Brazil, I used to look out the window and wonder what existed beyond the horizon. I just knew there was *something*. I had an inkling that I was somehow connected to the mystery of what lies beyond.

That was my starting point—one of the first dots.

What's yours?

If you have a feeling that there's more to life, I hope my story resonates and that you find the universality in my struggles, that you see your story, and begin to realize that most of us don't see who we truly are. Our vision is shrouded by traumas and the layers of armor we wrap around our hearts that obfuscate the truth.

My story's messy. It's also beautiful. In it are the clues that point to who I *really* am.

In reading my story, may you realize love. May you see your *true* self.

Mom

PROLOGUE: THE FIRST DOT

We were sitting on the couch, all three of us tangled together under the same blanket. A half-empty bowl of popcorn sat on the coffee table, the movie long finished, the room lit only by a soft glow from the kitchen.

"Mom," Helena said, twisting a piece of hair around her finger, "have you always been like this?"

"Like what?" I asked, smiling as I looked at her.

"I don't know, strong and brave. You know who you are."

I let the question hang there for a moment. Sophia turned toward me, too, curious.

"No," I said gently. "Not always. That part took time—a long time."

"You've always seemed so sure," Sophia added.

"That's because you've only ever known me after I stopped hiding."

"Hiding from what?" Helena asked.

"From myself," I said, "from who I really was."

They were quiet, waiting. It's a beautiful thing to have your children listen to you not just as a mother, but as a woman. I took a breath and continued.

"When I was little, I used to sit at the window of my bedroom in Brazil and just stare out. I didn't know what I was looking for. But I felt like there was something out there waiting for me—something bigger. I think that was the first moment I ever really *saw* myself, even if I didn't understand what I was seeing."

"Like a little version of you?" Sophia asked.

"More like a flicker," I said, "like I was remembering something I hadn't learned yet."

Helena leaned into my side. "So, what happened?"

"Well, life happened," I said, laughing softly. "Rules, expectations, people who wanted to keep me small. I became who I thought I *had* to be: quiet, obedient, afraid to speak up. I followed the lines drawn for me. But somewhere deep down, I kept that flicker alive."

"Was it hard?" Sophia asked.

I looked at her. "Very."

They both watched me.

"I lived through abuse. I stayed silent when I should've screamed. I chose people who didn't choose me. I wore masks so well that I even forgot what I looked like underneath. But one day, I remembered that little girl at the window. And I traced a new line from that moment to the one I was in."

They were both quiet again, thoughtful.

"So, this book," Helena said, "it's your story?"

"It's *our* story," I said. "It's the story of how I became the mother who could raise daughters like you. It's not perfect. Some parts might make you uncomfortable. There are things I've done and felt that might surprise you. But everything in these pages comes from love and from the truth."

"Even the hard parts?" Sophia asked.

"Especially the hard parts," I said, "because that's where we find out who we are."

Helena nodded slowly. "So, it's like you're drawing all the dots?"

"I'm connecting them," I said, "from the girl I was to the woman I am, to the mother sitting right here, holding your hands. And one day, you'll trace your lines. But maybe my story will help you see yours more clearly."

Sophia squeezed my hand. "Tell us, Mom."

And so, I did.

ACT I
THE DOTS

Os Degraus
Não desças os degraus do sonho
Para não despertar os monstros.
Não subas aos sótãos – onde
Os deuses, por trás das tuas máscaras,
Ocultam o proprio enigma.
Não desças, não subas, fica.
O mistério está na tua vida!
E é um sonho louco este nosso mundo…
Mario Quintana

••• 1 •••

CLINGING

CHRISTMAS IN BRAZIL is different from what it is in the movies. First, it's always hot, and we Brazilians celebrate it at the beach together as a reunion with family and friends, who often come from different states. We all wait an entire year to see each other at the same spot, creating memories of happiness and joy every time we meet. In Brazil, a country that borders the equator, beach season also coincides with the celebration of the end of another year.

Uncle Sergio, affectionately known as "Tets," was the king of the summer season, as all our friends knew. A beachfront bar and restaurant called Village was Tets's favorite place to sit all afternoon under an umbrella with his cooler full of water and beers.

"*Meus amores, está tudo muito lindo, mas eu vou me retirar para o meu espaço favorito: minha mesa no Village. Quem quiser, vem comigo.*" (My loves, everything is so much fun, but I am going to take my favorite spot at the Village. If you want to join me, just come.)

After we enjoyed the water and sand for a few hours, we'd exclaim, "It's Tets time!"

Then we'd head out together for the free ice cream, burgers, crab cakes (everyone's favorite), juices, and Cokes. My brothers, our friends, and I would sit around Tets as he smoked his Minister-brand cigarettes and sipped his beers. We were delighted with the goodies for our hungry bellies. Tets's favorite *passatempo* was telling us jokes to make us laugh, but in his heart, it was clear that he loved to see us happy, eating, and gathering with our friends.

On other occasions, he would prepare his favorite meal for us, *muqueca* (a kind of gumbo with a good mix of seafood and spices), that we'd eat with white rice and salad while stacks of beer cans would pile up in the kitchen trash can. He knew that my dad would never do the same for us. Dad and Tets were very different men, both capable of openly criticizing one another.

Almost like clockwork on such an occasion, my dad would enter from the front door, smell the food, and make a disgusted face, turning his eyes to the stove: "What the hell are you cooking, Sergio? It smells like old fish." He refused to let it go. "And it looks like you're going to clean out the beer case today."

Uncle Sergio would just raise his eyebrows toward Dad, and with a sarcastic laugh, he'd say, "It's something you probably can't eat because you seem to be allergic to good food. And please, don't worry about my beers; worry about your kids and what you'll leave them when you die. I already made my testament, and my nephews and nieces will be safe. I have doubts about what you'll leave behind."

From Tets's favorite *cervejaria*, we'd make our way back to the beach condominium, walking through the sandy streets in the 38–40°C heat. Then we'd assemble the umbrellas together, pretending that we were all in one house, until everyone left to go back to their destinations. Under the umbrellas in the shade, we listened to music with the small portable radio, and we played cards, staying there until we heard, "Kids! It's time for dinner!" The next day, we repeated the same routine. We all loved it, and we did this for about ten straight years.

Summers were a happy season for me.
Until fear took over.
It started when I began noticing changes in my body.
And so did the boys.

At school, at church, at the club—suddenly, I was seen differently. My breasts were developing, hair was growing in new places, and my heart fluttered in unfamiliar ways.

I was especially smitten with Osvaldinho, a boy two years older who wore the strongest cologne to Sunday Mass. I adored him from afar for years, until the night of my fifteenth birthday party when we kissed while dancing. For him, it ended as quickly as it began—not so much for me.

One night, he left his sweater at church, and I found it. I kept it hidden, breathing in his scent as I fell asleep, holding onto the fantasy of something more.

I didn't think much of the secrecy because I'd grown up in a house where emotions were hidden, and conversations about sex, love, and growing up were off-limits. Looking back, I realize I was simply trying to make sense of feelings I didn't yet understand.

On one Saturday morning before summer break, Mom invited me to go shopping for our upcoming beach vacation.

With fond memories of our vacations in my mind and excitement in my heart, I said to Mom, *"Oba mae! Vamos comprar os novos biquinis?"* (Are we going to get new bikinis?)

To which she replied, *"Sim, hora de renovar o que você vai usar no verão!"* (Time to get new bikinis for the summer!) Excited, I dressed up in shorts, a t-shirt, and tennis shoes.

I was ready to go when Mom said, *"Vamos de ônibus. Seu pai está trabalhando hoje."* (We're going by bus. Your dad has to work today.)

Mom never had a car; driving wasn't something that she and Dad could agree on. I never understood why, but later, it would all make sense.

Mom and I took the bus downtown. The destination for my summer clothing was a shop called Chiquitta, a kids' boutique that was like a modern-day Urban Outfitters if we'd lived in the United States. It featured many clothing racks throughout the store, offering a variety of colors and styles, and loud music that blared throughout the shop, celebrating the season.

I was holding Mom's hand while walking to Chiquitta, excited that I'd be in high school starting in February and itching to see my friends. I looked at Mom, and she seemed worried. However, because we never spoke about feelings, I just kept walking with her until we got to the shop.

We went straight to the credit line where she had to show her ID to obtain the authorization to use a line of credit for my clothes. She didn't have a checkbook, a credit card, or cash. That was the way Dad wanted it.

Credit approved, she felt relieved. She could finally make sure I'd have new bikinis for the upcoming summer season.

"What colors are you thinking of this year, *minha filha linda*?" she asked me with a very sweet and loving voice. "You can choose two this year."

The worried face I'd seen on Mom just a few minutes before had completely disappeared. Now, she was the woman who showed love and care for her children. That was my mom, the one I always looked up to for support and assistance when I needed it the most.

Calmly and making sweet eye contact, which was a big lesson and skill she always taught us, Mom bent over to be at my height and held both of my hands, reassuring me.

Deeply in my heart, I felt safe and excited, almost screaming as I bounced up and down. "Yes! I want a black one and a blue one," I said. These were the colors that were popular with the teenage girls at my school. My excitement was fueled by imagining all the fun I was going to have with the friends I hadn't seen in a year.

When we got home that afternoon, I was so excited about my new bikinis. Mom went to prepare dinner, and I went to my room. From helping me shop to making us dinner, she was always dedicating her time to us, her family.

It should have been a big night for me after getting my bikinis with Mom earlier in the day, my brothers returning home from tennis and soccer, and everyone gathered for dinner. And it began as a lovely evening. I was still bouncing up and down on my way to the dinner table after the morning's excursion. Mom and I looked at each other, and she blinked her right eye, giving me an "I've got you, Baby," nod of approval. I smiled back at Mom, feeling safe again.

I announced at the table that I had gone with Mom to shop for new bikinis for our upcoming beach trip.

Dad immediately looked at me and said, "Well, how much did that cost, Lígia?" While holding his stare at me, he was really asking Mom about the money.

She didn't make any eye contact with him but showed that worried expression again. She answered, "I got the credit line and used a little of it."

There was silence at the table—nothing from Dad, Mom, or my brothers. My stomach cramped. We all continued to eat, and the boys resumed making jokes about their day at sports, while Dad seemed tired from work.

As we finished eating, he looked at me across the table and said, "Tina, after dinner, I need to see the size of those pieces and how they fit on your body. I don't trust your mom for that. I know she always tries to squeeze in styles that are not appropriate for you."

Yet again, there was silence. Mom gently stood up and started to clean the table. We all helped her while my mind and my heart recoiled in terror. Suddenly, a memory knocked at my body, and I had the same sinking feeling I'd had the year before: *I have to go through this situation again?*

After Mom finished washing the dishes, my brothers went off to their rooms, and Dad brought some paperwork from the farm to complete at the dinner table. I was in my bedroom, terrified about what was to come. I nervously tried on the black one, noticing that it was just small enough to flatter my developing body, not revealing too much or too little. Mom hadn't said anything at Chiquitta; *maybe it was all right?* I had the feeling that if I could get the bikinis approved by Dad, it would be a temporary escape for Mom, a day passed out of prison. I didn't realize it at the time, but she needed me. Modeling my new bikinis for Dad was the last thing I wanted to do that day, but I had no choice.

"Are you ready?" bellowed Dad.

He was waiting to see the backside of my swimsuit, waiting to analyze every morsel of my bikini and judge whether it was suitable in his eyes. *How humiliating.* I felt it then, as I would today, the feeling of being diminished, ashamed, and ridiculed. His opinion was the law, and his thoughts governed what was appropriate for a fourteen-year-old girl.

Another summer, same fear.

I walked from my room after looking obsessively in the mirror, analyzing my body, before stepping into the dining room. I proceeded, ever so slowly, with the fear that my bottoms might shift, revealing my butt cheeks. I prepared myself for the humiliating comments that Dad might utter—and if not, the deadly silence.

I used everything in my power to manifest his approval, but never would there be a positive message or any form of praise. As I inched closer to where Dad sat, he removed his reading glasses, held them in his mouth, and inspected me with the scrutiny of a jeweler.

I froze.

"Turn around," he said. I had no choice but to comply, turning around to show him the bottom piece of my new bikini. He spent a few minutes looking at me, my butt specifically, almost stopping all sense of time, while I looked at Mom, who was also frozen on the other side of the couch. No one was allowed to say anything at that moment, except Dad.

"Ahem, next," meaning that the swimsuit bottoms were approved. "Not enough cover on this one," was a categorical *no*.

This scene, exactly as I describe here, was repeated throughout my entire pubescent life. After Dad's severe analysis, I would run to my room and cry quietly on my pillow, feeling extremely ashamed, insecure, unhappy, and angry. *Why does he need to be this way with me? Why such an invasion of my privacy, why such humiliation? What did I do wrong to have a dad like him?* Those moments represent my first memories of consciously feeling objectified, and by my dad.

Those occurrences usually happened at night, right after dinner, and most often during December. When other kids were feeling happy, safe, and joyful after ending another great school year and eager to celebrate Christmas, I was retreating into my shell, fearful of Dad's judgment.

"Mom," Helena's voice broke through the silence as I finished telling that part of the story.

I looked over. She was curled up at the edge of the couch, her arms wrapped tightly around her knees.

"That really happened?" she asked, her eyes wide, uncertain.

I nodded.

"It did—more than once."

Sophia frowned. "That's so messed up. Why didn't anyone stop him?"

"Yeah, the only thing Dad has ever said about our bathing suits is not to get into his truck if they're still a bit wet," Helena added.

I sighed, my chest heavy with the same question I'd asked myself for years. "Because in our house, silence was survival. Speaking up didn't feel safe. And honestly, I didn't even have the words to name what was happening. I just knew it felt wrong."

They were both quiet again.

"That must've made you hate your body," Helena said softly.

I paused.

"It made me confused about it—ashamed, even, like it didn't belong to me. But over time, I started reclaiming it—little by little. That's part of what this story is about."

Sophia reached for my hand. "You never made us feel that way."

"That was my vow," I whispered, "to end the pattern."

One day, I couldn't take it any longer and lashed out at Mom for not standing up to Dad's decisions. I looked at her and my three brothers, and I said, "I just can't accept that one man is capable of domesticating five humans to the point that we are absolutely unable to use our voices and speak for ourselves because of the fear of punishment. How can we let this happen? Please, tell me!"

But there were no answers. Mom just said, "*Seu Pai é somente um homem difícil.*" (Yes, your father is a difficult man.)

Mom had an ability to slide into silence, a signal of the obedient role she played in our family. Though my dad demanded respect, her subservience was anything but a display of respect, something I would discover later in life.

I was extremely angry at my family's passivity and complacency. It seemed as though there was a willingness to keep swallowing a reality that was slowly poisoning us all. I think that's because complacency had quietly crept into my life, threading itself through the walls of my cocoon at a time when I should have been building resilience and fire. Instead of cultivating inner strength, I folded inward. I wrapped myself in silence, not unlike my mother, not realizing that I was repeating the very patterns I resented.

They say people either run from pain or cling to it. I think I did both.

For years, I clung to identities that didn't match the woman I felt deep inside: the dutiful daughter, the perfect student, the quiet partner, the one who never made waves. That's what I call *clinging syndrome*: the impulse to hold on to roles, masks, and outdated versions of ourselves because we've mistaken them for safety.

Like a plant growing attached to a rock or another branch, we cling to the known, even when it no longer nourishes us, even when it hurts.

For me, it wasn't just about fear of the unknown. It was about survival. If I let go, who would I be? In a house where silence was currency and obedience was rewarded, I survived by clinging, first, to my father's rules, then to school and my perception of how a young woman should behave, and then to the illusion of perfection.

But clinging isn't living. It's a holding pattern that slowly strangles the soul. And like many lessons in my life, it took me years, and sometimes heartbreak, to loosen my grip.

Mom's actions and philosophy taught me that it was okay to accept the inevitable, even when it wasn't right. Even though I'm certain my mom didn't intend to champion complacency as the only way to handle a bully, she had to do what she could to survive. I'm grateful to have learned the lesson on my own that there are times when it's best to speak up and challenge, rather than simply roll along quietly, even if learning through Mom's pain was the path.

And so began my teenage years of fear, rejection, insecurity, and shame. I was domesticated by my dad, who largely controlled what I wore, what I said, and how I acted. All had to be in complete accordance with his expectations and tolerance.

But I was not the first one. Dad had domesticated Mom before me.

... 2 ...

FABIO'S LAUGH

EVEN AS A grown woman, I've never seen a picture of Mom and Dad as a bride and a groom or one of my mother in a wedding dress. Such a picture doesn't exist. They married secretly.

As a young lady in her late twenties, my mom, Lígia, was (and still is) a beauty—black hair, olive skin, brown eyes, five feet three inches tall. She still has the same captivating smile and impeccable extremities; her nails, toenails, hair, and teeth are always clean and shiny. She always presented herself in high heels, women's suits, and elegant purses. Mom prioritized her skin care and makeup, and she found exercising to be her favorite way to maintain a healthy mind and body.

When she turned 24, she met my Dad, Rogério, her next-door neighbor, who was five years older than her. They were married twelve months later. They were passionate about each other. Although Mom was shy and hesitated to admit the strength of her feelings, Dad was the opposite, always proud to say, "I hooked Lígia at first sight." Dad radiated power and charm.

They married in a secret ceremony at Igreja de São Pedro in Porto Alegre, a city in South Brazil, the Capital of Rio Grande do Sul State.

Dad was born in a different state, Santa Catarina, but moved to Porto Alegre at a young age. When he turned sixteen, his dad, João Maria, a farmer in the countryside of Santa Catarina, dispatched him to a boarding school. João Maria had bigger plans for Dad, maybe. Or he wanted more space for his private life as a widower, having lost his wife, Dad's mom, Dalila, in the early years of their marriage. Dad was only four when his mom passed, causing him to grow up without a mother figure, or any female presence, for that matter.

When they sent Dad away to boarding school, he lost his personal and emotional connection with his father and his younger sister, Clara Abigail, who remained on the farm to depend on and dote on her father. High expectations, periods of family detachment, and a lack of warmth or love shaped young Rogério's upbringing.

Although my father seemed singularly devoted to my mother, it quickly became obvious to everyone around them that the union would not be a peaceful one. Mom's family made it clear that they couldn't and wouldn't support a union that seemed so full of volatile passions.

"The two of them lived in a turbulent relationship; difficulties and your dad's controlling behaviors were constantly present. There were verbal fights, followed by romantic recovery dinners," my grandmother, Thereza, later shared with me. "Your mom tried to break up with your dad a few times, but I guess she really loved him."

Married, they made a plan. Dad asked Mom to quit her job and dedicate her time entirely to their marriage. Dad's insecurities played a role in this mutual decision, and Mom's beauty and charm might have provided a reason to establish some kind of control over her. She mustn't have known better. Her world became Dad's world.

Demonstrating her hesitation, Mom tried to defend her independence and keep her position at the bank and her dream of becoming a flight attendant at Varig, a respected commercial airline. However, in the end, she capitulated to Dad and inserted herself into the marriage bubble. In the bubble, she did what he did, went where he went, and his friends became her friends. She avoided close connections with her family, always feeling their disapproval. Bit by bit, her bubble shrank.

A piece had always been missing from her family picture: her father, who died of a heart attack when she was only four. Having him there during her struggles with a controlling partner might have offered the support she needed, but that presence was never part of her story.

In 1967, Mom became a full-time homemaker, learning how to cook and maintain the house impeccably. Dad became the provider, dedicating his working hours to making progress on his dreams of becoming a successful salesperson. He would try his hand first in the shoe industry, then in pharmaceuticals, and finally in the car and truck industry.

Two years into the marriage, Mom gave birth to my twin brothers, Fernando and Fabio, on October 15, 1969. They were premature, born seven months into Mom's pregnancy, and had to stay in an incubator for two months. Fernando was a healthy baby, feisty with sleeping and eating, while Fabio was calm and sweet. But Fabio was born with a chronic ear infection that was connected to his brain. Later in life, his condition morphed into a brain disease, producing constant seizures and resulting in what the medical community called seizure clusters. The condition would follow him quietly, shaping more of his life than anyone expected.

The initial commitment Mom made to her marriage, by this time, had become her entire life. Between cooking, cleaning, and feeding, Mom was on constant call with the twins. Meanwhile, Dad continued to expand his career as a salesperson, traveling to cities and states to find more clients and increase his income, making Mom more comfortable at home. Despite her family's unease with the relationship, Mom counted on the help of her mom and her brother whenever Dad traveled. Thereza and Sergio (Tets) became helpers for mom, taking on tasks like changing diapers, preparing bottles, and accompanying the kids to doctor appointments.

The days were all the same. Her life became her small apartment in Porto Alegre, next door to her mother's place. She felt exhausted and confined in her life and her space. She became a prisoner of her mind, too. Days and nights were becoming difficult to deal with as she looked back and felt miserable for letting her work opportunities slip away so easily. She felt as though she hadn't fought enough for her interests. Conflicted, she soldiered forward, believing that what she was doing was right for them as a couple. Plus, her husband was doing all that he could to be the provider, the one to make sure Mom had all her needs fulfilled, including the needs of the twins. For that, she at least felt that she should be grateful, though perhaps not necessarily happy or at peace. It was the reality in which she found herself.

It's a reality many women know all too well—a life that feels like a quiet prison, one they've lived, are still living, and long to break free from. It happened to my mom; it has happened to me, and it could happen to you. If we find ourselves in this place, we must summon the courage to ask, "What steps can I take to rise from this and to reclaim the life I truly want?" Because the first act of freedom is daring to believe we deserve it.

On a Saturday morning during the winter in South Brazil, with temperatures moving close to -7°C, Mom's discreet tears did all the talking. Her personal life had all but disappeared, replaced with the routine of changing diapers, making bottles, preparing for naps, waking them up, and repeating times two with the twins. Dad was traveling again that weekend, focused on his goal of becoming the top salesperson in the Southern region. Around that time, he was also considering a job offer from a company based in Curitiba, the capital of Paraná, another state in southern Brazil.

One more situation to handle, out of my control, Mom secretly told herself as she looked at her feminine, sad, and pale face in the bathroom mirror, as she refreshed herself with some gentle skin care for yet another morning. She reminded herself, *My life is his life, and I have to follow his dreams.* This meant that moving was an unquestionable step forward.

However, that day was especially sad. I can picture her sitting on her bed, still in pajamas.

The clock shows ten o'clock in the morning. The sun is bright outside, and she feels the warm sunlight on her legs as the sun enters the windows and permeates the white curtains of her bedroom. She finishes her second cup of coffee, and as she places her white cup on the nightstand table, she gently turns her face to the twin boys who are sleeping on her bed. She clenches her fists while the first physical signs of sadness drop to the hardwood floor. Releasing her head, chin coming closer to her chest, she squeezes her fists even tighter, fingernail imprints revealing themselves in the palms of her hands. Her chest is tight, full of sadness and desperation. The only audible sound is a gentle breeze infiltrating the crack between the window and its frame. As the teardrops pool, she realizes she hasn't shed a tear in years. She marvels in silence for a while, letting the tears run freely down her face. With the guidance of her right hand, she gently turns her emotions toward her womb, where I am located. And with her head down, tears flowing, heartbeat increasing, her twin boys peacefully sleeping, I feel the safety and warmth of her loving hands, but also the fear and sadness of her loving heart.

What did I do with my life? Mom asks herself. *I live in a prison; I'm a prisoner of this insignificant life I've created. I don't have anywhere to go or anything to do except to be here, at home, 24/7, on alert.*

Mom's feelings penetrate the womb, creating a sensation of heaviness, unwantedness, culpability, and shame. Mom's futile perception of reality transfers to me, a fetus forming inside her.

Perhaps that was the moment I inherited the emotions of sadness, guilt, and shame.

For the moment, though, it's dark, warm, and delightfully constrictive where I am. But I am safe. I have her love and strength holding me in her womb, secretly. Nobody knows she is expecting her third baby, including her husband. I can feel her heart beating faster every time the thought of having a new baby comes to her mind. Motherhood is her life, and so is being a prisoner. This time, she desperately wants to have a baby girl. A little pink would be splendid to accompany the sea of blue that colors the room of her twin boys. She already has a name for me, Maria Christina, and she uses her finest and most loving voice to whisper how much she already loves me without ever having seen my face.

"Christina, I discovered something as I read your map," my astrologist, Hilario, shared with me years ago. "You didn't want to be born. Did your mom ever tell you that? You felt unwanted and guilty for being created."

Mom stays in that moment until she hears a baby's laugh. It's my brother, Fabio, looking at my mom, smiling. She lifts her head and opens her eyes, and the sight of Fabio smiling at her captivates her. He wakes up from his nap, happy and ready to communicate with the world—the only world he knows: his mom. Fernando, having heard Fabio's noises, immediately cries, waking up from his nap, ready to eat again.

He was always starving. Fernando was born fifteen minutes earlier than Fabio and has cried ever since. Fabio was still in the womb while the doctors took care of Fernando, suddenly announcing to Mom and Dad that there was another baby in there. In 1969, it wasn't possible to know that a woman was expecting more than one baby. Thus, Fabio became the surprise twin, the one who was always calm, waiting for his time, as he had been inside the womb.

As Fernando cries, and Fabio smiles, Mom releases her clenched fists and places both hands over her pregnant belly, telling herself, *I need to find the force to continue.* She then takes the twins in her arms and walks to the living room porch, where the bassinets are fresh and ready for them, so the boys can experience some direct sunlight. She grabs the milk bottles that are ready on the kitchen counter and gives them to the twins. They grab the bottles with chubby little hands, eyes smiling, and make sounds of happiness, bouncing their legs and feet up and down, looking at their mom as milk drips delightfully onto their miniature faces. She looks down at them, more tears flowing, now expressing joy, gratitude, and love for the two young creatures in front of her. She lets the tears fall as her love abounds, the sun warming her skin, and her heart intensifying in force.

Then she looks up to the blue skies, straight to the bright sun, and tells herself, *How can I feel this way when I see these two precious faces smiling at me? I am being ungrateful for my life, for my babies, and for all that my husband does for me day after day. I must move away from this feeling of sadness and pressure and see the bright side of being a mom. Yes, this feels like a prison. But the reward of having these babies gives me hope.*

This is the force she needs.

••• 3 •••

BAIXINHA

I WAS BORN on a sunny Saturday morning in Curitiba, the capital of Parana, in the South of Brazil. Mom, Dad, and my brothers had moved from Porto Alegre when Dad got an offer to work for a pharmaceutical company. His dreams of becoming a decorated shoe sales director didn't come true, so he pursued a different dream and career. He accepted an offer to work for a pharmaceutical company, this time selling medications to doctors' offices. The field really didn't matter to Dad; he enjoyed working around people and making new contacts who could become friends for some occasional traveling, and perhaps new tennis partners.

Everything was new for Mom. She'd moved away from her beloved mom and brother in Porto Alegre, which contributed to her sense of isolation. The new challenge for her was to settle into a new city, to re-create a nest for her and her three children under four years old, and to find a community of friends to make it real. Porto Alegre had been the only place Mom had lived for twenty-nine years, and she was a social butterfly there. Mom loved to be around circles of people; she built connections wherever she went: the church, the country club, the neighborhood, her longtime friends from high school. Suddenly, in Curitiba, she found herself alone.

Despite the challenges, my mother again showed her strength, giving birth to me naturally, and finally receiving the little girl whose name had already been chosen years before my birth. As the doctor saw me coming out of the birth canal, he said, "Well, it's a girl, and she already pees!"

Thus, I came into the world with a splash on November 11, 1972. My father rushed to purchase a gift for his little girl: a "Suzie" doll, a kind of Barbie doll that was famous in Brazil. Mom and I bonded while breastfeeding.

My mom always tells the story this way: "When it was only you and I in the room, I looked into your eyes and said I love you so many times, giving you the sense of safety, love, and comfort, along with the soft touch of my hands on your beautiful face."

A new reality emerged for our family the day that I was born, six weeks before the height of our celebration season. Mom, Dad, and the twins were welcoming a baby girl, and a new story was about to be written. My life story feels like tracing lines between numerous dots, many of them belonging to others, forming an intricate pattern.

Inside the early lines of my life, I traced what felt like warmth, love, and, as I understood it then, happiness. These early dots, soft moments, familiar rhythms, and family rituals seemed to form a picture of contentment. When Fabiano arrived in 1974, the unexpected sixth dot in our Almeida constellation, the family line felt complete. With his birth, something shifted. I was no longer just one of five. I became Maria Christina, perched in the center of it all, the crowned queen in a house that spun around tradition, hierarchy, and unspoken rules. However, even then, I sensed that some lines I was following weren't fully mine.

I was the daughter they dreamed of, longed for, and wrapped in love even before I arrived. In those early years, they drew a simple line. It led directly to me, the girl who completed a vision, a hope, a prayer. That's when the little "Tina" emerged, her path marked with affection and expectation. My nickname, *Baixinha*, "the little one," became one of the first dots in my identity.

As Baixinha, I was always the one chosen to be first in the school lines. Short, amicable, and with a smile on my face, I made friends easily. Smiling meant feeling accepted, loved, and safe. In my younger years, my favorite way to enjoy free time was to be at home and create my own world, surrounded by my dolls and books. I played "mom" with my dolls, and one of my most playful moments as a little girl was imagining myself inside my little house: cooking, cleaning, and talking with the invisible members of my imagined family. My second favorite imaginative activity was being a teacher and using my dad's physics and chemistry books from his high school days. Finding myself able to solve the equations printed in those books, I would teach the concepts to my imaginary students. I was a very strict teacher and extremely smart, in my mind. This was the way I felt happy and safe in my house, living in my world.

We were the perfect example of Brazilian culture at the time: a nuclear family where Dad was the breadwinner, Mom the love maker, and four kids were being raised as Catholics. We had social and moral rules to follow and a home that should have reflected those values. Families of five, six, and even seven members were common. This was a time when life revolved around the interests of family members, typically centered on faith, love, food, and social engagements.

There are so many ways to describe what it means to be a Brazilian person, but there is one word that embodies the essence: *nurturing*. We are a nurturing culture with a focus on family, community, and personal well-being.

The Brazil that I know began as a colony of Portugal, as the Portuguese navigator Pedro Alvares Cabral discovered it in 1500. Being a European country with a strong Catholic background, Portugal influenced Brazil in the development of views on family, leisure, religion, and work. Brazilian families are often close-knit, loving, and warm, and enjoy spending time together. It's common for teenagers to live with their parents after high school and even into college, while extended family gatherings are the norm. Brazilians are very involved with each other and value living in a community.

We prioritize personal relationships and group identity over individual achievement. It's a culture in which leisure, social connections, and personal well-being are highly valued.

Flexibility is another dominant characteristic of Brazilians, especially regarding time; we don't place too much importance on punctuality. Late is better; late is chic. It's a culture of expressiveness with a vibrant mix of histories between indigenous peoples, Africans and Portuguese, forming the modern way of life. Brazil, however, has its own unique sense of style and swagger, more laid-back and relaxed, reflected in the way we speak, dress, and connect with others. We are the nation of the *Carnaval*, Christmas in summer; a vacation period of fifteen to thirty days; and a "the more, the merrier" philosophy in welcoming friends to a party. When Brazilians assemble at the table for a meal, there is no set departure time.

My family, the Almeida family, started as a nuclear family with traditional Catholic roots and a middle-class income. Having four kids under the age of seven in the early seventies in Brazil meant working hard every day. But that was the purpose of our lives because, of course, we are Brazilians, and family comes first.

Dad worked Monday through Saturday, and on the weekends, he indulged his love for tennis. Mom and Dad invested in a country club membership as soon as they moved to Curitiba, making the life transition a little easier with these new social connections. It seemed like we had it all: community values, well-being, and a solid sense of family. You might say we were all set to start a glorious life.

And life was sweet—at first. At home, Mom made sure the beds were always clean, smelling like fresh flowers and done in a tidy hotel style. The kitchen was always a warm and flavorful place, with Mom's recipes adorning the dining table. Mom continued to immerse herself in the household roles. Her love for us four children provided meaning to her life.

For years, Dad built his career in sales, eventually earning a law degree after much encouragement from Mom, who believed it would benefit the family's future. She was proud when he finally achieved it, but the legal profession, sitting behind a desk, writing case files, and defending clients, never suited him. He remained drawn to the world of sales until, years later, he shifted course entirely, following in his father's footsteps by becoming a farmer. The move proved profitable, thanks to a valuable piece of land in southern Brazil that he inherited. Still, it clashed with the life Mom had imagined for their family. But in our home, Dad was the one to be obeyed, not questioned.

In the early years, I felt that life was simple. I was a cute, smiley girl, a little shy, but confident. I believed wholeheartedly that living was about love, family, and friends. I didn't feel the need to compare myself to anyone and cared little about money. I had a good life. I was part of a sweet family, I thought. And yet, all along, there were indications that things were not as they appeared.

••• 4 •••

GOD, GUILT, AND GOOD HAIR

EVEN TO THIS day, an impression sticks with me: Mom is sitting on her side of the bed, crying, covering her face with her hands, while her beautiful, black, long, and messy hair hangs like the cascading leaves of a willow tree. I get closer to her, and my face levels with hers.

As a petite five- or six-year-old, I ask, "Mom, why are you crying?"

She continues to cover her face with both hands, her long hair dripping over her fingers as she bends forward, her head sinking lower with the weight of it all. Even at that age, I could see she was suffering—hurt.

"Mom, you're bleeding," I say.

She moves her hands and lifts her face toward mine. She looks straight into my eyes as her tears continue to dampen her well-cared-for skin and says, "Nothing to worry about, my angel." And then she hugs me. But the sign of physical aggression is imprinted into my memory. I don't believe it can ever be erased.

Who did that to her? I ask myself.

By the time I was in my teenage years, I was well aware of who was making my mother cry. My bewilderment and horror were immense. But soon, I would be on the receiving end of physical and mental abuse, which allowed me to relate more to Mom.

Dad didn't allow Mom to drive. So, she took the public bus, accepted rides from friends, or walked to church and the grocery store. She adapted to the rules he set, quietly navigating a life shaped by someone else's control. Beneath her obedience lived a woman in survival mode, her spirit forced to shield itself from the constant wear of emotional harm. The brain remembers these patterns most: the fight-or-flight instincts triggered by persistent threats, by a home that didn't always feel safe. Moments of genuine joy were rare, brief flashes scattered like glittering specks in the dark. They came at Christmas, Easter, and summer visits from Grandma Thereza and Uncle Sergio, when, for a few short days, Mom could exhale. With her family around, the tension eased just enough for her to experience a version of peace. It never disappeared, but sometimes, it softened.

"I was wrong about my reality," I told myself the first time Dad hit me in the face. I was only fourteen years old, and my internal world had been spiraling under the constant tension because of Dad's reign. I remember bloodied lips and a battered sense of identity.

"Dad! Tina's singing a song that has inappropriate words!" one of my brothers pointed out.

"I don't understand why things have to be so hard on me, Dad," I said. "The boys get to do whatever they want, and I'm the one stuck at home. I have rules about what to wear, how to act, and who I can or can't go out with. I don't like it; it's not fair."

I remember the occasion because it was one of the rare times I dared raise my voice, despite the tears flowing down my face.

"Come here, Maria Christina, and lie on the couch," my dad responded.

I did what he said, absolutely shaking. I was a little girl, and the imposing form of a giant approached me as I rested my head on one side of the couch. He then grabbed my cheek with his left-hand fingers, looked me in my eyes, and asked me to keep looking at him.

He said out loud, "You don't listen to inappropriate songs, and you don't raise your voice to me. I am the authority in this house. You do what I tell you to do. Do you understand?"

I nodded desperately, knowing that what was about to come was going to hurt. He implored me to close my mouth, and with his index and middle right fingers, he struck my lips once, twice, three times, until they bled.

"Now, go to your room and reflect on this lesson," he said.

In my room, I wanted to disappear under my covers. I cried until I fell asleep—the only way to end the nightmare.

Dad had beautiful hands, but the beauty was the beast. My cheeks were his target when he felt that his authority was being disrespected.

Eventually, I would receive permission from Dad to date boys, but I wish I could say that the physical abuse ended. There were a lot of rules, though, including always having one of my brothers with me on dates. This was usually Fabiano (we all called him "Bano"), who was always ready to listen to my point of view, to party, and to have a good time. He was always in the back seat of my boyfriend's car whenever we went anywhere. He was also present at restaurants, parties, and any other event I attended with my boyfriend.

I enjoyed the little freedom I had, but I secretly knew it came with conditions. Another chance for Dad to assert control. When the rules finally loosened enough that I could go on dates without my brother tagging along as a chaperone, my curfew became the next point of domination. If I were even ten minutes late, let alone thirty or an hour, his fury erupted.

I slipped up a few times. And when I did, the consequences were swift and humiliating. In front of my boyfriend, Dad would raise his voice, lashing out in anger. Then, without hesitation, he'd strike me across the face. He directed the punishment at me, but often aimed his words at my boyfriend, like a warning or a performance, a twisted assertion of power for all to witness.

No one could say anything in the house while Dad exacted his punishments. After one particularly heavy-handed strike, I remember running to my room to retreat under my covers, wanting to disappear. Bano was there for me, though, as he always was. Silently, I would cry while he'd whisper words of support until I fell asleep.

These moments sculpted me, and my teen years were, without a doubt, the most difficult years of my life. Witnessing the loss of joy and freedom, and living in fear every moment, marked the passage of my teenage years.

But it got worse.

Dad was also a stalker, secretly following me to the club as I hung out with my friends, constantly watching me from a distance.

Sometimes, he watched from above. Climbing on a tree branch was one of his favorite ways to spy on me as I arrived home after being out on a date. I have such vivid and traumatic memories, the shivering sensation of getting close to my parents' house, usually late, and missing the curfew that was given to me.

I can remember those instances as though they happened yesterday. Sitting in the car, my hands would sweat. It would be just past midnight, the deadline to be home.

It's going to happen again. These thoughts would dominate my mind. My mouth would get dry, and I wouldn't have any more words to say to my boyfriend, who drove me home.

One night, I was with someone new. He didn't yet know what happened when I walked in late. I couldn't bring myself to tell him. But in my mind, the spine-chilling scene was already unfolding. And yet, love, or maybe the rush of it, often outweighed my fear of humiliation. So yes, I was late more than once. And each time, I braced myself for what I knew would follow.

On this occasion, my date slowed the car and pulled up in front of Estoril, the building where I had lived with my parents since I was seven years old. Just before I leaned in to give him a goodnight kiss, I pretended to look off to the right, scanning the shadows to see if my father was already there. He wasn't. So, I turned and kissed my date.

But then, my date noticed something through the passenger window and suddenly said, "Your dad's jumping out of that tree!"

I whipped my head to the right, and there he was. My father yelled at me to get out of the car, demanding to know if I had any idea what time it was. He began berating my date, who sat frozen, blindsided by the scene unraveling in front of him. We were thirty minutes late, and that alone triggered the chaos. My dad slapped me hard across the face, sent me upstairs, and continued his tirade on the poor boy, who likely went home and decided never to call me again.

That scene, exactly as I describe it, was part of my formative years of life. However, it didn't end there. Even after college, when I was already a young adult, the humiliation and aggression continued. I imprinted shame and fear on my soul. This shaped in me the self-image of a fragile, small, and shameful girl, when in truth, I was just a young woman trying to understand what it meant to grow up, to feel seen, and to go on a simple date with someone I liked.

Dad was a physical and mental aggressor, using violence without a second thought, against his only daughter to teach her about respect and authority.

At first, all I felt was fear of my dad. Then I felt hate—and, finally, remoteness. I remember asking God to end his life because of all the suffering I felt. My pain was deep; I felt constantly ashamed around my friends and even my acquaintances. Dad punished me mercilessly in front of whoever I was with and in whatever situation, according to his rules of what he deemed was "not appropriate."

I felt like a prisoner in a horrible story. *Why did God choose this family for me?* was what I asked in church as I knelt down in the pews at Igreja Santa Teresinha. "Jesus, please, take my dad away. He hurts me too much," was another common refrain.

Dad maintained his strict rules toward my three brothers, as well. He expected top grades in school, and if the *boletim* (Portuguese for report card) ever showed any red marks, it was bathroom time. Red grades were poor, and blue grades were good. From the bathroom, everyone could hear the belt thrashing anyone with red grades.

Fabiano, the last child, received the least amount of thrashings from Dad, but he still got into a fair amount of trouble. Once, Mom found a pack of cigarettes—lost or hidden—between Bano's bed and the wall. She was making his bed one morning, and as she straightened the cover over the side of the bed, she felt something. It was a pack of Camels. Mom showed Dad and, in his traditional way of lecturing us, invited everyone to the family table. Before lunch, on a weekday, he asked Bano to stand up. No one understood what was going on. We remained silent.

"Your mom found this next to your bed," said Dad. "Is this yours?"

Fabiano, only a thirteen-year-old premature smoker, replied without hesitation: "Yes, Dad, it's mine."

"So, this means that you are smoking, correct?"

"Yes, I am smoking," said Bano.

Dad and Mom were also longtime smokers. Though we were never educated about the ill effects of smoking, Dad decided this would be the right moment.

"Well, cigarettes are not good for you," said Dad. "You are too young to be a smoker, and in my house, my kids may not use these. And as a lesson for all of you, Bano is going to eat one cigarette in front of all of us. After tasting it, he'll always remember how bad they are for you."

Dad gave one cigarette from the pack of Camels to Bano, who took it and put it in his mouth, slowly beginning to chew. Surrounding him in all his misery, we remained quiet, staring at him, until he swallowed the whole thing.

"Now," Dad continued, "I hope Bano and all of you understand how bad this is. The lesson is done. Let's all eat our lunch."

That humiliating scene has remained imprinted in my memory, just as much as the bikini runway episodes from my childhood. Whether it was lashings from the belt in the bathroom or public humiliation, Dad employed a variety of tactics designed to keep us caged and fearful. It drew my siblings and me closer together, sharing the same cage.

Meanwhile, Mom never quite seemed able to utter the words, "This is not acceptable," to Dad. She was immersed in her fears and forced into submission by Dad. While we kids could ultimately escape from his abusive ways, Mom remained a prisoner until the end.

Interestingly, both Fabiano and Mom still smoke. Go figure!

Perhaps no one had taught my dad any better. Perhaps his abuse stemmed from being a prisoner of his parents' lives; he lost his mother young, and his father sent him away at sixteen. I often wonder, *How were my dad's teenage years?* And the answer is: I don't know. I don't have anyone to ask who would have known him during those formative years. Was someone teaching him to lead by example, putting him down, or even using physical force to impose their will on him? If I knew, it might explain things. However, even recent attempts to get answers from his sister, my Aunt Clara, have revealed no insights.

Another area where Dad influenced my choices was my education. By the time I was ready for high school, Dad decided that the best place for his daughter was an all-girls Catholic school. My oldest brothers were already in high school, at Nossa Senhora Medianeira, a prestigious school where the popular kids and traditional families attended. It was also academically renowned. Their friends from Medianeira were the hot guys of that era, and my dream was to be with my brothers, taking the bus in the early mornings, joining the fun, making new friends, and experiencing high school with the hotties. Though my interest in boys blossomed at that point in my life, I had a more serious reality to face.

One evening during dinner time, when I'd just finished middle school, Dad mentioned he had spoken with Mom about my next steps.

I excitedly asked Dad, "Am I going to Medianeira?"

He continued to taste his fresh bread with ham and cheese and took one more sip of his coffee before he looked at me, raising his eyebrows and said, "I have a better plan for you—a plan that is more appropriate for a young girl. Nuns in an environment that is safe should educate girls. Your Mom and I discussed your next school, and we've chosen Sagrado Coracao de Jesus. You will study to be a teacher in an all-girls school."

It was a defining moment in my young life. Upon hearing those words, I felt frustrated and desolate inside.

"Be a teacher? Why? I never wanted to be a teacher, and I never told you I wanted to study to be a teacher," I replied to Dad.

"Christina," he said with a raised voice, putting both of his hands on the table while the boys and Mom were staring at me, "this is my decision, not yours. I know what is best for you as your father. Your brothers have a different plan. They are in the right place for boys, but it's not the right place for girls, especially my daughter."

My father's refusal to let me express my feelings, desires, and dreams devastated and disappointed me.

"I don't want to be a teacher, and I don't want to be with all girls," I secretly told my youngest brother, Fabiano, when we were in bed.

I shared a bedroom with Fabiano, and nighttime was an important time for us to exchange confidences. We were always so close to each other and have remained so ever since. Bano is the brother that everyone would love to have in life: the guy who's always ready to listen, who talks only when he thinks it's the right time, and is always up for a good time. He's very social, but not so outspoken. He has been the charm of my family. He graduated in economic science and worked for years for the Bank of Boston, but his dream was always to explore the world. So, he traveled to Indonesia, Australia, and the United States with a little money he'd saved from the years on and off in different banks. He is a lover, and today, he owns one of the most famous pet shops in my hometown, taking care of over six hundred dogs a month for grooming. He is still the one I call the most when I need help.

When we'd go to bed, all I could dream of was Osvaldinho, the boy with whom I was in love and so desperately wanted to kiss. I wanted nothing more than to be his girlfriend. But he was at Medianeira, along with his two sisters. Other boys had their sisters there, too. In my mind, I was the only one left out. From time to time, I even wore my brother's uniform when going to the club or hanging out with my friends, pretending I belonged to the cool Medianeira. My last attempt was to write a letter to my dad at Christmas. It was 1988.

Dad, the only thing I want for Christmas this year is to transfer schools. Please, Dad, please, I wrote.

But it didn't resonate for him. Perhaps his heart was closed. He had already decided, and my only choice was to continue the journey that had nothing to do with my desires.

It must have been my dad's deepest fears that fueled his behavior, fears he never spoke of, but acted out in control and anger. He couldn't see me as my own person, and try as I might to oppose this conditioning, I grew up clinging to someone else's ideas for me for a long time. In trying to protect me from the world, Dad treated me as an extension of himself—as his property, his shadow. But the very patterns he used to contain me were the same ones that imprisoned him. We were both captives of his conditioning, trapped by the legacy he couldn't escape, and for a long time, neither could I.

••• 5 •••
GRAFFITI AND SHAME

AT THE TIME, the environment at Colegio Sagrado Coracao de Jesus, where I was enrolled, was toxic—one might say, harmful. I went from my oppressive, tiny hive right into a swarm of frustrated bees. Many of the girls—predominantly white—of the Catholic School of the Sacred Heart Organization, were similarly domesticated young women. If their parents hadn't domesticated them, they were bound to be groomed by some of the nuns who, from experience, were particularly damaging to my personal development. The school was made up of a mix of families with traditional last names and non-traditional ones, such as mine. Many of the students had middle-class working parents, while others had high-profile elite ones. For different reasons, many of these families had something in common: They wanted to prepare their daughters to become teachers, then wives, and finally mothers. This was not my plan at all. I wanted more from life, and I knew it.

I had been quietly formulating an image of motherhood, and it wasn't enticing. The mother figure, for me, represented submission. Witnessing my mom's experience created a force in me that sought the opposite of her life. I would often catch myself saying, *Christina, do something totally different than your mom.*

A few times, when Mom and I were in the kitchen doing dishes after a meal that she'd prepared impeccably, I was reminded that every dish she made was imbued with love. On one occasion, we were next to each other as she washed the dishes, and I dried them. Without stopping and without making eye contact, as though she resented sharing such a heartfelt message, she softly said, "Tininha, earn your independence, financially, and as a woman. Don't do the same as I did. You have the potential to do and be much more than I. I don't regret my choices because I have you and your brothers, but I want to see you tracing different lines than mine."

It was a defining moment.

So, I followed her heart, as well as mine. My dreams were to become a strong, successful, and independent attorney, perhaps a judge one day. Marriage and kids weren't in my spectrum of dreams. But finding love? Always. A husband? Not necessarily.

One of my favorite habits on Sunday afternoons was sitting at my bedroom window, alone, looking outside at the grandiose world. Living on the ninth floor, I had a unique viewpoint from above, closer to the sky and away from the ground. I felt that I was closer to my imagination and would ask myself, *What else is there?*

Mom would often see me at the window and ask me the same question every time: "Where is your mind today?"

"Mom," I would answer, "I am just wondering what is out there that I can't see but would love to experience."

Needless to say, my education at Sagrado was not a great experience. Because we were a mix of social classes, it was a constant exercise to get to know people for who they really were. It shouldn't have been so difficult; we were simply high school girls. However, many of the girls had last-name baggage, status, and attitudes to accompany their rank. I never felt confident being vulnerable, always unsure of who to trust, and as the years went by, I only found three or four girls with whom I was able to connect and be friends. I played volleyball, ran track, and got good grades. I behaved appropriately, treating everyone—nuns, regular teachers, staff, and classmates—with respect and kindness. Academically, the school was enjoyable, but the environment was the real issue for me. It began to feel like an extension of the hostility, secrets, and tension that existed at home, becoming more vivid as I entered my teens.

Despite the challenges, I made good memories with the few girlfriends I made at Sagrado. One of them was Maria Eugenia, an outsider like me, except her last name had more status in Curitiba than mine. We became good friends. We were not popular or the leaders of the pack, but we enjoyed one another's company, and we had good conversations.

Commuting to school always started early because Dad couldn't (or didn't) ever take me to school (he was too busy with work), and Mom didn't drive. This meant that I had to walk about thirty minutes every day to get to school. I did the walk for a while, whether it was cold or hot, carrying my little briefcase (not a backpack in those days), going and coming back, rain or shine. Occasionally, other kids would join me on the way, so I wasn't always by myself. In the 1980s, a sense of safety still lingered, enough that a fourteen-year-old could walk to school alone in the early morning, and her parents could trust she'd arrive on time without worry or incident.

However, Maria Eugenia was my neighbor, and she had a private chauffeur. As we became closer, she said, "Tina, I can pick you up and bring you home every day." So, by my second and third years of high school, Maria Eugenia and I became close buddies as we commuted every morning, enjoying conversations about life, friends, and dreams.

One early morning, I jumped into the white, four-door Passat that waited for me. Maria Eugenia was in the front seat next to Edgard, her private chauffeur. He was a sweet old man, in his sixties, with glasses and a mustache, a white shirt, and a black tie. The days were always brighter around Eugenia. She would greet me with a sweet smile, always happy with our tradition of riding together. With no seatbelts, at that time, and windows open, Maria Eugenia would turn her body toward me in the back seat and start a conversation about something going on in her life. "Tina, you won't believe…" and the story would go on. I was her listener and could feel her affection for me as a friend, and I knew she appreciated me being her confidante. We were, in certain ways, the same: two prisoners of their stories. Her life's story was fought privately, with her own struggles. But we felt safe with one another. My friend was always funny and warm-hearted, and she routinely brightened my days.

On the way to Sagrado, she would usually be the only one who talked. Edgard and I would listen as she shared her thoughts and feelings about anything that came to mind. Sweet Edgard would just move his head side to side and provide a shy smile, whispering the words, "Oh, Maria Eugenia, you are a storyteller."

That morning, we were feeling light, and the conversations were bouncing all over the red interior upholstery. As Edgard approached the school entrance, we got ready with our briefcases, Maria Eugenia with her big one. Edgard slowed down the Passat to park in front of the main gate entrance, as usual. When the car stopped, our heads turned to the school's white exterior wall, just next to the gate, and we read in black graffiti paint in large letters: "*Tina, pare de dar o cu,*" which translated into English meant, "Tina, stop giving your ass."

The horror.

"Mom," Sophia's voice broke the silence. "Why? Why would they do that? *Who* did that?" You could almost feel the heat coming off her from where she sat.

I looked at her, not surprised that she'd articulated the very questions I had myself all those years ago. I was also a little heartbroken by what the memory still stirred in me. Helena's eyes were wide, too, waiting.

"I don't know. I never knew." It felt good to share this out loud. "People can be cruel," I continued. "Especially when someone doesn't fit the mold, when they shine in a way others don't know how to handle. Back then, I was growing into my body, into my voice, and that made me a target."

Helena shifted closer. "But to say something like that—and for everyone to see it."

"It was humiliating," I admitted. "I didn't even know how to process it. I just felt this deep shame, like I was suddenly exposed and wrong, without ever having done anything."

Sophia tilted her head. "Did anyone stand up for you?"

I paused. "Yes—and no. Eugenia was there for me, but only to the extent that she could comfort me. That was the hardest part, feeling so alone in it."

They were quiet for a moment.

Then Helena asked, almost in a whisper, "Is that why you always tell us to speak up—even when it's hard?"

I nodded. "Exactly. Because silence can turn pain into a secret, and secrets turn into stories we start believing about ourselves. I don't want that for you. I want you to know your worth, even when the world tries to write something else on the wall."

Sophia reached for my hand. "You didn't deserve that."

"No," I said, brushing a strand of hair from her cheek, "and neither do you. That's why I'm telling you these things, not to make you sad, but to show you how we survive and how we heal together."

Who could have done something so awful to me? My head dropped, and I froze, gripped by fear. I couldn't move. I couldn't speak. My whole body shook. I was just a young girl, and I couldn't understand why anyone would direct such cruelty my way. At only fifteen years old, I didn't have any sexual experience, let alone what I was being accused of.

With my hands and legs shaking, I grabbed my stuff and got out of the car. Edgard stayed quiet, head drooped in silence. He couldn't look at me.

Maria Eugenia, without a moment's hesitation, bravely put her arms around my shoulders and said, "Let's go to the principal's office right now."

I could barely walk, my heart racing. *What do I say to my parents about this? Are they going to think that I am having sex at this young age?* I was unable to maintain my breath. I was in complete shock at the words written for everyone, parents and girls, to see as they all pulled in to be dropped off at school.

We met Irma Giselda, our principal, a nun in her sixties who was five feet tall and had blue eyes, pale skin, and gray hair. She was known for being rigid, strict, and on top of all future teachers' behaviors. Usually quiet, with slow rhythmic steps, always checking her surroundings, she had a blank face. We entered her office, and I stayed there while Maria Eugenia left for class. I sat in front of Ms. Giselda's desk, feeling shorter than her and in a completely frozen state.

Our eyes made contact, and after a deep breath, she said to me, "What a terrible message on the school wall. Do you have any idea who did it?"

I tried desperately to find my voice, forcing the connection of my thoughts to my feelings, and responded that I had no idea who had done it, that I was feeling devastated and humiliated, and timidly inquired what she was going to do.

"We are going to clean up that mess, and you should forget this day and go back to class. It's hard to know who did it, but for sure, it's a big humiliation. By the end of the school day, the wall will be clean."

"Thank you, Irma Giselda," was all I could muster as I left her office, heading straight to the classroom where I had to face my classmates.

I remained quiet for the rest of the school day, insecure and fearful, imagining who could hate me so much that they would hurt me so cruelly.

The author was never revealed. My parents never found out about the attack. I went back home that day with Maria Eugenia and Edgard, and they both said to me, "Forget what happened today. Someone is just very jealous of who you are."

As I gratefully got into the white Passat parked on the street near the scene of the crime, I saw the white wall restored to a blank canvas, covered by a fresh coat of paint. The wall may have been cleaned, but the stain of those words still made me feel dirty and ashamed. I wondered, *What's next?* I surveyed the wall, looked around at the three hundred-plus girls getting out at the same time as me, and thought, *Which one of you did this?*

I went home that day and didn't eat dinner. I crawled under my covers, eyes wide open, wishing I could disappear. It was the first time I remember feeling like my body didn't belong to me, like someone had stolen a part of it by writing those words in public.

Without realizing it, I started clinging to that story, trying to outrun it, disprove it, erase it. But all the while, I was feeding it. That's the thing about clinging syndrome: Sometimes, we hold onto the version of ourselves we most want to escape.

Those words are still impressed in my mind forty years later. What affected me more, however, is that I could not use my voice to tell Mom and Dad what happened or demand an investigation from the school administration. Motivated by fear and shame, I remained quiet inside my prison—my head. It was a pattern I wouldn't recognize until much later in life: bullied at home, bullied at school. At five feet tall, I must have looked like an easy target, and maybe I was, in the beginning. I didn't know how to do it, but I had to break out.

High school graduation finally occurred in December of 1989. I was done with the oppressive and toxic environment at school and at home. And this time, I was intent on making a decision for myself. So, I decided I would apply to law school. I didn't have a precise reason for this choice, but it wasn't teaching, and it seemed that choosing law meant that I would escape all the girls who harassed me in high school.

Of course, Maria Eugenia and I remained friends outside of school, and I am proud to report that she, too, broke the mold and became a well-known and respected psychologist in my hometown.

••• 6 •••

INVISIBLE GIRL
WITH RED RIBBONS

PERHAPS I WAS subconsciously pursuing the path of my aggressor by choosing to become a lawyer, hoping I would someday have the power he seemed to hold, though he wasn't the conscious inspiration for me to pursue law. However, when I look back, I can see the lines that connect the dots between high school and law school. You might say that my life depended on making something happen, something that was uniquely my doing. I needed to escape the "incarceration," first at home, and subsequently at the hands of the nuns. It made sense to want to be a litigator, a fighter, without even realizing the choice I'd made.

Acceptance to law school came as one of the biggest surprises of my life. After high school, I was so depleted by my family and academic life that I felt a sense of hopelessness about getting into law school. In January of 1990, during the high summer season in Brazil, I was preparing myself to be rejected by the most prestigious law college in my hometown: Faculdade de Direito de Curitiba, or FDC. Against Dad's wishes, I had applied to FDC. He had wanted me to enroll at the Catholic institution he'd once attended, Pontifícia

Universidade Católica do Paraná, or PUC. But this was my quiet rebellion, another small act of defiance, another way I claimed my right to choose.

I was sitting outside of FDC one Saturday at lunch hour, waiting for the application results to be placed on the gray wall. The school was old and classic in its architecture. The walls were white and gray, the concourse made of rocks, a traditional technique that involves setting small, hand-cut stones, usually white limestone and black basalt, into mosaic patterns on sidewalks and public squares. It's called *calçada portuguesa*, a style common in both Brazil and Portugal. The school had three floors full of classrooms. Downstairs was the cafeteria and the teachers' rooms, along with the administration. On top was the auditorium. Heavy curtains, dark furniture, and marble columns made up the rest of the architecture and design. It was my dream school. Alone, I gazed at the gray wall, waiting for the results.

It's so difficult and so competitive to get in here. There's no way I will get accepted, I told myself. So, there I was, just waiting to accept my fate. I knew that as soon as I faced the rejection, Dad would have other plans for me.

It so happened that a friend of my oldest brothers (the twins) was also there, awaiting his results. We knew each other, but we had no idea we'd applied to the same place.

"*Olá Gustavo, o que você está fazendo aqui?*" I asked him what he was doing there. He replied that he'd come to check the results and asked if I already knew about mine. "No, I'm just waiting here for them," I said.

He quickly responded, "They just placed them on the wall. Did you check?"

"No," I said, discouraged and fearing my fate.

"Do you want me to have a look for you?" he asked.

"Yes," I responded, feeling that having someone else see the crappy results would lessen the hurt. He walked toward the wall, and I waited.

"Is your name Maria Christina de Almeida?" he asked when he returned.

"Yes," I replied, wondering why he was asking such a silly question.

"Your name is there. You got in!"

"What? No way!" I shrieked. "Are you serious?"

His smile gave it away, but his words, "Yes, you're in," caused me to be momentarily paralyzed.

A few seconds after that, my heart started beating again. I heard a voice deep inside my heart say, *"My life is going to change right here, right now." This is my new beginning. I did it. I got accepted because of my efforts. Dad didn't put me here. This came from me!*

I stood up on my tiptoes (he was a tall guy) and gave him a giant hug of gratitude. "Thank you. I just can't believe it," I said.

He replied with a sweet smile. "Congratulations. You deserve it. I didn't get in, but I'm happy for you." He shrugged as he turned to leave. "Say hi to your brothers."

I got home that afternoon, and my heart was exploding with pride. Despite the slim possibility that I'd entertained being accepted, it had happened. In my mind, I could envision the hours, days, and nights studying out loud on my bed—my favorite way to memorize concepts, understand subjects, and focus my concentration. The essay writing component of the admission process required many hours of out-loud thinking. But for the first time in my life, I had accomplished a monumental achievement on my own.

"Mom, Dad, you're not going to believe it! I got admitted to Curitiba [yet another shortened version of the school's name]." They were both in the family room at home, the *copa*, watching TV and eating fresh oranges. It was Dad's favorite way to relax on a Saturday after a round of tennis with his buddies. Mom had spent time in the sun with her friends. I could see Dad peeling the oranges, gently, and passing the *gomos* to Mom.

"Mom, Dad, did you hear me?"

Mom jumped up to hug me and began crying. "You are so brave, so incredible, *minha filha amada*. I am so proud of you." Locked in an embrace, we both began crying. "I saw you in your room day and night, nonstop, preparing yourself for this," she said.

"I know, Mom. I studied so hard. I'm so happy."

Dad never flinched and continued to methodically peel his oranges, finally looking in my direction. "When does the PUC release its results?" he asked, passively displaying his dismay with my choice of schools.

"I'm not sure, Dad," I said. "But I don't care about PUC. I want to be in Curitiba. It's the best law school in town."

His beautiful and violent fingers stopped peeling oranges, and he looked at me and said, "I think you did great, congratulations. But your best choice is going to be PUC. I went there, and I know you'll like it, too."

"No, Dad, I am not going to PUC," I said forcefully. "Please, respect my desire to attend the place that I've dreamt about."

Mom remained silent, and Dad said, "You are going to wait for the PUC results."

Yet again, Mom reverted to complacency, saying, "I know you don't agree with him, but he has the final word on this."

"On this and on everything, everyone, and everywhere, Mom," the tears were now streaming from my eyes for an entirely different reason than the joy I'd experienced earlier in the day. She followed me to my room to comfort me.

The PUC results came a few days later. To Dad's surprise, I was not accepted. "Wait until the last group gets the call; you might still have a chance. No registration to Curitiba will be made until the last group of names comes in," he said.

It's typical in Brazil for college acceptance results to change as students make their choices. After seven groups were called, Dad realized he'd lost his hope, and I'd found mine. It was time to move forward and begin to build my story—the one that I'd chosen, the one that I would create, the one that was meant to be.

One thing was for sure, though: I would be paying for the bulk of my tuition, despite Tets paying for the older boys' college. Even

Fabiano had his tuition paid for by the Catholic Diocese, something Mom had been able to coordinate. I wouldn't be so lucky.

When I examine the dots between that moment in Curitiba, Parana, Brazil, when I was sitting outside of the building waiting for the application results, and the writing spot in which I sit at the present moment, one thing is clear to me: The Universe plants the dots, like seeds, before we're able to trace the lines that connect them and long before we take action. I contend that even before we are born, the stars are aligned, and the dots exist: a complex puzzle solved with simple line art that serves to render the image of the beauty and intricacy of what we call life.

My birth, my home, my college, and my experiences are all dots. So is the friend I met at college. That friend offered me a job—another dot. The job took me to Mexico, dot. What Cancun gifted me in the most unexpected way was another dot. The United States, my husband, and my daughters are all beautiful dots. Connect them, and the most unique and incredible picture emerges from the pixels. What an incredible way to visualize the synchronicities of life's crucial moments.

By February of 1990, I was finally fully registered at Faculdade de Direito de Curitiba. I was seventeen years old and ready to connect new dots that would reveal a new routine, new forms of living, and opportunities yet to be discovered. The domesticated little girl was about to learn how to enhance her world vision and become aware of a much bigger spectrum of reality. Everything that was about to unfold made those quiet moments at my window even more meaningful. Now, those dreams were beginning to take form. For the first time, it wasn't about Dad. It was about me. And I was ready to step beyond the frame and run with my newfound freedom.

Not long after, Mom got a phone call from Sagrado, my old high school, the intense and toxic environment from which I'd finally gained my freedom.

"Tininha, Sagrado called, and they are asking for you to be there next week for a special presentation. As an alumni member, they would like to introduce you to their current students as a form of inspiration. They'd like you to share your college plans with the student body."

"Really, Mom?" I asked gleefully. "I can't miss this opportunity." It also provided Maria Eugenia and me an opportunity to connect and for Edgard, her beloved driver, to pick me up one more time.

When the morning arrived, there were no uniforms. Instead, we dressed in fancy clothing, wore makeup, and flashed our bright smiles. Maria Eugenia was just as excited as I was. She was accepted at PUC to study psychology. I was happy for her, and she was happy for me. And, of course, Edgard was happy for both of us. Though he didn't say anything, his smile was always a sign of acceptance, happiness, and support.

When we arrived at Sagrado, we entered the main office. As former students, entering through the main office was a sign of respect. The principal, Irma Giselda, greeted all of us—the ones who were going to college. She offered each of us a beautiful cross and a medal from the Sacred Heart Organization.

"Beautiful work, young ladies. Are you ready? We want to introduce each of you to the whole school as part of our commitment to recognizing your efforts after having been here for three years," she said.

As she talked to us, I looked around her office and experienced a flashback that was accompanied by a strange feeling. The last time I'd been in her office, I was ashamed. It was on that horrific early morning when my name was graffitied on the entrance wall. I could recall all my feelings as I looked at the school principal, now happy and proud of us. However, as I contemplated her face, suddenly her voice faded, and my mind traveled back to the experience that occurred a mere two years prior.

I felt a tear drop onto my face. The unexpected emotions made me feel like I was fracturing into a million tiny pieces. It occurred to me, at that moment, that a trauma was awakened inside of me, never having had the opportunity to exorcize my hurt and pain as a child normally would with compassionate parents. At the time, I knew nothing about therapy. Talking about feelings, where I grew up, had always been taboo. The graffiti episode was a secret between me and every other girl at the school. As Irma Giselda gave all the girls their gifts, I cried on the inside, maintaining my composure as I had been taught to do, while feeling immense pain for what a younger me had endured.

As I received my gift, she looked me in the eyes and placed her soft hand on my face, saying, "You made it here. You must be proud of yourself. Go up to the balcony and share with all the girls that you will be joining a law school."

As we stared into one another's eyes, we knew without saying a word what that moment meant for us: me as a young girl, a victim of bullying and aggression, and for her as a principal nun of a prestigious school in Curitiba. She didn't know my home reality, and my parents didn't know my school reality. I was the keeper of both.

We young college-bound girls took the steps to the school balcony and formed a line. The principal stood by the microphone and said good morning to the younger girls who were all seated by grades in the assembly below.

"Today, we are here to present to you the 1989 graduates, and now young ladies on their way to college. I am very proud of each of them for what they have chosen to pursue in their lives. Please, help me to welcome each of them as they introduce themselves and share with you the college and field of study of their choice."

I was in line behind about ten girls. I felt proud of myself, salivating at the opportunity to reveal that I had been accepted to law school. I waited nervously for my turn, my hands sweating, and my heart beating fast. Finally, my shot at redemption arrived.

"*Meu nome é Maria Christina*. I am going to law school at Faculdade de Direito de Curitiba."

Each word that escaped my mouth took every bit of energy to say; it was my body communicating the news, not just my mind. I felt *grandiosa* for the first time in my life. I'd chosen a simple blouse, low heels, and a pencil skirt for my appearance at the school. I wanted to look as different as possible from the bullied student in a uniform that I'd been wearing when I used to attend. It was one of many small acts that communicated my need to break out and break free. I didn't know it at the time, but small acts, such as this, were like breaking out of a jail cell and not realizing that the prison itself has locked doors and a moat surrounding the entire building. I would later learn that I'd have to break out repeatedly. However, at that moment, I heard the applause and accepted it wholeheartedly.

I was the only young lady going to study law; the others were going to study the "*gias*," which were more traditional areas of study for women, such as *fisioterapia, fonoaudiologia, psicologia,* and *pedagogia*. I was going to study *direito*, and this word, *direito*, at that moment specifically, felt extremely prestigious, empowering, and, yes, different. I was different. Different had become my identity. I wanted to be an outsider—a wild one—doing things differently, doing things outside of the box, always the opposite of what was trendy.

Perhaps that outsider mentality was baked into my family history, stemming from my mother's decision to marry my father even though her parents didn't approve. We were never trendy in terms of doing what other families were doing or even being included amongst them; we were us, the six of us, plus Grandma Teresa and Uncle Sergio. We had our little nest—sometimes a positive space with nurturing, love, and acceptance, and sometimes a negative space filled with repression, compression, censorship, and shame. Such was the duality of my existence; sometimes, my home was one of comfort, and sometimes, it felt oppressive. As a result of this constant need to shapeshift, I never quite knew how to fit in.

... 7 ...

ONE DOT AT A TIME

THE 1990S ARRIVED. So did the wild in me, the personality of a molded creature emerged, secretly, in the sacredness of our sweet home. No one knew except Mom and me.

Around the world, many institutions were being dissolved and reinvented. The dissolution of the Soviet Union marked the end of Russia's status as a superpower, the end of a multipolar world, and the rise of anti-Western sentiment. China was still recovering from a politically and economically turbulent period. This allowed the United States to emerge as the world's sole superpower, creating relative peace and prosperity for many Western countries. During this decade, the world population grew from 5.3 to 6.1 billion people.

The decade was also a space for greater attention to multiculturalism. Generation X bonded over musical tastes and alternative music movements like Grunge, Reggaeton, Eurodance, and Hip-hop, all of which became popular, aided by the rise in satellite and cable television and the internet. The Human Genome Project was launched in 1990, while building the Large Hadron Collider commenced in 1998. The Nasdaq became the first US stock market to trade online. Network cultures were enhanced by the proliferation of new media and a new ability to self-publish web pages and make connections on professional, political, and hobby topics.

Meanwhile, in Brazil, our President resigned due to corruption, and the country was mired in economic uncertainty, facing crises such as the Mexican crisis and the Asian crisis. I mention all of this because I went through my discovery and also navigated a crisis or two.

As the world buzzed around me with challenges, innovations, and change, my inner world began to shift, too—subtly at first, then with growing momentum. The "Tininha" once targeted by high school bullies was now a more confident woman, standing at the edge of a new story—one that would no longer be written for her, but *by* her. The moments of her life, past pains, present realizations, and future hopes, were like scattered dots. And for the first time, she was beginning to trace the lines that connected them.

What she didn't yet fully grasp was that she held the pen. Still, she knew something wasn't right. Beneath her awakening was a heaviness, the weight of false beliefs about her worth, her image, and the limited choices she had made because of them. Emotionally and socially, she was still limping. But she had begun to draw.

Nevertheless, the signs of a hidden human were emerging. My college years were good ones. I began to remake myself during the span between February 1990 and December 1994.

FDC offered evening classes only, starting at 6:50 p.m. and ending at 10:30 p.m., with some courses on Saturday afternoons. Truth be told, the Saturday classes were a lot of fun. Who in the world was going to go to classes on a beautiful Saturday afternoon to hear lectures about criminology, finance, civil code, or the appeal process? I did. And most of the time, it was a spirited gathering full of learning, chatting, and meeting others.

Dad wasn't too happy with his little Tina going to school at night. The environment was predominantly male, and that angered Dad. But he had no choice except to accept it. Despite my newfound freedoms, he still managed to hold power over me. One of the ways was by finding me a job in a law firm owned by one of his friends. He didn't ask me if I wanted the job; he just proceeded.

Mom simply told me, "He has the final word on this, Tininha."

Complacently, I agreed—same old me, but different. Thus began the long journey of working eight hours a day as an intern and going to school at night. I took the bus to work in the mornings, and my brother Fernando gave me a ride home for lunch nearly every day. He and Fabio had been gifted cars from our Uncle Tets. I was never given a car, and I never asked why. But I worked hard to purchase my own car when I was older. Until I got my car, I relied on the bus, friends, or my brothers for rides.

At the same time, Dad became more involved with a farm he'd purchased. The dream of owning "big land" was born in 1982. Now that my brothers and I were all in college, with Fabiano following behind closely, Dad felt that he could leave us with Mom. It was yet another self-centered, impulsive decision on his part because he now made his kids responsible for Mom's needs and the house payments, so that he could enjoy his dream, three hundred miles away from Curitiba. And that's precisely what he did.

We Brazilians experience college differently from Americans. Now that I have two daughters preparing for college in the US, I can feel the vibrancy that comes with the process of applying and planning for college life here in the States. For many, attending college in the US provides an opportunity to detach from home, from parents, and old friends; it's a time to move away from the place you were born and live the full spectrum of studying, fun, joy, and adventure.

By contrast, in Brazil, due to a more family-focused, nurturing ideal, we stay together as long as possible. Growing up, I lived with six people in a 1,291-square-foot apartment for about twenty years. I shared a bathroom with my three brothers and a bedroom with my youngest brother. When I was in college, we all lived together in the same space, the four of us working as we studied. Dad was on the farm, building his dream of becoming a "rich farmer," while Mom was the loving one, taking care of her kids, who were all building their futures.

For about five years, life was about *becoming*. I aimed to leave behind all that had been challenging, instead focusing my efforts on the next chapter. *I hope life gets easier,* was my prayer to the Universe.

We sacrificed our time, money, and fun for the promise of graduating and moving toward our dream jobs. *Becoming.* I wasn't so sure I wanted to be an attorney, a judge, a prosecutor, or any other label that might exist for a law graduate. But I knew I was in the right place. I enjoyed the often challenging routine, and I began to feel more emancipated at home. Dad being at the farm, for the most part, helped a lot. It resulted in a lot more freedom with only one parent at home. It allowed me to meet potential boyfriends and go out (but still with my younger brother in the backseat).

Meanwhile, Mom and I blossomed in Dad's absence, sharing our feelings, secrets, and dreams. "Dad is away, yes! Let's party!" It was our freedom chant. We had all been incarcerated by Dad's unrelenting mindset.

Fittingly, the *wild* in me emerged whenever Dad was gone. I started to feel like somewhere inside me was another woman waiting to be revealed.

In high heels, makeup, suits with glasses, and my hair done, I spent long days at my legal internship; meetings, greetings, learning, and experiencing were how I discovered the real world. This was college for me. I was experiencing life outside of the cage.

On one summer day, I walked to the courts with one of the other interns. She was a little older than I was; she'd entered law school later in life. Her name was Sandra. Sandra enjoyed the responsibility of fulfilling an important role in the firm and, as such, was acting the part of my boss as we carried papers and documents to complete the day's tasks. We had taken the bus to the court; she was in jeans and shoes, and I was in a suit and high heels. She had no makeup, wore a white shirt, and had naturally curly hair. She carried a simple cross-body purse while I carried a brand-name purse that I'd purchased with my first paycheck.

As we walked to the building in a fast-paced rhythm, as was her signature, she said, "Come on, Tina; we need to get things done."

We marched forward with determination, and out of the blue, she asked me, "Why are you working at such a young age? You should be with your mom at the club, enjoying the swimming pool. You'll have plenty of time in the future to do this. I've almost graduated, but I spent a lot of my early college days simply enjoying life."

Her comments stunned me. I grew quiet, and in my heart, I could feel she had a point. It was 95° outside, my body was hurting, and my feet in those high heels were most uncomfortable. Yet there I was, disguised in my lawyer identity costume that I'd envisioned since the age of seventeen.

Why? I wondered.

I don't know, came the answer.

Unconsciously, I was probably trying to survive the lack of safety I felt at home. Even though Dad was gone, Mom needed help, my brothers were working, and I couldn't be the "queen" enjoying life. I had to work, too, I figured.

I knew I wanted something different for myself. I didn't yet know how I'd make it happen, but I remember feeling it deep inside, an instinct, a quiet certainty: *I can rise out of this heaviness.* I wouldn't have used those exact words back then, but the feeling had been with me for as long as I could remember.

I want to do something completely different with my life was a common thought pattern of mine, *different from what most of the other girls in school are inevitably going to do.*

I didn't want to be generating another domesticated Brazilian family unit, and I certainly didn't want to be a teacher. *That's not for me*, I knew.

"You know what, Sandra? I think you're right," I said. "I would love to be with Mom, enjoying the days of freedom. But I think I want more from this life, and I want to start it now." Though I could easily have said, "I am running away from a predator, so the earlier I start, the better." But I couldn't see my situation clearly, yet.

She didn't agree with me, and I think that, deep down, she was sad to see me dressed in a costume—so pretty, so fancy, and so unsure of my place in the world. Deep down, I yearned for the freedom

Sandra spoke of, but I knew I couldn't rest until I'd achieved something for myself. In my gorgeous, pinching stilts, I lifted my chin and clogged forward.

••• 8 •••

THE FIRST YES

THERE'S A WORLD *outside my window*, I thought as I entered the college experience, and doubly so when I graduated. The little girl who was once so insecure and ashamed was starting to experience life in different ways, allowing herself to make choices without having so much clarity of consequences ahead of time. Someone had always thought for her, made decisions on her behalf, and established her next steps, so much so that the little girl didn't know how to think for herself.

After so many years of being controlled, I found myself enjoying the perceived freedom of being reckless. It was a time of experimentation and discovering my edges for the first time, without my dad's physical corrections—that is to say, without my dad's influence, at least as often as before.

"Dad is going to the farm for ten days," Mom used to announce with a sense of joy.

With those words, my brothers and I knew it was time to live a few days without the fear of physical and mental abuse. In these moments, I often felt a sense of relief and a paradoxical feeling: *I feel happier and safer when my dad is not around.* Isn't it supposed to be the opposite? It certainly wasn't in my reality.

The First Yes

Using my freedom, I escaped. It was time, and I was feeling ready.

My first real taste of freedom, the kind that stirs from within and seeks connection, came through a boy named David. It began with energy and presence—the way he listened and the way his eyes met mine without hesitation. David was nearing the end of law school in Santa Catarina, a coastal state in southern Brazil. My oldest brother, Fabio, one of the twins, was dating Patricia, a ballerina who lived in Florianópolis, the island capital. David was part of Patricia's circle there.

She was thrilled at the idea of introducing us. "Tininha, you're going to love David," she said, beaming. "He's finishing law school, too, just like you. You already have so much in common; he loves the beach, he's bright, and honestly, he's incredibly charming."

At the time, I didn't realize how much I was craving something more than conversation. I was craving a connection that might offer me a different reflection of myself than the one I'd been taught to see.

By my twenties, a few "handsome and smart" boyfriends had already come and gone, each relationship bringing me a little closer to the edge of something I both craved and feared. We didn't go all the way, but the moments brimmed with tension and intimacy. There were kisses that lingered, hands that explored, heartbeats that quickened against mine. My body was learning its language, how it responded to warmth, to pressure, to closeness.

What I didn't yet have the words for, I could still feel: a building hunger, not just for sex, but for permission to want, to enjoy, and to know myself through another. The sensations were real, even the peaks of pleasure, though I didn't yet understand them fully. I only knew they made me feel more alive, more curious, and more certain that something within me was awakening.

At this age and time, sex was on my mind, but there was a barrier stopping me: At home, sex was a taboo topic, a "bad thing," a "not appropriate thing" that I was not allowed to talk about, think about, or experience. Dad had struck my mouth hard whenever he caught me singing songs about sex, which I did naturally, as did others of the same age. My daughters do the same today, and we talk about it, instead of blocking the conversation. But for me, such a taboo was part of a mystery that occurred behind the doors in our house. My brothers and I knew, silently aware, that when Dad closed and locked his bedroom door with Mom inside at night, it was time for them to have sex. Fabiano and I would whisper, "Did you hear that?"

Despite the censoring atmosphere around the topic of sex, I didn't feel any barriers anymore. I met David, and we liked each other. The fact that he lived far away attracted me even more, not only because it was interesting to recognize the "missing" feeling of living apart, but also because having private moments with him was possible, thanks to having my brother and Patricia as alibis. If I was with my brothers, I was safe, inaccessible to dad's restrictions or violence. It provided a perfect recipe for experimentation for the little girl who had always been so ashamed of her choices. Finally, with this opportunity, she could choose the guy, the time, and the place to discover one of the most beautiful, magical, and profound life experiences. Of course, I'm talking about sex, orgasms, and the intimacy that accompanies those activities.

I finally experienced it on a sunny Sunday afternoon, when Fabio and Pati were on a bike ride to the park. We had plenty of time to experience sex and each other. He was leaving town the next morning and would be going back to his life in Florianopolis. Our encounter didn't involve much conversation; it was clearly about our bodies, enabled by our common interests in law, philosophy, and the near future. Conversations were good. He was a very interesting young guy who had golden skin, green eyes, and blond hair. He was a little taller than me, had an incredible body shape, large shoulders and chest, big lips and smile, and smelled like a real man. My hormones were finally saying, "This is the one."

His hugs were enveloping, and I felt desired. He had an interesting life story: a young beach man, an only child, with parents much older than mine. He came late in their lives. He shared details about his lifestyle at the beach and with his parents, the freedom in the afternoons to surf, run, read, and party. It didn't take long after we first made love for me to see David more clearly—not just as the confident, sun-kissed man who lit up every room but as someone still swept up in the rhythm of beach parties, youth, and freedom. He wasn't unkind or careless, just not yet rooted, not ready to stay still. But none of that bothered me. Our realities were completely opposite. I lived in a prison, and he was on perma-vacation; I worked all day and attended school at night, with almost zero time for philosophy by the beach, while he didn't need to work. Simply attending school was good enough for his older parents, who wanted to provide the best, most comfortable life for the miraculous child who came late in their lives. The young man was their treasure. He was treated as a spoiled brat, albeit a charming spoiled brat. I don't know for certain, but I feel that charming, spoiled brats tend to look alike. None of those signs were a problem for me, though. I felt safe, and the moment finally arrived.

With the apartment windows completely open on a beautiful sunny afternoon, we started to kiss and moved to Pati's bedroom. *Weird*, I thought, *my brother and Patti probably have sex here, too.* The moment, however, was delicious. I was ready, and I let all my negative and preconceived thoughts evaporate in the heat of our passion. We continued to kiss, and suddenly, our clothes came off. I felt the body that I'd already felt with clothes on, but now completely naked, lips and tongues unable to be separated, as we nestled onto the bed and into the beautiful white sheets. I felt as though I was moved into the clouds, covered by peace, love, and joy. There was a little (okay, a lot) of blood, too, and it spilled onto the white sheets. I looked, and rather than feel ashamed, I saw its beauty. Looking at David, and my privates soaked in blood, I felt that I was becoming a woman that day, still observing the red stain as it touched the softness of the sheets. I felt my orgasms starting to run all throughout my body, and we continued enjoying the experience. He didn't know it was my first time, and I wasn't brave enough to share it with him. I let the flow take me to the most incredible sensations, the first orgasm arriving when he was deep inside me. There was an explosion of oxytocin and dopamine. My whole body shook, my legs were numb for a minute, and I felt incredibly alive. In the throes of such an intimate moment, Dad flashed through my mind. *Darn it!* But how could he not? For all those years, he'd been so protective, to the point that I knew practically nothing about sex. Fortunately, I was able to let go of the image while David was on top of me, continuing with the intention of giving me more orgasms as he whispered in my ear, "*Goza mais, Tininha.*" For a second, I saw Dad's image in my head as I experienced my next orgasm, and silently, I told him, "This is not a bad thing, Dad."

❧❧❧

Helena shifted beside me, hugging her knees to her chest.
"So, that was your first time?" she asked.
I nodded slowly. "Yes, it was."
Sophia looked at me with wide eyes. "You didn't tell him?"
"No," I said, my voice soft. "I didn't know how. I think I was afraid that naming it would make it too fragile. I needed to keep that moment for myself, something that belonged to me for once."
"But weren't you scared?" Helena asked.
"A little," I admitted, "but more than anything, I felt ready. For so long, I'd been watched, judged—especially when it came to my body. That moment felt like the first time I truly lived inside my skin, that it wasn't wrong, and that *I* wasn't wrong."
Sophia hesitated. "And you thought of your dad during it?"
I let out a slow breath. "I did—just for a second. His voice had been in my head for so long; it was almost automatic. Even beauty came with shadows back then. That's what I now call clinging syndrome. I held onto old ideas of who I was supposed to be, even when they didn't serve me, even when they hurt."
I looked at them both.
"But that day marked the beginning of my release, a shift. I told myself that if I ever had daughters, I'd help them grow up with less fear in their bodies, less shame, and more freedom to choose, to feel, and to ask questions."
Helena leaned into my side.

"You're doing that, Mom," she said softly.

"That's all I ever wanted: that you both get to live fully, bravely, and free."

Sophia then eyed me mischievously. "So, you're saying we can have sex anytime, then?"

Helena's eyes popped open in shock.

"Girls, you know that's not what I mean! The time and the situation have to *feel* right…"

"We know, Mom. Just teasing."

My relationship with David lasted about three months. I visited him in Florianópolis with Fabio and Pati, and during that trip, I saw a different side of him—the soft, playful, untethered side. He lived with his family in a charming cottage facing the Atlantic Ocean. His mother, a warm-hearted German woman, loved to cook for him, and his father, a college professor, had inspired David's love of law, philosophy, books, and history. Their home was filled with conversation and quiet encouragement, so unlike the rigid, rule-bound atmosphere I came from.

As I stepped into their world, I couldn't help but compare it to mine. And in that comparison, I shrank. Shame rose to the surface, and the little girl trapped in my mind, the one who had learned to stay small, quiet, and good, burst forth with full force. *I wish I lived here. I wish I had this life. I feel miserable,* the thoughts echoed.

David's free spirit clashed with the confinement I still carried inside me. My negative self-image distorted everything. I couldn't relax or let myself simply enjoy being with him. Instead of appreciating what we had, I spiraled, projecting my insecurities, shame, and fear onto him. The emotional distance between us only deepened as we lived in different cities, and what began as attraction slowly warped into something else—not rejection of him, exactly, but of myself. I was writing a painful story in my mind, one where I wasn't enough, where I couldn't belong, and where love was something that I wasn't quite ready to receive.

On one occasion, David was driving us around the city, and he made a funny comment about my sunglasses, which I didn't take graciously. I felt diminished by his comments about the style I was wearing, something that could be taken as a normal comment from a young beach man toward a young city woman. However, because of my domestication, I interpreted his words as a rejection of my style. From that lone instance, I created a negative view of David, which would signify to my unsafe mind that he was dangerous and not right for me. After all, we had opposite lifestyles: freedom versus incarceration, laid back parents with a positive communication style versus mine, who lacked in dialogue and created a sense of tension at all times.

All of it led to the creation of a story that I would tell myself: *I don't belong to him, to what he has and who he is. I am the problem, not him. But which problem?* I wondered. I wasn't quite sure, but that moment marked a significant turning point in my life, when I started creating stories in my mind about not deserving someone who loved me unconditionally. It wouldn't be long until I'd see how far down a dangerous path that type of thinking would lead me.

Soon after, we broke up, and I never saw David again. Pati and Fabio ended their relationship as a couple as well, even after being engaged for a year. She was an artist, and her love was ballet, dance, and her relationships with dancers. Fabio was a businessman who wanted to build a career with a woman who wanted to be married, become a mother, and be by his side.

However, that Sunday afternoon, with David and the white sheets covered in blood, I felt an exuberant sensation that stayed in my heart forever. With my first sexual experience under my belt, it was time for more. I was a young attorney—hot, sexy, fun, and full of traumas, with a prominent career, a high-paying, desirable job, and gaining visibility in the world of law. Nothing could contain me anymore, I figured. I felt my wild nature flourishing, and I was ready to write a new chapter in my life. A season of hunting was born:

Instead of chasing my dad's expectations and being incarcerated, I felt like it was time to break the cage and go wild. *There has to be something out there*, I thought, *that will save me and deliver me to my destiny.*

So, I jumped to higher experiences. The adrenaline felt good. I wanted more.

••• 9 •••
THE HOUSE ON RUA XV

BY 1993, FOUR years into law school and having experienced different opportunities working as an intern, I managed to create a modicum of distance from Dad's direct influence. He spent more time at the farm, and I was making my journey a meaningful one. It was now time to find a permanent job.

There was a firm in town named Garcia Pereira Advogados Associados. In my mind, this was the premier place to work. They were all refined professionals, respected by the legal community, and I had heard incredible things about their work environment. I kept my eyes and ears open for an opportunity to apply, but there was always a steady stream of candidates vying for the same positions at the esteemed firm. Once again, I felt substandard and left out, unable or incapable of being seen or valued. As a result, I never asked for an application, but the dream remained in my head.

Meanwhile, opportunities were popping up here and there, and I was applying for those that I felt were good fits for me. During my four years of articling, I had experienced four different firms, jobs, and groups of people. None were really right for me, but they were what was available at the time.

One of my classmates in law school was already working at Garcia Pereira. His name was Andre Goncalves, but everyone called him Andi. His father was one of the firm's main partners, and Andi carried himself like a full-fledged attorney long before we even graduated. Always impeccably dressed from head to toe, he had a way of being in the right place at the right time with the right people. And as the years went on, he only grew into that image, becoming highly successful and building a strong reputation and fortune through his talents.

One day, we met by accident at Rua XV de Novembro, the main tourist street in downtown Curitiba. We were both walking, and there we were.

"Oi, Andi!" I said.

"Hey, Maria!" He always called me Maria. "How are things with you?"

I explained to him that I was doing well, but I was just trying to find the right place to work. I was in the middle of transitioning jobs, having been offered to work for one of my then professors in civil law, which could be a good step forward as the end of my college life approached. I mentioned that it could potentially lead to an opportunity to become an associate.

Andi listened to me intently, looking directly into my eyes. When I'd finished recounting my prospects, he smiled from the corner of his mouth, his signature, and slowly said, "Maria, I have an offer for you. There is an open spot at Dad's firm right now. You should come and apply. Try it, come on. Let's work together. I know you'll get the job."

"Andi, *serio*? My dream job opportunity!"

"Yes," he replied enthusiastically. "Call tomorrow and ask for Dr. Rubens. He's the one conducting the interviews, and I'll talk with him. Just do it. I want you with us."

I called the next day and scheduled the interview.

And I got the job. It was November of 1993.

That moment on Rua XV de Novembro changed everything. It's incredible how a single instant can shift the course of an entire life. The next eleven years were, in many ways, magical. I made lifelong friends, people I still consider part of my inner circle, and I discovered a powerful gift: my ability to defend and protect others. Just two years in, when Andi's father was nominated to the bench and his position at the firm opened, I was offered the chance to lead the family law department. I accepted without hesitation. It became more than a job. It was a calling.

On paper, those years looked golden—a steady climb, a woman coming into her own. However, deep beneath the success, the old programming ran wild and unchecked. The roots planted by my father's influence hadn't been unearthed, only covered. Before long, I would make choices, subtle at first, then seismic, that would threaten everything I had worked so hard to build.

···10···

THE POWER SUIT

IT'S ALWAYS POSSIBLE to find light in the darkness, though sometimes that light looks nothing like what we expected. Darkness can be obscure, enigmatic, even seductive in its ambiguity. But then, all at once, it can split open into something startlingly clear.

"Deixe a vida viver como é para ser vivida," my astrologer Hilário once told me. (Let life live as it's meant to be lived.) A poetic version of "Let it Be," as The Beatles sang. That phrase would come to define the next chapter of my life, a journey from shadow to understanding, from illusion to clarity.

Motherhood was never a dream I carried as a girl. Neither was marriage. Not even in the private, imagined stories that so many children act out in their heads. Instead, my early life was shaped by a fixation on how I looked and on being pleasing to the eye. Somewhere along the way, I bought into the lie that beauty would open doors for me, or at the very least, help me avoid being noticed in ways that felt dangerous. I didn't yet realize that beauty could be its own form of captivity.

By my early twenties, newly minted as a lawyer, I had begun to weaponize that beauty. I understood its currency. I learned how to leverage my appearance, the shape of my body, the softness of my voice, and the arch of my eyebrow as a tool to gain influence. It became part of the unspoken strategy: deepen connections with judges, sway prosecutors, smooth the edges of systems built to resist women like me. Every morning became a calculation. *Which suit will catch Judge A's attention today? What color will disarm just enough to make space for persuasion?*

It was power, but it came at a cost. And soon, I'd have to reckon with the line between using what I had and losing who I was.

As the years passed, I began to harness the courtroom not just as a space for legal argument but as a stage, one where beauty, irreverence, power, and a touch of rebellion could all be part of the performance. I approached each case like a game, constantly reading the room, evaluating who was winning and who was losing.

Gradually, my style began to reflect this shift. The reserved, formally suited Christina gave way to someone bolder. *I'm going to start wearing tight blue jeans, high heels, and tops that show a little more skin,* I told myself. It was more than a fashion statement; it was a declaration of identity.

The effect was immediate. I created a ripple in the otherwise conservative culture of the law firm. Whispers turned into nicknames. Soon, I was being called "Dr. Spicy," or *Dr. Pimenta*, a nod to both my fiery appearance and the unapologetic presence I brought into every room. In Brazil, attorneys carry the title of "doctor," but I had taken it somewhere entirely new. The timid girl at the window had transformed into a woman who owned the spotlight.

Although I was achieving so much professionally, I was still struggling to find the timbre of my voice. As I grappled with the power I had at work, I was impatient and sometimes exercised poor judgment. I'd come a long way, but I'd not yet stepped into my true divine feminine power, one that is equal parts strength and grace.

It was early morning in the summertime, another hot and sunny day in Curitiba. Mom liked to keep the windows in the apartment open to receive the sunlight and the fresh breeze of the early morning. She had just come back from her walk. Dad was in town that week and had left to play tennis at the club. When away from the farm work, his favorite place to be was at the tennis court. Mom would meet him at Clube Curitibano, the country club where my parents were so proud to have been members. They joined in 1972, the year I was born, and always told us that it was a great place to raise kids and have a social life.

I stepped out of the shower, vibrant and awake, as the sparkling morning light poured in through the wide-open windows and the fresh air kissed my skin. *Today, a white linen suit will be perfect.*

I took a quick look in the mirror in the hallway between the bathroom that I shared with my three brothers and the bedroom I shared with Fabiano, and then went straight to my closet. The right side was mine; the left was his. We loved living and sharing the space.

I opened the closet door and placed my hands into the suit section. I also loved to keep my clothing organized by colors and style (something I still do). Looking toward the off-white and then the white ones, I couldn't locate my white linen suit. I kept rapidly moving right and left, going through all the hangers to be sure I wasn't missing the white one. This type of frenetic pace was a speed I'd become accustomed to since joining the law firm. For a second, I panicked, visualizing myself not wearing what I'd planned on wearing that crisp summer morning.

Why in the world are my clothes not ready in the closet? I thought. *What does she do all day that what I need the most is not here for me?*

"Mom! Mom!" I raised my voice as I ran toward the kitchen, where Mom was preparing our light breakfast and already organizing lunch. I still had my shower towel around me, and my hair was all messy and wet. "I am going to be late today, Mom, and I can't find my white linen suit!"

Noticing my agony, she replied gently, "You and your brothers are everything to me. It still has to be ironed, *Tininha*. I'll do it quickly for you." Ironing everything from clothes to bed sheets to underwear is a cultural norm in Brazil.

"No, Mom, no. I can't wait one more minute. I have to choose another one, or I will be late to the office today. We have a meeting this morning, and I must be early to prepare for it."

I marched back to my room, feeling very disappointed with Mom, as her services were failing to meet my busy schedule. Completely blind to my selfish way of being, I got another suit, which completely changed my mood for the day. It was a black suit for the dead of summer, which reflected the darkness that was building inside my body. With the new choice of clothing, I took off from the house and made my way to the bus station.

I deliberately held back on a kiss and a hug for Mom. I was mad. Later that day, after a long list of meetings, phone calls, and visits to the court, I came home exhausted. My white linen suit was waiting for me, finely ironed on top of my bed, with a note from Mom: *Forgive me for making your day hard this morning. Here is your favorite clothing, ironed with all my love this morning. Eu te amo filha, Mamãe.*

Her note broke my heart, and I went to the family room where she was watching her favorite soap opera while eating oranges with Dad. "Are you ready for your dinner?" she asked me.

I was starving, and I replied, "Yes, Mom," but not before hugging her to show her my gratitude and offer her my forgiveness.

The hunt for control and the need to have things ready for me were small examples of how my wiring was faulty. I was living a life of impatience, high demand, and acceleration. Doing, being, and feeling fast was the tone, all for the glory of getting somewhere. *Where?* I didn't know, but I continued my pursuit of power and recognition.

ACT II
THE LINES

Cada escolha, por menor que seja, é uma forma de semente que lançamos sobre o canteiro que somos. Um dia, tudo que agora silenciosamente plantamos, ou deixamos plantar em nós, será uma plantação que poderá ser vista de longe...
Padre Fabio de Melo

• • • 1 • • •

SKIRTING THE REAL ISSUES

IT'S HIGHLY PROBABLE that the years spent in a house watching my dad attempt to improve his professional status made an imprint on me. It's also likely that our family routine of squeezing time, making plans, and having busy schedules set the tone for my future life. I guess you might say that I was programmed that way.

After two years of long days and late nights as an intern at Garcia Pereira, I was offered a position to lead the family law department inside the prestigious law firm. My sense of achievement erupted; I felt I was in the right place with the right people at the right time. A feeling of success and satisfaction, joy and cheerfulness, fulfillment and contentment filled my soul.

What could possibly go wrong? I may have asked myself.

It wouldn't be long until the answer to that question revealed itself. I had no idea at the time that I was about to enter a different prison than the one I'd endured with Dad. This time, however, there would be different oppressors.

Every morning, I continued to dress up to go to war. I entered the realm of disputes, litigation, and accusations. Minors, money, and couples. Hate, disputes, and sadness. It was all about who won and who lost. But I was engaged in it, able to separate myself and my battle stories from the ones that were in front of me—the ones who were counting on, trusting, and paying me to win their arguments.

My routine was based on setting up to win. Like a knight who goes into battle, the first line of defense was my armor. Mine consisted of high heels, well-pressed linen suits (courtesy of Mom), and a leather suitcase. My hair was always tinted, and I wore shiny makeup. Before leaving for the battlefield, I always conducted one last check in the mirror before I power-walked my way to the bus station. Though I didn't have a car in which to place all the beauty I was feeling, I didn't allow it to be an obstacle. I just lived the way I was supposed to, or so I thought. Just like when I used to look out the window from my bedroom, I knew there was something out there for me. But I'd have to go through the challenges first. These were my thoughts.

Subconsciously, I was trying to bolster my fragile confidence through my appearance. In fact, I used my appearance to help make me feel strong and capable. I became known as the "Christmas Tree Attorney" by the court clerks, many of them young men, who looked at me as a piece of entertainment, seeing so much glitter from head to toe. Sometimes, people would jokingly say, "Tina, it looks like you just got out of the oven," because my skin was so tanned.

Needless to say, my presence became notable, and I liked the way it felt. I was, at least, unforgettable. I thought that was an advantage.

Leading the family law department at Garcia Pereira Advogados Associados, the top-ranked firm registered with the Paraná Bar Association (Ordem dos Advogados do Brasil), placed me in an enviable and prestigious position. What made it even more distinct was that I was the only woman among a team of seven attorneys. My name appeared last on the official roster, just beneath six men, headed by the firm's founder, Gilberto Garcez, who, remarkably, still practices law today at ninety-two years old. Andi, my former classmate who had first offered me the internship, and I were the youngest on the team, both fresh graduates. Together, our names rounded out a highly respected and tightly knit circle of legal professionals.

"Today, the new plaque will be placed at the entrance of the firm," Gilberto announced that morning. "I would like to invite all of you to the ceremony to unveil the piece."

At five o'clock that afternoon, we were all called to the front entrance as he unveiled the plaque from beneath a white cloth. Immediately, I saw my name in bright gold letters—*Maria Christina de Almeida*—below six reputable and respectable attorneys.

My time is arriving. I will make history. The little high schooler who was once ashamed and bullied is here, representing a powerful organization. Those were the words I told myself quietly as I looked incessantly at the gold letters pressed into the brown wood plaque located on the white walled entrance. Once again, my name was featured prominently on a white wall. The irony of the situation doesn't escape me.

Hunting was my pace. "Doctor Pimentinha is on a mission," my senior partner and boss, Gilberto, would joke as he watched me dart through the firm's hallways in high heels, papers clutched in hand, always prepared for a court hearing or ready to greet a new client.

I was constantly in motion—chasing time, chasing goals, chasing the thrill of opportunity. That was the rhythm of that decade: fast, focused, relentless. I had grown accustomed to operating under pressure, especially from something deceptively beautiful called time, a force I now see with entirely different eyes. Back then, I believed that pressure would lead to reward; if I pushed hard enough, someone would eventually recognize my worth. I was hunting for validation, hoping to be seen and acknowledged. Deep down, I thought I deserved a trophy just for surviving the grind.

Ironically, free of my dad the jailor, the years in law only served to deepen the impressions caused by traumas and feelings of inferiority, shame, and fear. I couldn't have known, but those negative feelings had implanted themselves during my teenage years. I had created an armor, insulating myself from having to deal with the pain of my childhood. The armor consisted mainly of my appearance, which I felt would create a buffer between the image of respectability and professionalism that I was attempting to cultivate and the insecurity I felt beneath my physical appearance.

••• 2 •••

DOCTOR PIMENTINHA ON A MISSION

THE CHASE STARTED in earnest in 1995. If it was not in court, it was in the classroom where I was teaching law.

Just after my college graduation in December of 1994, I heard rumors in the legal community that having a master's degree would take me to higher levels as an attorney, and it could open doors to other job opportunities. As a result, I engaged in a master's program in civil law in January 1995 at the Universidade Federal do Paraná (UFPR), with no breaks between my first degree and this next master's degree. I continued the chase and engaged in a nonstop rhythm of accomplishments, eventually earning a doctorate in civil law. That part of the journey lasted from 1994 until 2002. In effect, I added seven years to my sentence, the trauma accumulating somewhere in my unconscious mind. It must have been so ingrained that I dreamt, a few times, that I was unable to conclude my doctoral thesis and had woken up questioning whether I actually had the title in real life. That's trauma!

Working eight to ten hours a day to produce numbers and results for the law firm was not a normal routine for a woman in her early twenties. But I did it, realizing that not every woman my age was given the same opportunity; some were traveling after college graduation, and some were still wondering what to do with their graduation certificates. However, I was sure about what I wanted: my freedom, my independence, and financial success. I felt I was doing the right thing at the right time with the right people, and I also felt lucky whenever I looked around and saw that my college mates weren't as far along as I was.

This was when the prison cell began to reveal itself.

Every first Friday of the month, there was a meeting in the library at the law firm—attorneys only. Andi was the one responsible for handling the meeting as the anointed young, new, fresh spirit who had a brilliant mind for numbers and strategies. The older partners had years of experience, but seeing a young man introduce new ideas and approaches was a source of relief for the partners. "Just bring the results to us, Andi," was a sentiment that was often echoed at these Friday meetings. It was customary for Andi to go over all current and recent cases, evaluating clients, win-loss results, and, of course, analyzing the monthly numbers.

Each attorney had a different track record. Some of them demonstrated a solid progression in their work, while others stagnated. No words were ever said about the differences, but I could feel a certain hostility in the air. Being the only woman in the room, the testosterone was always flowing and filled every crevice of the library. It seemed to be a competition of who wielded the most power. It was an indoctrination into the deeply competitive landscape of corporate life.

I soon recognized my responsibility to be a winner and to contribute economically to the firm—an absolute must if I was to maintain my position and image of a powerful attorney. I was learning how to be a man in a woman's body.

Production became my mantra, and the first oppressor was numbers. *When will I be able to hit six-digit revenue?* I asked myself every time Beto shared each department's monthly contribution.

"Family law continues to lag behind all the departments from a revenue perspective, but Tina's doing a great job," was something I'd hear often in those meetings. The support was there, but the solemn nods of condolence from the senior partners permeated the library air. *It might be because I'm a woman*, I thought—a legacy of rejection and shame deeply planted in my psyche.

However, I had something else that money couldn't buy: I had my appearance, and I recognized that it could be used to bring results in different ways—namely, as a source of power and influence. As I began to grasp the intricacies of the legal system and court programs, I increased my focus on self-promotion. I met with judges, prosecutors, and the people who wielded the most power, always playing the role of the mascot of our firm. My plan worked, and I became the attorney who opened gates, doors, and access to the courts when our cases needed a little finessing. *This is the way the system operates* is how I justified dinners, lunches, and meetings with judges, all of which became an important part of my contribution to the firm. As I worked to build the numbers for my department, I fought to prove my worth during our Friday meetings, insisting that my connections held real value.

Yet, despite my efforts, I faced a significant setback when I lost a crucial case for a client. Even so, one of the presiding judges took notice, not for the verdict, but for the integrity and dedication I brought to the courtroom.

The story revolves around a particularly challenging hearing. On the occasion, I walked to the courts with purpose, dressed in blue jeans with a fashionably torn patch on the right leg, a black belt cinched at the waist, shiny black heels clicking against the pavement, and a silk pink-and-gray polka dot top that revealed just enough of my sun-kissed skin. My black leather briefcase swung at my side, a blend of rebellion and professionalism. Once inside, I headed straight to the attorneys' lounge to grab the standard-issue black tunic required for courtroom appearances.

I met my client in the hearing room, a man in his sixties, retired from a logistics company he'd built himself. He was divorced from his third wife, and the case for which I was defending him was about the money his wife requested him to pay as alimony. He had already tried his luck, but his previous attorneys had failed to save him from owing her a substantial amount. I came to the picture on fire. Perhaps it was because his last name was prominent in my hometown; his Italian family had made a fortune and garnered much fame in business and politics.

"Alfredo, we must win today. I have all the arguments ready to defend you from having to pay such an exorbitant amount for the rest of your life," I said before heading into the court together. I felt a personal connection to his case; the woman was much younger than he was, and it was clear she intended to live off his fortune indefinitely. I was indignant at the situation, and under my skin, I was furious, craving justice.

As we stepped into the hearing room, I had my black tunic open at the front, and I walked in feeling ten feet tall. (I am five feet tall, in reality.) I looked around the room to perceive the energy, and as Alfredo and I sat down, we waited for the session to begin.

The court was overseen by five judges, all of whom were men. *They will all vote in my favor,* I believed, *whether they support my arguments or not.* The woman's attorney, by contrast, was an old man in a dark suit with gray hair and a large belly—traditional, predictable. *No match for my powerful presence and well-prepared case,* I thought.

The arguments began. I stood up at the pulpit designed exclusively for attorneys, and I started my presentation, absolutely convinced of my arguments and Alfredo's rights. The other attorney did his part, and the judges came to a decision: three for her, two for Alfredo. To my surprise, the alimony was upheld.

I felt humiliated in front of my client. I'd told him, insisted, that his situation was a case of pure injustice. However, justice didn't see it the same way I had.

I lost that day, or so I believed.

Yet, as I walked out of the hearing court after some time spent with Alfredo discussing our next plan, one of the judges came out of the room and approached me.

He held my arm strongly.

"Doutora Maria Christina," he pulled me close to him as he spoke, "I voted against your client today. A difficult situation you have on your hands to defend, but his ex-wife has reached a certain age that makes it difficult for her to find an occupation to support her livelihood; plus, her delicate health presents to us as part of her needs."

I looked into his eyes, still angry and disappointed with the unjust way of keeping a man linked to a woman financially, and I said: "Judge Oliveira, I still believe in his rights. I will appeal."

He continued: "You must. But what I really want to tell you is that if I ever get divorced from my wife, I will hire you to defend me. You are impeccable in all senses."

And just like that, he released my arm that he'd been gripping the whole time and left.

Was it my beauty, my fashion, or my intelligence—or perhaps my voice and my personality—that made such an impression on the judge? To this day, I don't know. But I know that my presence was there in the room that day, and it was an inkling that I was something more than my clothes, my looks, and my fashion. I felt I was becoming a woman of substance.

Yet despite the momentary realization of confidence during that episode, I was unaware that all the emphasis I placed on looks was just the manifestation of my insecurity. The bulk of my confidence, at that time, stemmed from an ego being built out of accessories, representations, and external validation. This is what formulated the foundation of my identity. I learned to be that way, which was influenced by my impression of how a woman acts and functions. In reality, all of it was my armor, my protection against the prison that surrounded me at home and inside my head. An identity that triggered behaviors for the next few decades, from my teens to my thirties, and perhaps into my forties.

I can remember that transition happening during my teen years, when the sparkle of my little girl spirit began to dissipate. Insecurities that never existed started to show up; comparison became the lens through which I measured my worth, and fear and courage were constantly at war with one another. My early internal sweetness was lost at the beach, at school, at the club pool, and in Sunday masses, places where I once created friendships and felt happy. In those happy places, life had been lived with no expectations, no worries about the next day or the previous day's sorrows. In those days, life was about experiencing the present moment and living life as it was. Now, I was different. My choices were based upon a subconscious lesson from my Dad: that power was worth having. And I was using every ounce of my 110-pound frame to wield it.

"Mom?" Sophia broke the silence gently, her head resting on my shoulder.

"Yes, *filha*?"

"Was there ever a time when you really felt like… you?"

I looked over at her, then to Helena, who was tracing invisible lines on the fabric of the couch. The question landed like a soft thud in my chest. I exhaled.

"There were moments," I said, "flashes. But for a long time, I wasn't sure who I was without the performance—without the heels, the suits, the validation."

"You mean, like, you were pretending?" Helena asked.

"Not pretending, exactly. I was surviving. I clung to an identity that looked strong from the outside but was built on fear. I thought if I could just control how the world saw me, if I was beautiful enough, accomplished enough, charming enough, then maybe I'd be safe."

Sophia looked up at me. "Safe from what?"

"From feeling small," I said, "from being overlooked. I didn't know how to name them. Dad taught me that power mattered more than softness, more than joy. So, I sharpened myself to match the world I thought I had to survive in."

Helena's voice was quiet. "That's what you mean by clinging syndrome, isn't it?"

I nodded. "Exactly. I clung to the version of me that looked invincible, even when I was hurting inside. And when you hold on too tightly to a false identity, it becomes a cage."

"Do you think we do that, too?" Sophia asked.

"We all do, sometimes," I said. "But the difference is, now I see it. And I'll help you notice it, too, when you're shrinking or performing or forgetting who you are. You don't have to armor up to be loved."

Helena leaned against me. "You teach us how to be brave without pretending."

I smiled, pressing a kiss to her forehead. "And you remind me how to be soft without breaking."

Having access to power can mean different things in different countries. In Brazil, gaining access to those who decide cases can represent visibility for the firm. It can also speed up processes since the Brazilian system is notoriously plagued by inefficiency and procrastination. Access to power can also be the difference between a favorable decision and an unfavorable one, especially when corruption is a factor. Judges or prosecutors could make a decision based on money or influence at their discretion. I learned the game quickly and played it silently and subtly, growing my reputation as someone who was deeply connected to the highest levels of power. I leveraged my charisma to present rock-solid cases and utilized my charm to expedite the evaluation and advancement of these cases, moving them forward at a pace that was significantly faster than the traditionally slow Brazilian legal system.

It was a game I enjoyed playing, but I had no idea it was concealing the insecure young woman who was playing with power and importance in a male-dominated landscape. Had I thought deeply about it, I might have recognized similarities between my new manipulation tactics and those that were used against me as a child in my home.

••• 3 •••
FASANO'S SMILE

LACKING CONSCIOUSNESS ABOUT my real identity, I became a self-manufactured persona with the appearance of efficiency and effectiveness. However, my soul was hidden, buried somewhere. And because of this duality, my chase became a hunt, and the stakes kept getting higher. Each choice was more dangerous and riskier than the last one. At times, the feeling was numbing, a vague feeling that everything happening was being controlled by someone other than the real me.

It all started when I met a guy at the country club in Curitiba during the summer of 1995.

I'd graduated from college and had a wicked "What's next?" attitude. I had a feeling that I'd accomplished something monumental, looking back at the prison I used to inhabit. I felt that the law degree was my trophy, a symbol of my victory over domestication. I was educated by the years in law school, which honored my desires, intentions, and purposes. This was the opposite of having honored my Dad's purposes for nearly twenty years.

The guy at the club was named Fasano. He was ten years older than I, a well-known and respected doctor in my hometown. Single at the age of thirty-two, with an established career in Curitiba,

Fasano was hanging out at the pool club that Sunday afternoon on his own. I was there with Mom and her girlfriends—*a turma da piscina*, they were called. They were a group of twelve women who occupied the same seats at the same spot, on the corner of the main pool, for over thirty years. Twelve chairs were aligned by the first staff member to arrive at the club, and no one, absolutely no other member, could ever touch those spots. Mom was the queen of that group, and I loved to see her leading those special women during the sunny days as they drank beers, ate pastries, talked about their marriages, their husbands, fashion, kids, and their respective plans for the future. They were all household women who were created to be wives, moms, and grandmothers. They had the appearance of being happy with their realities as they fulfilled their purpose.

Fasano looked handsome—sunglasses on, great body shape, and alone. I loved it. I was attracted to men who enjoyed spending time alone. I noticed him, and he noticed me. I could feel it. He didn't waste any time and decided to approach me as I went to the water. After a short introduction, it became clear that we were both single, attractive, and possibly looking for a date.

He invited me to go out for dinner. But Dad was home that weekend, so the first thing that jumped into my mind was, *Fuck, he has to meet Dad for me to be able to go out with him.* But he'd met Mom at the pool after we'd talked for a while. And since Mom had met him, I felt I had a partner to help me ease any doubts Dad may have had. *Dad will allow me to go out with Fasano,* I figured. *Mom will vouch for me and say that I'm safe.* All these thoughts were racing through my mind. It was the trauma pattern asking, "What do I say? How do I behave? Where can I hide?" All of this sprang forth out of my memory of past experiences with Dad stalking me as a teenager.

At 6:30 p.m., Fasano rang the bell at my parents' apartment. I felt excited. Mom shared with Dad all the details of meeting the young doctor at the pool. She relayed that he was ten years older than I, single, and interested in knowing their daughter. The picture was perfect.

"What a great candidate for Maria Christina," Mom said. It's even possible that they imagined him to be my future husband. For once, we all had something in common: We were all interested. I was, of course, most interested in his personality, his appearance, and our potential future. *Why not allow the date to happen?* my parents must have wondered.

I opened the door, and there he was—Fasano—grinning like he'd just won a carnival contest, dressed as if he were still in the parade. His hair was slicked back, still wet, and his nose—how had I missed it before? It was the size of a small car. His appearance gave me a jolt: an aggressively bright shirt, loud shorts, and sandals that flapped with every step, not exactly the look that would stop me in my tracks, unless I was trying to cross the street. Had I met him under normal circumstances, say, in the hotel elevator, I probably would've looked away. But since our first encounter involved him strutting around in a Speedo, I chalked up his style to eccentric flair.

My family felt the same. My brothers emerged one by one, like judges at a talent show. My dad gave him a once-over. Mom said hello again, trying to be polite. In our house, any guy taking me out had to pass through a gauntlet: greet Dad, acknowledge Mom, survive the brothers, and only then were we allowed to leave. Oh, and my youngest brother often had to tag along, for "safety," according to Dad. That was his unwritten code for dating his daughter: full exposure to the family and a built-in chaperone. Fortunately, the chaperone wasn't required this time.

After meeting the family upstairs, permission was given. I was free to go out for a few hours, but Fasano had to bring me back by ten o'clock, all the way upstairs.

He suggested a popular Tex-Mex restaurant near my house. We lived on the same street: I was in a high-rise, and he was still living with his parents in a house a few blocks down. Driving a sports car, he drove us to the restaurant where he'd made reservations. As a twenty-two-year-old recent college graduate, this date with an older man intrigued me in the sense that marriage might be an option, and it could be an innovative way to break out of prison. That was a lightning thought that crossed my mind as I visualized myself in the new situation. As we engaged in conversation, getting to know each other, a side of me that I hadn't explored started to emerge: *I wonder what it would be like to have an established man as a boyfriend. Maybe it's time to settle—and escape.*

As the conversation shifted effortlessly between personal details and colloquial talk, Fasano asked me if I enjoyed drugs. Not hesitating for a second, I said, "No, I don't do drugs."

"I like drugs. You should try them," he responded. The bell didn't ring. I didn't even see a red light. He seemed to be too nice and settled to pose any danger to me. His appearance, status, and age created an ideal for me, on which I stayed transfixed. Consequently, he won my trust. About two months later, after he had Dad's approval and I'd met his delightfully big family, lots of siblings, nieces, and nephews, I tried cocaine.

Helena's eyes widened. "Wait—what? Cocaine?"

Sophia sat up straighter on the couch. "With your *dad's* approval?"

I nodded slowly, the memory like a bitter aftertaste. "Not the drug, of course, but he approved the man. Fasano came off as respectable, charming, even safe."

"But he *wasn't*," Helena said, incredulous.

"No," I admitted. "But when you're craving approval, when you're still clinging to the idea that someone older and more established can protect you, you ignore the signs—even the flashing ones."

Sophia exhaled. "That's so scary."

"It was," I said. "But sometimes it takes getting lost to realize how far you've strayed from yourself."

••• 4 •••

COCAINE AND COMPROMISE

IT WAS A Friday night, and we were at an upscale wedding reception. A girl from college was getting married, and it was a night when all my graduated friends would see me with Fasano, officially my boyfriend. I was dressed up in a tight, shiny green dress, and he was the charming doctor standing next to me.

It was an amazing and extravagant wedding that tickled my dreams of having one too, though that would be impossible on my dad's budget. The girl was getting married to a local millionaire. She was one hour and thirty minutes late for the church ceremony, a sign in Brazil of extreme elegance, but in most places on Earth, a display of pure disrespect and insult. But not at Igreja Santa Teresinha in Curitiba, where the rich and famous would marry, always arriving fashionably late.

As the guests all waited for the couple to arrive, we enjoyed seeing and being seen—me, especially. Finally, the bride and the groom arrived, and a luxury reception ensued at the Clube Curitibano, the local country club for the privileged. I enjoyed the party with my former college friends, and everyone enjoyed meeting Fasano; they all seemed happy and excited for me. The idea of dating a man of his stature and being able to show off to my community of colleagues made me feel important. The once ashamed and fearful girl had finally arrived. I felt I deserved recognition.

As I fantasized about the idea, Fasano asked me to leave the party. Up until then, we hadn't had sex. I felt his words were an invitation, and I felt ready. David's experience was still in my veins, and I was emotionally compelled to feel an orgasm again. Before that, we'd been dancing, singing, and drinking. We left and had sex right away in his car. Then he showed me a white powder that he was carrying in a tube called a *torneirinha* (a little faucet). He opened it, allowing the powder to run into one of his nostrils.

"This is cocaine. Let's try it, Tina," he said, as he poured some fresh powder out of a plastic bag he had in his other pocket. He used a CD as a plate and a *real* bill to snort the drug. (Real is the currency in Brazil, and CDs were what we used to listen to music in cars during the nineties.) Feeling excited, I tried.

I snorted cocaine for the first time in my life that night, inside my boyfriend's car—a doctor, after midnight, on a summer evening in Brazil. We both got very high. It was a new concept and sensation for me: My legs were shaking, my mind was racing, and my whole body was on high alert.

"I love this feeling," I said. "It's crazy!"

"Let's continue the fun at my office," he replied.

That night was long. Dad was away at the farm, which mentally gave me permission to stay longer with zero worries about coming home late and being physically attacked by my dad in front of Fasano. Mom trusted me with the young doctor, as well. While waiting at home, she probably thought, *She's with a nice man, a respectable doctor from a good family. She's in good hands.*

At his office, full of pictures and high-end furniture, I could see the evidence of his reputation plastered around the walls with certifications. We had sex again, this time on the floor, and continued to do cocaine from his desk. The summer of 1995 was a high season of experiences, and it lasted for almost three years. I used cocaine with

Fasano for three years, weekly, during our nights out. Nobody knew it, but the physical stress started to show.

Cocaine—that was the first drug. The second was marijuana, and I even tried Ecstasy once. Cocaine was a recreational addiction, perfect for moments when I wanted to feel numb. Marijuana, I never enjoyed. I never liked the smell, and it was always hard for me to inhale. Ecstasy was pure peer pressure; I took it once and never did again. It was the one that made me lose all control. It made me feel like I was flying. All shreds of modesty disappeared that evening—along with my clothes.

However, cocaine was an intriguing stimulant for me. I was never physically addicted, but I enjoyed its effects.

That is, until my life became compartmentalized. All at once, I was a polite and contained daughter, a brave young attorney succeeding and winning, a sweet and trustful sister and friend, and a wild woman on weeknights and weekends. There were weekend trips to the beach, where he had his boat at the country club, and nights out on Thursdays and Fridays to the bars where we would meet his longtime friends and then drink and snort. I had become a collection of fragmented selves, each reflecting a life out of sync. Drugs had never been a need or even on my radar, but suddenly, snorting cocaine became a frequent habit.

Numbed by the situation, I stayed in the relationship for three years. My colleagues at the law firm noticed that I was becoming too thin. Mom was concerned that I was losing my appetite and looked perpetually tired. My skin was pale, and I was introverted at home, once again locked into a relationship that was imprisoning my mind. I couldn't extricate myself. Sex wasn't even the same anymore. My orgasms were gone, and I came to discover that cocaine would cut the sensitivity of my clitoris. At least for me, it did. Sex had become *a do-it, not a feeling for it.* The good feelings had all but disappeared.

Things started to become complicated.

Fasano and Dad got into an argument one night; actually, it was quite early in the morning. It was about 4:30 a.m. After a night out where wine and cocaine were our companions, Fasano took me home. Dad was waiting for us in front of the building. My body froze, just like it had almost ten years before. However, this time, he wasn't up in the trees. Dad looked furious, waiting for us with his arms crossed and legs wide open. He was ready to attack.

"Get out of the car," said Dad, as Fasano parked the vehicle. "I want to talk with you both upstairs," he fumed.

Dad's reaction was different this time. *What's coming next? I wondered*. With my mind and body full of chemicals from the drugs and slightly tipsy from all the wine, a surge of dread coursed through my body. I was unable to walk, talk, or think clearly. *What's going to happen upstairs?* I wondered.

Dad got in the elevator first. Fasano finished parking the car, and together, we went upstairs. We didn't talk in the elevator, which is one of the side effects of cocaine use: You can't talk, or you talk too much. The ninth floor seemed like the nineteenth as time became malleable. Entering the apartment, Mom and my three brothers were waiting for me in the family room. Dad had ordered them to stay awake before starting the show.

"Don't say a word," he said to Fasano as he pointed his right finger at our faces, addressing the absurdity of being out so late. "I am wondering what you were doing out until this time. Where is your mind, Maria Christina? Your entire family is here, worried about you. We thought that you were both dead somewhere. You have never been this way, *filha*. What's happening to you? And your appearance has changed."

Except for Dad's booming voice, silence dominated the room. All at once, I could see myself depleted. It was obvious to me, and to everyone in the room, that I was killing myself with such an unhealthy lifestyle.

And then it was all words. As Dad lectured us, Mom and my brothers sat in silence around the family table, their eyes heavy with exhaustion and worry. Then the unthinkable happened: Fasano decided to lecture my father.

Cocaine coursing through his veins, he turned the tables, blaming Dad for his absence in our family, especially in Mom's life. He brought up the unspoken, the very things no one dared to say in front of my father. But Fasano did.

He accused Dad of being distant, authoritarian, and consumed only by himself, his farm, and his tennis passion. The words landed like punches. My father's face darkened, his chest rose, and his body tensed. Then, in a flash, he lunged.

Fernando jumped between them, shoving Fasano backward before fists could fly. The room held its breath.

And then Dad said something that made my blood freeze.

"Get my gun."

A collective gasp. We hadn't even known he had one.

"I'll shoot you right here!" he roared, his voice shaking the walls and the neighbors'.

It was past 5:00 in the morning. The ninth floor of the Estoril residence—our home since 1979—had become a battlefield. My family's desperation hung thick in the air, drowning out even my breath.

I ran to Mom, burying myself in her arms. "Please, Mom, ask Fasano to leave."

My brothers did. Fernando led Dad back to his room, shaking. The gun—hidden inside his closet when in the city and on his belt when at the farm, we found out—never made it into his hands.

Fasano left.

And I broke.

In tears, resting my head on my pillow, was a scene of desperation, sadness, and fear. I felt it in the back of my heart. Years before, I'd endured the bikini humiliation, bleeding lips, and finger marks on my face. But this time, it was different.

With my face buried in my soft pillow, I was washed with love by Mom. Even the smell of her care comforted me. Yes, this was still my home, my family, and my safe place, but I felt scared inside my head. Though there was no blood or physical harm, an invisible pain of desperation, uncertainty, and shame permeated the apartment at almost 6:00 in the morning. *I am responsible for this inferno*, I told myself. But perhaps Fasano was right about all he had said to Dad.

The next morning, breakfast was cold for the first time. Everyone was called to the table by eight o'clock. No one had slept. I watched my entire family—worn, silent, drained—while my body still reeled from the night's toxins. I felt something deeper than shame. I felt ruined.

No one spoke while we drank our coffee. Nothing was left to say.

Dad finally broke the silence and looked at me, almost crying out of sadness and disappointment for his daughter that he'd tried to protect in the only way he ever knew. Shaking as he spoke, he used a gentle voice for the first time in my life.

"I saw another side of your boyfriend last night—a side that I didn't like, disrespectful and offensive. I don't feel he is the man for you, *minha filha*. If he can disrespect our family and me with such words and actions, then he can disrespect you, as well. Late nights are not healthy for you. Today, I want you to put your hands on your heart and think about whether what you are doing with this doctor is something that you enjoy. From the outside, it doesn't look like it. You are different. Maybe your Mom can find out better than I can, since I am away most of the time. But I will leave the matter at this table as we start a new day. I want to say that I am sad with you. I never imagined in my life having my daughter involved in a scene like we had last night."

After breakfast, everyone got ready for work. Dad left for the farm again. A blank space replaced the thoughts that usually occupied my mind. Mom remained silent for the weekend, and so did my brothers. There was an Atlantic Ocean between all of us, a mix of disappointment, fear, and rejection. I felt that my family had lost their confidence in me due to my choices. And they didn't even know the whole truth.

Fasano and I didn't communicate for a few days. I was lost between Dad's compassion, Mom's sadness—she was quieter than usual—and Fasano's brashness. I foolishly believed that what he did that evening was the action of a brave man. I was blind about many things, including his bravery.

We reconnected and got engaged one year later on November 11, 1997. It was my twenty-fifth birthday, and that evening, Fasano and I exchanged rings.

At that moment, I pondered the idea of love: *Maybe this is what happens when a woman finds a man and she thinks it's the right thing to do.* Families on both sides were cheering on my engagement, even at such a young age, and with a doctor ten years older than me. *It must be the right relationship*, I thought. We had overcome deep obstacles, like the confrontation at my parents' house, presenting ourselves that evening as happy and engaged. I couldn't get it out of my mind. *It must be real—or surreal.*

The engagement party happened shortly after we exchanged rings. The party was at Fasano's parents' house when suddenly the lights went off and the whole ceremony went dark. We improvised with candles to illuminate the space. *Was it a sign of something broken? What did it signify?* If only I'd listened to my heart. Comments were made here and there about the meaning of it, but the night went on, and I had a ring on my finger. I had been asked to be married, a sign of status, in my mind.

Cocaine remained a companion on our nights out and weekends away on his boat—his other addiction. I was squeezing time between my dreams of evolving into a prominent attorney, dedicating hours and days to my master's program, and in my free time, I partied with a drug dealer. Yes, he was also selling the white dime.

… 5 …

SILENCE AND THE MIRROR

MISERY SLOWLY REVEALED herself. I began to drift from my girlfriends, avoiding nights out with them. Being with friends meant no cocaine, and Fasano didn't like to be alone on nights we were supposed to be together, mostly Thursdays and Fridays. Mom was missing me too during the weekends, when we had our pool time, mass, or movies together. I was often absent—sometimes physically, but always mentally and emotionally. I'd sold myself a story that was a fantasy in my mind.

At the law firm, Dr. Spicy had become bland and tasteless. Two of the oldest attorneys began noticing my changes. Both were about my dad's age; one of them, Dr. William, treated me with the affection accorded to his daughter. Every morning, he arrived at the office, and his first stop would always be at my desk. "*Bom dia, Tina. Como voce esta hoje?*" as his sweet eyes would meet mine—no hugs, no kisses, just warm body language with deep eye connection. *He's checking in on me*, I always felt.

One day, he said, "Tina, come to my office, please."

"Tina, my daughter is getting a new car," he said. "She has an old Volkswagen that's in very good condition. I would like to offer it to you, and if you want it, you can pay me per month according to your budget."

"Dr. William, are you serious?" I asked. After he nodded, I accepted with deep gratitude.

"No more early or late buses. Now you can drive. Stop at my house this Saturday to get your new car."

I'll never forget the license plate of that silver Volkswagen Golf. It was ADF-4575.

That Saturday, Fasano drove me to pick up my new car. Dr. William was in front of his building, where the car was parked, shining under the unbroken Curitiba sun. The silver car was spotless. He'd taken care to ensure it was washed and looked brand new. When I saw it, I felt like a happy child. And there it was again: his unconditional smile as he took in my happiness while I turned on the car and drove away.

I looked upon that same face on the very day of my engagement with Fasano as I stopped by his office to say goodbye before going home to get ready for the ceremony.

"Tina, are you sure about what you are doing tonight?" he asked.

My throat seized, and I didn't have an answer for a minute or two. Then I replied, pretending to be excited but afraid of what he might be seeing, "Yes, of course, I am. I think he's the right guy, and it all looks so perfect for us."

I didn't dare ask why he asked me that question because I didn't want to hear what he was thinking. But my soul knew that the wise Dr. William had made some connections between my appearance, my behavior, and what he'd observed about Fasano over the few times they'd met. That moment stuck in my mind. This father figure knew me, he loved me, and he cared for me. Though he was worried about something, he allowed me to move forward and live the experience myself – a direct opposite of Dad's constant interventions that did nothing to provide me with real-world experiences.

Dr. Gilberto noticed as well, but he was more straightforward with his questions. One day, he called me into his office. "Tina, you must know how important you are to us. You have talent, but above all else, we value you as a person. Make sure this man, Fasano, is not taking you away from your values, the ones that we saw in you when we hired you to become one of our firm's leaders. I heard at the beach club that he cultivates strange habits, and I am wondering if he is tempting you to do the same."

Of course, he knew the whole story, and he knew that I was enjoying the same habits as Fasano. More guilt and shame filled my heart. But I dismissed all the advice in the name of being engaged, in love, and about to be married.

It will look good on me was the central idea behind my supposed fairytale story.

••• 6 •••

RUNNING IN HEELS

SEX HAD ALWAYS played a powerful card in the game of my twenties. It was sex that ultimately severed my attachment to cocaine and my engagement to Fasano.

Two months after I got engaged, I was invited to deliver a speech in Porto Alegre, the city where Mom and Dad had first met. As part of my master's program, I was working on my *dissertação*, a required thesis. My research on DNA and paternity in the Brazilian legal system after the 1988 Federal Constitution had caught the attention of the family law community, and I had been asked to present my findings at an international convention in Minas Gerais.

That conference opened an entirely new world for me. It shifted my vision of what my career could be. I met experienced attorneys, judges, and prosecutors, people with knowledge far beyond my own. Some of those connections turned into lifelong friendships.

One of them became a lover.

He saw the ring on my finger. I saw the one on his.

As I stood at the podium, addressing an audience of seventy professionals, my eyes kept drifting to him, *front row, watching me.*

There was something in the way he looked at me, unwavering, intrigued. He wore dark jeans, a charcoal-gray shirt, glasses, and had thick, dark hair. He sat with one leg crossed over the other, a slight, knowing smile playing on his lips.

I kept my focus on my speech, ignoring the pulse of awareness building inside me.

When I finished, I took a few questions, including one from him. Then, as I gathered my papers, he approached the table, navigating through the lingering crowd.

He introduced himself. *"Meu nome é Carlos. Que prazer ouvir tu falares. Tu tens ideias fantásticas e me interessa muito saber mais sobre o teu trabalho."* (My name is Carlos. It's a pleasure to meet you. You have fantastic ideas, and I'm very interested in learning more about your research.)

I took him in fully then—his scent, his presence, the way his voice settled into me. He was a man. And something inside me, long dormant, stirred. *Was my sex appetite coming back?*

I had not felt this way in years. I had not had an orgasm in years.

We went to dinner with the other attendees. The hosts of the event knew Carlos well. He was respected, accomplished, and one of Porto Alegre's most prominent attorneys. By the time I arrived at the restaurant, he was already seated. We exchanged glances throughout the evening, a delicate, unspoken language unfolding between us.

At some point, he leaned in and asked where I was staying. I told him.

The night stretched into deep conversations, a table of twenty family law professionals bound by a shared purpose: how to serve those who relied on us in a legal system struggling with divorce rates, custody battles, and systemic inefficiencies.

It was nearly 2:00 in the morning when I returned to my hotel.

Out of a sense of duty, the first thing I did was call Fasano.

There were no cell phones in 1997, so I used the room's landline. He answered but barely spoke. I knew why—cocaine. It freezes the brain.

The weight of that conversation settled over me, a stark contrast to the energy I had felt just an hour before. I went to the bathroom, removed my makeup, and stepped into the shower.

As the water streamed over me, I looked in the mirror.

And I saw him.

Carlos.

His face was clear in my mind, a reflection of something stirring deep inside me. I imagined his presence, his touch, the electricity running through me.

What is this?

You're engaged. You're getting married. Stop this, Tina.

Then, the phone rang. Loudly.

I froze.

It was past 2:00 in the morning. Who would call me at this hour? I had already spoken to Fasano. It wasn't my parents.

Still dripping from the shower, I ran to the bed and picked up the receiver.

"Hello?"

"Maria Christina, it's Carlos. I'm downstairs. I want to see you."

I was naked, lying on the bed, and my body hummed with an almost volcanic energy.

"Carlos, what are you doing here? It's so late."

"I can't get you out of my mind," he said, without pretense. "I need to see you again—just for a moment."

And I wanted the same. Desperately.

But the ring on my finger held me back. I had just spoken to Fasano. What's right needs to stay right.

"Carlos, I would like to see you, too, but it's late. I'm leaving for Curitiba in the morning. I have to sleep."

He hesitated. But finally, he relented.

I hung up.

But sleep didn't come.

His scent lingered in my imagination—the way his lips moved when he spoke, the thick waves of his hair. I allowed myself to dream of the feeling of his hands on me—large, warm, and strong—and the image of him above me.

It didn't happen that night. I remained resolute.

However, one month later, it did.

That was December 1997. Then Christmas and New Year's happened, and I was in constant phone conversations with Carlos while preparing for the upcoming summer weeks away with Fasano. On New Year's Eve, Carlos told me he was coming to see me in Curitiba. He was going away with his family, his wife, and two kids, to the beach. After his vacation, he would come to Curitiba. It was almost like a New Year's resolution for both of us.

We made the plan.

He reserved the hotel.

He arrived.

January was hot in Curitiba, and that day, I was on fire. I'd seen Carlos once in my life, spoken with him over the phone, and felt an undeniable attraction. But that wasn't it. He had an interesting mind. He represented the opposite of Fasano, who had lost his mind to his addiction and his desires for material things: a new car, a new boat, a new apartment, a new watch. There was always something new to be purchased. And not for me, necessarily, but for him.

Carlos stayed at a hotel close to the office. It was lunchtime, and I was dressed to kill: a long skirt, high heels, and a tight top showing off my belly, my tiny body, and my back.

He told me his room number.

I went straight up, and he opened the door. I jumped into his arms, and for about two hours, there was no speaking. We kissed and made love the entire time. Without knowing it, I'd longed for the powerful effect of having skin on skin, tongues entwined, kissing all over, and one orgasm after another.

When we finally stopped, we talked. He shared his life, and I shared mine. We reflected in the moment, realizing that we were both missing things from our respective relationships. The ensuing conversations were honest (yes, I see the irony), yet there was plenty of humor that served as a great intermission between passionate sex.

Carlos left for Porto Alegre the next day. My mind was upside down. He told me I would be making a mistake getting married to a man with whom I didn't share any sexual chemistry. But mostly, it would be a mistake to marry a cocaine addict.

"Christina," he liked to call me by my middle name, "this man will never leave his white dime. It's his toy, his disease. You will be married to it."

Carlos had marriage issues, the ones that many married couples have, mostly revolving around routine. Our affair was an adventure for him, simply a break from the routine. But he never divorced his wife despite the challenges they faced. Though I wondered if he might be inclined to leave her for me, that wouldn't end up being my destiny.

I, on the other hand, left Fasano.

In February 1998, I went to spend a Saturday at his house. His parents were out of town, and we had the house to ourselves. Mom was at home, and Dad was at the farm that weekend. I had plans to try to reconnect with Fasano, despite the intense adventure with Carlos. I figured that Carlos must have been an angel sent to open my eyes.

Fasano and I spent Saturday around his house. Most of the time was spent in the pool, drinking, and watching movies. Cocaine was plentiful, and he kept serving himself. I wasn't partaking because it had begun to make me sick every time I did it. Years ago, I couldn't wait to snort one more rail because the physical sensation was so intensely fun, but by that time, it would often make me throw up.

I was present, but I wasn't. I had emotionally signed myself out of the relationship at the end of the previous year, I realized. But as the night came, he wanted to have sex with me, veins coursing with cocaine. I snorted once, and then twice, to numb my mind. And then we had sex. I closed my eyes on purpose because all I could see was Carlos on top of me, not Fasano. Desire was gone; libido was dead. Tina had left, and all that remained was my body. I stayed next to him until he decided to go to sleep. Because the cocaine was keeping me awake, I couldn't fall asleep until early the next morning.

The next morning, I woke up, and Fasano was already gone from the bed.

Craving a nice Sunday breakfast, or perhaps even a brunch in a special neighborhood place, I went to the kitchen to make my coffee. As I entered the family room, there was Fasano with a white plate, snorting more cocaine at 9:00 a.m.

I was shocked. I felt that it was finally time to say something about the bizarre, sad, and disgusting situation in which I found myself. I settled onto the couch while he remained standing next to the wood cabinet, where the television and books were located. He was in his pajamas, barefoot, with a white dinner plate next to him. On the plate was a mound of white powder. He crossed his arms and looked at me while I sat on the couch with an unhappy face.

"We must talk about this, Fasano," I said.

With a blank, numb look, he replied, "Talk about what?"

"I can't live with you and all this cocaine. It's early morning, and you're back at it again. You did this all day yesterday, last night until the late hours, and now you're doing it again, first thing in the morning."

I kept going. It felt good to get the words out after so much time. "I was expecting to have a normal Sunday morning in your house since we have the extra space—have some breakfast, talk a little. But that won't happen because of your addiction."

My hand waved toward the plate. "This won't work for me."

As though he were a frozen statue, he looked straight at me, keeping his arms and legs crossed, and in a cold tone, stated, "This came before you, Tina. I am not going to let you change what I like about this."

Inspired by my previous conversation with Carlos, I said, "Well, then I am ending this engagement with you, right here and now."

I took the ring off my finger, placed it on the coffee table, put my shoes on, grabbed my purse, and left his house.

He didn't say a word.

He didn't follow me.

He stayed stuck in that same place with his beloved addiction, where, for all I know, he may be to this day.

"Mom?" Helena's voice was soft this time, almost hesitant.

"Yes, *meu amor*?"

"Why did you stay with him for so long? Fasano."

The room fell quiet except for the hum of the dishwasher in the distance. I let the question settle. It didn't sting—not anymore. I turned to look at her, then at Sophia, who was curled beside me, listening.

"Because I didn't realize I was clinging to a version of myself that needed to be chosen to feel worthy. I thought if I could just be perfect enough, patient enough, fun enough, then maybe I'd be enough. I thought I was supposed to be married—"

Their brows furrowed in unison.

"I mean, of course, I could have walked away physically," I continued, "but emotionally, I was trapped in a story I didn't even realize I was still telling myself."

"What story?" Sophia asked.

"That I had to earn love. That I had to prove myself. That if someone chose me, even if they didn't treat me well, I should be grateful because that meant I was worthy. And when you grow up doubting your worth, you mistake pain for passion and control for care."

Helena's lips pressed into a line. "I hate that for you."

"I hated it, too," I said. "But leaving him—that was the beginning of remembering who I was, not just who I wanted to be, but who I had always been underneath the fear."

Sophia touched my arm. "That's when the book changes, right?"

I smiled. "Yes. That's when the line I'd been tracing started to bend toward me, not away."

"And now you teach us to walk away when we need to," Helena said, "to not shrink."

"Exactly," I whispered, pressing a kiss to the top of her head. "You get to write your story—even if it takes a few messy chapters to realize that."

••• 7 •••

MOM'S HANDS

IT WASN'T EASY to walk away from Fasano. He offered just enough to keep me hoping. But I finally understood that the hunger I felt wasn't for him. It was for something inside me I hadn't claimed yet. I wasn't going to wait anymore. I was done clinging to people who only saw pieces of me.

I headed home, where Mom was enjoying a beautiful summer morning. The skies were cloudy, so there was no pool time that day. Dad was away, and my brothers were out and about on their Sunday habits: biking, playing tennis, and washing their cars.

There was about a mile between my home and Fasano's. I walked that mile uphill, my eyes fixed on the concrete, analyzing each step I took—forward, back to my roots, back to my family, back to my life. The walk in my tennis shoes under the cloudy skies felt heavy on my legs. Each stride felt as though I was trudging through mud. I was tired, physically and mentally, from what I had left behind. *It's finally over*, I told myself. As the hill came to an end, I felt myself emerging from the mud, feeling lighter, braver, and ready to continue the journey toward home and myself, who had been lost in the white-powder power.

I had left Fasano. But more than that, I had reclaimed myself.

I was never a cocaine addict. I never had been, and I never would be. I had been consumed by the idea of love, a love that came with a fungus—one I had ignored for too long. But when the time came, I killed it.

I lived through experiences that could have destroyed me. But they didn't.

They could have broken me. But they didn't.

They shaped me. And because of that, I had to let go.

When I got home, Mom was on the couch, enjoying a rare moment of quiet. She had just returned from 9:30 a.m. Mass, and with all the boys out of the house, it was the perfect time to tell her what I had just done.

"Hi, Mom!" I rushed to hug her, and as always, she was ready—one to give, two to receive.

"*Oi, filha, tudo bem?* How was it at Fasano's?" She asked.

I sat beside her, meeting her gaze. I needed one more hug before I could say it.

Then, suddenly, the tears came—raw, deep, uncontrollable.

"What happened, *minha filha*?" Mom pulled me in, squeezing me tight against her heart but also searching my face, trying to understand.

I took a deep breath. "Mom, I ended my engagement with Fasano this morning." I held up my right hand, bare.

She pulled back slightly, studying me, her hands still wrapped around mine. "What happened? Why did you decide this?"

I was too drained to explain everything—mentally, physically, and emotionally. I had spent nearly three years losing myself in that relationship, not just to him but to the sickness of that habit, the pull of a life I no longer wanted.

"Mom, it's a long story. But I just knew that I was making a mistake. And I need to change."

She exhaled, nodding slowly. "*Filha*, I understand you. And whatever you decide, know that I am here to support you."

Then, with the gentle wisdom only a mother possesses, she placed her hands on my face. "For now, let's leave it at that and enjoy a good meal. Your brothers will be home soon. Why don't you shower, put on fresh pajamas, and rest on the couch? I'll finish preparing lunch. I love you more than you know."

At long last, the white powder was gone from my life.

The white man with the big nose, the one who obsessed over wealth and excess—he was gone, too.

I spent weekends at home again. With Mom. With normalcy. Slowly encasing my life in healthy habits, finding comfort in the rhythm of ordinary days.

That Sunday afternoon, as I lay on the couch, my tears sinking into the soft cotton of a sweet, clean pillow, I felt something I hadn't felt in years.

Safety. Freedom. Release.

But now, a new question loomed: How would I live my life with no addiction and no man's leash?

• • • 8 • • •

WHITE SHEETS AND RED STAINS

THAT SUNDAY SCENE represented an end and a new beginning.

Internally, it was clear I had chosen myself and my health over a relationship that was killing me.

A few weeks before the breakup, I was lying on my bed on a Friday morning, hesitating to get ready for work, again. Tiredness had imprinted on my body. Hesitation to face reality had become a chronic feeling for me, someone who was always known to be a latent spark ready to ignite. Dr. Spicy had transformed into Dr. Lazy, first in my mind, and perhaps in my partners' eyes, too. They had been watching me, and I had been disappearing.

I got out of bed, went to the bathroom, pointed my face toward the mirror, opened my eyes, and noticed the pale skin, the hair with no volume, and eyes with no light.

Who am I? Who have I become?

The questions echoed as I stood before the mirror, staring at a face I barely recognized. *Where had my light gone? What happened to the spark—the joyful expression of the little girl I used to be?* The reflection staring back at me felt foreign, hollowed by a story that wasn't mine. Once again, I had been folded into someone else's narrative, this time under the shadow of a different man.

However, this time, I got out.

And with that, I knew that it was finally time to write my own story.

When I saw Fasano and his white plate that Sunday morning, I saw my fate. As I continued to stare at my face, it may as well have been Fasano's. I was becoming him. Seeing the path and knowing that I had a say in my destiny, it was time to shatter the image of the face that stared back at me from the mirror. It was time to bring back the light.

Breaking up with Fasano was an easy decision, but dealing with others who were involved in our story was a different matter. Nobody understood my decision, and I didn't want to share my reasons with the world. The reasons were mine, and it was enough for me. It became a secret of mine for many years. Neither my parents, brothers, partners, nor friends knew why.

"It just didn't feel right," was the statement I used to anyone who questioned me.

Fasano knew the secret, but it wasn't enough for him to change. "I can't believe you're doing this to me and my family," he said when I met him one last time to collect my share of the gifts that were given to us at our engagement party.

He berated me as I filled the last of the toys into my car, imagining how they would look in my future home. I didn't acknowledge his comments but left one last piece of advice before driving away: "Fasano, take care of your life. Take care of your business and your health."

With that, I drove away and never saw him again.

You might say that, in that moment, I woke up for life.

In the years following my uncaging from yet another restricting male relationship, I indulged the freedom to explore new destinations and experiences that would shape my life in different ways. Admittedly, I had chosen Fasano. No one forced me into that story. For reasons both conscious and hidden, I walked willingly into that chapter. While the confines of our relationship eventually felt like another form of incarceration, I couldn't ignore my role in constructing those walls. That truth was uncomfortable but liberating.

Because if I had helped build the prison, I could also dismantle it.

••• 9 •••

DOTS KEEP FALLING

THE YEAR 2000 was approaching, and with it, a new future was in the making. Some were saying, "I'm going to the end," and others were praying for a new beginning. However, "What's coming?" was the question everyone was asking. I was, too, as the new century barreled toward my reality. Not one to wait anymore, I started to build opportunities and a life of fulfillment.

At around the same time that the world failed to explode with Y2K, I was invited to teach in a college recently founded by one of the most respected attorneys of constitutional law in Brazil. The invitation occurred over the phone, and I almost couldn't believe what I was hearing: "Maria Christina, we've heard great things about you, and we know you don't have any experience teaching, but we want you here as we form our college teachers board in our brand-new institution. We want you to be part of this story."

I accepted the job. It was an interesting moment for me because the school Dad had insisted I attend all those years ago, designed to train me to be a teacher, was about to come in handy. It's tragically comical that what once hurt me so badly would serve me in such an unpredictable way.

As I've learned throughout my life, not everything goes well all the time; some disruptions and setbacks are created to shape us. We learn from difficulties, disappointments, and fears. Often, the challenges represent true ways of discovering our capacities, strengths, and value.

As a college professor, I faced adversity related to my gender, my age, and my reputation. I had male students who were significantly older than I was. I had female students who were much younger than I was.

Despite being an accomplished professional in her late twenties with a master's degree and a doctorate in civil law, two books published, and a partner in a prestigious law firm, I was being attacked by all sides.

On one occasion, I faced hostility from a young female college student who said I ought to be happy for her presence in class because she was paying my salary. This was after I demanded better behavior from her. And then there was the young man who was running for office. As he inched closer to winning the campaign, he invited me for a drink and beckoned me to spend the night at his apartment. All of it represented the epitome of objectification.

To shift my self-image and identity, I changed my hair color and style a few times throughout that tumultuous decade. But I kept going. It was a blur of discovery, imagination, creation, and reconciliation.

Around this time, as I was flying on a plane from Foz do Iguaçu to Curitiba, a hijacking happened at thirty-five thousand feet in the air. Four criminals were looking to steal the money that was being transported on the plane.

I survived, but that day, I thought my life was going to end in the air. Fortunately, it didn't. What it did do, however, was fuel my belief that I alone was responsible for filling my life with meaningful choices.

It was that realization that gave me the courage to finally act on a childhood dream: to see the world beyond the narrow frame of my bedroom window. I moved briefly to Paris, France, drawn to the city's beauty and possibilities. It wasn't just about charm or curiosity; it was about freedom. I was living away from home for the first time, navigating a new language, walking unfamiliar streets. The trip was also part of my Master of Law studies, and to my surprise, my law firm partners encouraged me—emotionally and financially—to go. It was the beginning of a new chapter, where I could study, explore, and rediscover myself in equal measure.

I'd spent years accomplishing what many thought I couldn't do. All told, I spent eleven years in the court system. The little, ashamed girl learned how to fight for her position, and I reached heights that were previously unattainable. For instance, I became the first attorney under thirty in our acclaimed firm to earn a doctorate title in civil law and publish two books (one on paternity DNA and the other on descendancy). I taught law students in college and traveled around Brazil giving speeches and signing books. It was a first amongst any woman in the industry at the time.

The young woman had been rescued. These positive and invigorating experiences allowed me to go back to living life. As I continued to thrive and heal, people stopped asking me about Fasano and my plans for getting married. My older partners in the law firm, who once worried about me, came to embrace my decision with love, discretion, and support, only saying, "You made the right decision." They knew what had been happening behind the scenes.

Dr. Spicy was back.

···10···

THE SUITCASE AND FREEDOM

AT THE AGE of twenty-eight, I moved out of my parents' house. I rented a space where I could build a nest. (Years later, I would purchase my own home at the age of thirty-one, an accomplishment that filled me with pride.) I'd made a solemn promise to myself that I would not be living under my parents' roof as I reached a new decade. As a *mulher balzaquiana*, I couldn't continue living with Mom and Dad after I turned thirty. *Balzaquiana* is an adjective used to denote a woman in her thirties; it's synonymous with maturity and beauty. I didn't really feel I embodied this until I was in my fifties, but I was moving in that direction. *It would be a sign of immaturity and a lack of confidence and value if I continue to live with Mom and Dad,* I thought. *And it won't be a good look for me as a woman.*

Renting a very cute little apartment in downtown Curitiba, with a kitchen bar and a balcony with a *churrasqueira* (a Brazilian spot made of brick to barbecue on the weekends) facing the main avenue, I found my freedom spot. It only took me twenty-eight years to honor my voice and my choices. It wasn't an easy decision. I had to cross several hurdles in my mind on how to share the news with my dad.

First, I made the decision internally. *Yes, Maria Christina. You can. You work hard, and it's time to find your own space*, I told myself. Once I found that special space, I had to work on the finances, and my brother Fabio helped greatly. Always there for me, he signed up as the guarantor for my lease. Then it was time to tell Mom and Dad.

First, I told Mom. I did it in a straightforward manner on a weekend when Dad was away at the farm. I approached her on the couch, lay down on her lap, and rested my face close to her heart, giving her a huge hug.

"I need to share something with you, Mom," I said. "I made a decision. I am moving out of your house."

That would make me the second person in the family to move out; Fabio was already married, and Fernando and Fabiano were single and still living under Dad's roof. The *balzaquiana* was going to do something different, not because of a marriage but because she was ready to find her own space, an important step in her emancipation.

Mom looked at me and, with her sweet, supportive eyes, gave me a gentle smile and said, "I will miss you, but I understand that this is what you want to do. You have my support." At that, we hugged and squeezed as we did anytime we cheered for one another. "Tell me more!" she said. "Where, when, and what do your plans look like?"

As I shared the details, she suddenly paused and said, "But now comes your dad. I think I need to be the one to share your decision with him. Let me call him tomorrow and tell him."

And that's exactly what she did. Surprisingly, there was no punishment, no rejection, and no consequences. When he came back from the farm the following weekend, we had a talk. There was more silence than words, but I felt that he was happy and supportive of me, maybe even scared to let me leave what he deemed to be the security of his house and what I deemed to be my prison. Though I didn't realize it at the time, it might have been an important moment had I been able to see it as clearly as I do today. I might have realized the love my dad had for me, despite his behavior. But I didn't—not then.

I didn't move alone, mind you. I bought a puppy. It was a first for me. A fluffy Maltese, I named Yanick, white as snow and nearly as loud as I. I am a loud woman, despite loving the silence, but I have a loud voice and a loud spirit. All my new neighbors tolerated his barks, and I had to learn how to create a relationship between a free woman and a small dog. *Had I just imprisoned myself again? No, this time, it would be different.*

Living in solitude with Yanick, I had a full schedule, with Sundays being my only days off. Well, they were technically my day off, but not really. I used Sundays to prepare the classes I would teach during the upcoming week. Teaching in college absorbed three nights of my week; the firm and court took up every waking weekday, while Fridays were for traveling to other states to teach graduate and master's programs around Brazil. As one of the few lawyers with a doctorate and two published books in the country, I was offered high-paid positions to teach in many emerging programs. Those classes were mainly on the weekends, starting Friday nights and ending on Saturday afternoons.

Nonstop speeding was the tone of my life during that decade: high heels from Monday through Saturday, makeup, talking, teaching and studying, traveling, and medicating myself to sleep—zero self-care, no exercise, no pauses.

Sunday syndrome started to develop, a feeling of dread and anxiety as an exhausting weekend came to a close and the nerves of the coming week lay ahead. I overworked myself, and resentment became my default state of mind. I kept telling myself, *One day my life will be different.* But perhaps I was praying more than I believed that to be the case.

On Fridays, the younger attorneys decided to create a new habit of closing the work week a little earlier and having lunch together, where wine was allowed at the table. "It's Friday, let's cheer as a group for all the work we do together." This was the spirit and the appropriate time for more relaxed conversations and an opportunity to get closer to one another. I enjoyed those moments, but I was constantly struggling to stay relaxed because it was always a reality that in a few short hours after the get-together, I'd have to catch a plane to another destination in the country, where I would be working Friday nights, Saturday mornings, and afternoons.

"No wine for me, bummer," was my regular response, already feeling the exhaustion of the work weekend ahead. When I should or could have been relaxing, Fridays and Saturdays simply became a continuation of my week. *But the money is amazing*, I would tell myself every time I was on the way to the airport.

I paid for everything in cash, and the high respect and honor I felt were priceless to me at the time. I became trusted and admired by college boards and students alike. The admiration was everything to me, a woman who grew up under pressure and was always unsure about who loved her, who might respect her, and who valued her. In the law firm, the college in Curitiba, and the organizations I worked for, I received the treatment I'd always desired.

As a result, I determined that the high speed combined with the high heels was worthy of the sacrifice.

All of this is how I justified sitting alone on Sundays after heavy and relentless weeks of work. Tears would come from time to time, and I sometimes wondered, *How long will I have to live this life?*

I continued to work, travel, and make money—and date the wrong guys. Nonstop was my rhythm, and *busy* was my favorite word.

Pausing would mean missing an opportunity to do more. Once again, I was an addict. This time, however, I was addicted to a lifestyle I had created.

Around this time, there was an incident at the firm that astonished me. Despite my accomplishments, it seemed that my right to claim them was still owned by another.

One day, I answered the phone at my desk at the law firm and heard the following words: "Too much light shining."

"*Sim, Lourdes, não estou entendendo,*" I replied. I didn't understand her statement.

"Tina, come to my office; I need to talk with you in person," she said. Lourdes was the main secretary of the law firm, responsible for handling numerous logistics-related decisions.

"What happened?" I asked as I tried to glean some information from her, holding the phone between my shoulder and right ear while looking at the computer to finish the petition that I needed to deliver that afternoon.

"Just come to my office, please," she said calmly. Something was not right. Lourdes was a quiet lady and had an intimate knowledge of the male-female office equilibrium she was managing. For her to call me must have meant that something was wrong.

I went downstairs to the second floor where her desk was located. At the time, the law firm had grown in numbers, so much so that three of the four floors were occupied with attorneys. I was still the only female partner, but we were bringing on more young ladies who were finishing college and dreaming of being invited to join the firm.

"What happened, Lou?" I asked as I opened her office door. She had my business card order in hand. I looked at her, and she squeezed her lips, something she did habitually when there was a problem to solve.

"Doctor Gilberto doesn't approve of your business card with the title, *Professor and Doctor in Civil Law*. He said to remove the title and maintain only your name as partner," she said.

I sat down in the grey chair in front of her desk, gently looking at the proof of the business card. I saw a big slash, perpetrated by a red pen, striking right through my title as effectively as the sharp knife I'd seen my mother use to cut through succulent *picanha* so many times.

"Did he do that?" I asked.

"Yes," she said. "And he dropped it off on my desk this morning."

I remained quiet for a minute, trying to digest the slaughter of the hard work that represented my title at the hands of the oldest man in the firm. I gently picked up the card and told her not to worry about it.

"Just keep it as he's requested. Thank you, Lou."

In a voice that tried its best to comfort my disappointment, she said, "I guess he can't admit you rose higher academically than anybody else here in the firm."

I looked in her eyes and gave her an amicable smile, a gesture of gratitude for so delicately handling my humiliation.

Back at my office on the fourth floor, Doctor Gilberto passed by my door and with a dry voice said, "I saw your suggestion for your business card. No one else at the firm is publicizing their academic achievements. I'm not going to allow you to do it. I hope you understand we all have the same position."

And just as I'd learned how to obey orders from a young age, from an older man, from a person who believed he could control me, it was happening all over again. But this time, it was coming from my boss. Now, the oldest partner in the firm was demanding that I behave a certain way. It all felt so familiar. But instead of standing up for myself, I silently agreed to remain little, to retreat into my shell of fear and shame.

"Yes, Doctor Gilberto." Those were the only words I could find to answer him. I may as well have been saying, "Yes, Dad" or "Yes, Irma Giselda." It was a day to forget, but one that I will always remember.

• • • 11 • • •

BAIXINHA BUT BOUNDLESS

ONE MORNING, I looked into my bathroom mirror and was surprised to see a pale, empty face looking back. My eye sockets were deep; my hair was thinning. It was a sure sign that what I was seeing reflected my mind.

Today, that image makes me think of a book entitled *The Body Keeps the Score* by Bessel van der Kolk. The thesis is that the mind makes the commands while our bodies listen and obey—until they collapse. In Portuguese, we say *"A mente, mente. O corpo, chora."* (The mind lies; the body cries.) Mine was crying from symptoms of chronic pain and stress. My addiction penetrated my body, this time through a different vehicle.

Struggles in life, dualities, dreams—what do we do with them? Just live it. Let it be. The signs will show me when to turn, when to stop, and when to continue. Physical signs, mental or emotional, will come.

The identity I created as a thirty-year-old woman felt more like a woman in her fifties, at least from a biological perspective. Today, fifty, well-lived, is the new thirty, now my personal mantra. A *balzaquiana*, the mature woman, turns out to be her best version at the age of fifty. That's how I feel.

However, twenty years ago, the story was different. I didn't know how to pause; all I knew was to keep going to the next invitation, legal case, destination trip, or new car. My mind was fixated on what came next, while my body attempted to hang on to the present.

Sleeping became difficult, so much agony. Chronic pain invaded my lower back and my sciatica nerve, all the way down to my leg and foot, particularly on the right side, the one that was always focused on moving, driving, and picking up the next suitcase to catch a flight. I was exhausted due to a lack of sleep. The suffering emanated from my back, making its way up to my head; daily headaches became my partner in crime.

I enlisted Mom's help, who subscribed to the popular Brazilian belief in Rivotril sleeping drops. I started with two drops at night and quickly increased the dosage to six. It helped put me to sleep. However, it was band-aiding the pain, numbing me to the point of being knocked out on a nightly basis. That was my way of living. I lived in high heels, pacing myself like a sprinter, moving from one project to the next, and then medicating myself to sleep. It was my lifestyle, and I didn't know any better.

Body pain, sleeping drops, and running seven days a week while always chasing more had me on the brink of crashing. And that's what I did. I crashed. Only this time, what I crashed into would eventually save my life.

...12...

BENDING LINES

IT WAS ANOTHER beautiful summer in Brazil. The sun was out in Curitiba, which was rare. The city is well known for being "the London city" due to its frequent clouds and rain, which had a way of messing with people's moods. "*Curitibanos são muito antipáticos e fechados,*" so the saying goes. (Curitibanos are unkind and unsociable.) I always felt that the saying was unjust and had to be related to the weather. But cold or hot, Curitibanos are some of the most loyal people. The friends I made almost forty years ago are still my good friends. My childhood neighbors, college mates, and old professional colleagues are all still dear to me.

That day, a warm Sunday, I was at the club basking by the pool with my pack of besties. With beers and skin oil to fry under the sun, it was our favorite way to nurture impressive tan lines while grooving to the beats of Latin music. Conversations were always plenty, and eye contact kept the mood spicy. Brazilians love basking, relaxing, and living in the moment. One Brazilian is good, but two are a party. We are known for our positive vibes, warm approach to life, social gatherings, and a deep fascination with red meat–churrasco. We also take our holidays seriously; every other month, we have one. We love our time off work, soccer, and family traditions. Indeed, family comes first for Brazilians. Sunday lunches, Christmas evening dinners, and Easter brunches are among the most traditional. Besides those events, birthdays, and pretty much any small reason, are good reasons to celebrate with food, drinks, and music.

Sitting in one of the white chairs by the pool that day (Mom had already left after having spent time with her friends), I decided to stay a little longer and engage in conversation with a guy named Paulo. Paulo was a swimmer at the club, and he loved to bask in the sun, as well. Always clad in a black Speedo, his torso was phenomenal. His long legs were equally as stunning. He was a tall guy, especially for me, as a five-foot woman. Paulo and I got to talking about health, lifestyle, and other elements of being energetic and vital. Though we were two good-looking specimens sipping on beers, there was no physical attraction on my end, not for sex or even dating. He was quiet about his private life, and conversations with him were usually deep. I loved my time by the pool with Paulo whenever we met. It was always refreshing, reflection-worthy, and inspiring.

In fact, during one of those talks, he inspired me to try something I'd never imagined doing.

I mentioned that I was having chronic back and leg pain, omitting my Mom's Rivotril medication routine (something I've never divulged until now). I told him it was difficult to sleep and move. He looked at me and said, "Tininha, you should try yoga. It's good for pain relief. There is a studio owned by a couple named Francisco and Luciana Kaiut, and I have been several times, especially for my back. It really helped."

"Yoga?" I said. "I've never heard of it." I had no idea what yoga was. What it might do for my back sounded mysterious.

"Here's *Xico's* phone number," said Paulo. I called the very next day.

I met Luciana, Xico's partner, that same week after a long day at work. Pulling up to the studio, I got out of my Mercedes-Benz in a white suit, pink high heels, and a luxury purse. From the outside, I probably looked healthy. However, from the inside, not so much.

In tremendous pain, I walked into her office, where she asked me to take off my jacket. I had a top on underneath, and I lay down on a maca, which is a stretcher bed.

"Where is your pain, Christina?" asked Luciana.

I showed her.

In silence, she asked me to breathe and proceeded to touch my lower back and spine down to my sacrum. Sometimes, she squeezed, putting pressure on a specific area, asking me to breathe deeper.

Without making any diagnoses, she asked me to sit on the bed and said, "Would you like to see the yoga room? I think it'll be a good place to start."

"Yes," I replied.

Together, we walked toward the back area of the little house where the studio was located. As we approached the space, she placed her index finger over her mouth. Then, before she opened the door, she held me back, putting her hands on my shoulders, and said, "This is yoga."

With her hands still on my shoulders, she moved me gently into the yoga practice area. It was deadly silent, and I saw around twenty people, all lying with their backs on mats, legs up to the wall, and two white sandbags on top of their feet.

What is this? I thought to myself, but I was already too curious to step back. She continued to guide me with her hands on my shoulders, presenting me to the teacher, her husband, Francisco, who was also in silence. She then placed me in a spot between two people. She guided me into the same position as the class, stacking two white sandbags on my feet, and asked me to interlock my fingers and place my hands under my head. I followed her instructions and kept my eyes open, distinctively different from the other twenty people in the room who were… *napping?*

As I observed my feet and legs perched on the white wall, I was stunned. I thought, *Well, this is fucking different from everything else I've experienced.* After a few minutes in that position, Francisco directed the group to remove the bags and their bodies away from the wall. I didn't have the courage to say "oi" to anyone in that room;

they all left quietly, saying bye to the teacher, after which I heard Francisco say, "See you on Thursday." I took that to mean that they were all going to do the same strange thing again on Thursday.

I stood up, and Luciana introduced me to Francisco. Briefly, she explained my physical situation to him. The solution was clear: "You need yoga. Your body is crying for help. Don't be surprised if in a few months you start to crack down on your lifestyle and make some significant changes."

Wow, talk about a straightforward truth. They were known for being no-nonsense teachers, and without me saying anything about my situation, they'd already figured me out. To this day, I have Paulo to thank for that introduction. Perhaps he had me figured out as well.

Next week, I was there as a *new student*. "Students, because we want to educate all of you on your lifestyle habits and how they are either positively or negatively affecting your health," said one of my new teachers.

That's how I came to learn yoga as an educational process of lifestyle habits, based on the philosophy of pursuing a long-term relationship of living in harmony with body and mind. I would learn that the equitable balance creates a sustainable way of life.

That was in the summer of 2001. Since then, I have never stopped practicing yoga. My last asana and last breath will be synchronized. This is my intention.

However, it wasn't always smooth sailing. There was a degree of misalignment when I started my yoga journey. I was in hunting mode, aiming to ascend to the highest levels of professional excellence—translation: money. It was the nature of my reality at the time. However, yoga was presented to me as the opposite: "a descending mode in which we must turn off our motors and shut down our minds when we lie down on the mat. Only then can we truly enter our systems, our bodies, and our minds," said my teachers.

But I resisted.
The poses are painful.
It's hard for me to get to class after a long day at the office.
I don't have time.

I have to teach.

It's lunchtime; I have to eat.

I was registered to attend two classes a week, as they recommended, but I usually missed one of them—or both.

The pain wasn't missing me, though.

More Rivotril, please. When will this headache go away, Jesus? became my refrain.

Yoga is not for me, I told myself loudly in the car after a particularly stressful day at the office, and more pain than I could tolerate. So, I avoided the studio. *I'm going home!*

••• 13 •••

TRACING IT BACK

DO YOU BELIEVE the events of your life's experience, each of them represented by a dot, formulate the image of your life? Are they pre-aligned, and are you responsible for connecting them? Or do you believe that everything is just a coincidence and destiny? How much of our willpower translates to real power?

I'd accomplished all my professional milestones. "I've earned all this success," was something I might have said. As a leader of Brazilian family law in my state, I was recognized as "one of the best names" in litigation in my hometown, Curitiba. Dr. Spicy could often be seen wearing her elegant hat and standing tall. She may have been in pain, but she was pretty and successful while experiencing it.

I was also still partying pretty hard. When not at work or focusing on the next event, I had fun with my brothers. We were best friends and alibis in our adventures—sometimes drinking too much, kissing the wrong people, and staying out too late.

Between working and partying, I managed to live. By that time, at the age of thirty-one, I had purchased an apartment for myself and my Maltese, Yanick, despite Dad's preference for the dog to stay at the farm because of his love for animals. I finally agreed to release him, and he became Dad's best friend.

The apartment was a project crafted by my best friend and architect, Jocymara, or Jo. I was living a single and busy life, and changing boyfriends was as common a habit as changing clothing. However, Jo was always looking to the future. As such, she designed the master bathroom for me. I told her my dream was to have a white bathtub. She delivered, but she also insisted that I have two sinks.

"But Jo, it's only me. I don't need two sinks in my new place," I said. She winked at the engineer in front of us and said with a sweet smile, "Tina, you never know what's ahead. Let's put in two sinks." And because I always followed her ideas, I agreed. Not even a year later, I understood why.

Jo also created a special corner in the new place where she envisioned a crafted chair with a special design—something that would call you at the end of the day, after a warm shower, to lie down and rest, perhaps with a glass of wine in hand and soft music playing. Again, Jo was creating a habitat to suit the person I would become. That chair became my reflection spot. Next to it, I had the wood cabinet where the wine glasses were, and in front of the chair was my music station. Always incredible with the details, Jo still transforms dreams into reality as an architect and designer today.

Each day, after turning the lights down, taking a hot shower, and donning my soft white robe, my favorite spot was always that chair. Sometimes, it would be late at night; other times, it would be after my last class at the Unibrasil. But it wasn't uncommon to find myself in that beloved chair a little earlier on occasion, after dinner with my girlfriends or on Saturdays after teaching. Whether there was soft music playing or it was completely silent, it was my safe spot where I could breathe and connect with my feelings. Those moments became habits of solitude, silence, and connection, similar to what I would come to feel at the yoga studio.

Symbolically, the chair ushered in a new way of being. Until then, I was living life as a hunter. However, a different philosophy began to emerge. It wasn't emanating from the outside; instead, it was driven by an inner knowledge, slowly revealing itself in those quiet and contemplative moments. Interestingly, a chair forces the user into a semi-fetal position, perhaps more conducive to introspection.

Today, I return to a simple mantra: *One can receive it as long as one is ready. Yoga can make sense for one as long as one is ready.*

Sitting in that chair, the silence seemed to wrap around me, stirring a curiosity I hadn't felt before. I became increasingly curious about my feelings.

The yoga practice I'd been avoiding began to make sense, mentally and emotionally. Slowing down felt like a good thing for me, starting with sitting in a chair and then lying on the mat. Though the pain persisted in my body, my mind started to flush away the heaviness, and I experienced moments without a headache for the first time in ages. Paulo, my pool buddy, had told me that yoga was a powerful way to heal.

Maybe he was right.

Once skeptical or unsure, I became a believer. In my first few sessions, I broke down and cried like a baby. According to my teachers at the time, it was perfectly normal; I was coming to a deep release.

"Tininha, if you don't stop, your body is going to break," they'd say. Thankfully, before it broke, I began to mentally and emotionally release the pressure that had built up inside me.

All of it spilled onto the mat.

I began to make space for yoga in my schedule, quickly developing a preference for the evenings, especially Mondays and Wednesdays, after work. Mondays proved to be a great way to start the week. Wednesdays were terrific, as well, because between Unibrasil, the college, and the law firm, I took a lot of steps in high heels. Yoga turned out to be the most effective way to decompress my sciatica from all the walking and long-distance driving. It was also a marvelous way to quiet my mind, given all the teaching and communication required of me as an attorney.

Something was changing. I wasn't sure how and why, but Tininha was transforming. However, not in the way you might imagine. I was softening, but at the same time, I began to exhibit signs of being short-tempered. I became unimpressed by bureaucracy and other aspects of my profession.

Dr. Spicy was becoming irritable with clients, attorneys, and judges. The legal system's procrastination, laziness, and scent of corruption were draining me.

Around that time, one of the older bosses told me, "You are using your voice too loudly," implying that I should go back to being the polite and obliging lawyer he desired—or worse, go back to my cage.

His comment led to a profound discovery. *My voice—do I have a voice?* That was news to me. Before then, I used my voice when necessary, but I'd never owned it. It seemed to frighten the older men and women in court. *Maybe it was time to shake up the system.*

I became the wild attorney at the firm. At first, I did it through my body; I got a belly button piercing.

"Christina, you must cover this," one of the attorneys once said.

But I continued to dress my way.

··· 14 ···

DR. SPICY, REDEEMED

MY LAST CLIENT in the firm was the biggest contract the family law department had ever received at the time. He was a high-profile client who was a neurosurgeon in Curitiba. He was getting divorced, dealing with personal accusations and money matters, and there was custody and property to negotiate, not to mention two teenagers who had to be protected. The case took off in the winter of 2003, and on my birthday that year, I was able to purchase my first property with the money I made from that contract. I finally came to a Friday meeting with numbers, and for once, I was not only a pretty appearance but someone who could produce revenue for the firm.

As I prepared to meet the new client, I worked tirelessly to ensure our first meeting was a success. I felt excited and eager for the challenge of defending someone famous. Before the meeting, I checked my appearance in the bathroom mirror and made sure I looked striking. My partners were aware of *who* was going to be in the building that afternoon, and everyone was on high alert.

Dressed for war (war is what we lawyers are trained to do), I moved to the entrance to receive my new client.

"*Ola, Dr. Manoel,*" I said as I extended my right arm and hand to give him a handshake.

"Are you the attorney?" He backed off a bit in body language. I replied that I was the attorney, and he quickly said he was expecting some old lady dressed in a traditional suit with gray hair and glasses. We both laughed for a minute, yet I felt more pressure to impress him than I had five minutes earlier.

Manoel's case took all my energy for about a year and a half. It turned out that a former judge was his ex-wife's attorney, which may have provided an advantage in terms of access to the presiding judge. Throughout the case, I faced numerous instances of injustice that forced difficult decisions. In one instance, my holidays were interrupted due to a custody dispute that resulted from one of the parties not following custody rules. I recall having to file a contentious petition to reverse a challenging situation. This case also moved into criminal law since the ex-partners had become aggressive toward one another.

On one summer day, I was spending my limited hours of vacation time on a break at the beach, basking and breathing, when my phone rang. Dr. Manoel was screaming into the phone because the custody rule wasn't being observed.

In that exact moment, a bright bolt of sunlight pierced my heart, like clarity shining down on me. That clarity asked me, "Why are you working like this?"

All I could say to myself was, *Yes, I have my own apartment now, but I don't have my own time anymore. My life is now about Dr. Manoel's life. Have I sold my soul to the devil?*

The disappointment reached a plateau when I read the decision made by a judge in the High Court of appeals. I worked for that petition with six hands—mine and two of my partners'—since the case of Dr. Manoel had since spilled into the areas of corporate and financial law. We dedicated six hands to this task and endured seven weeks of nonstop work, developing the theory for the rights we wanted to secure for my client. I was utterly convinced of my client's rights. At the same time, I'd been teaching in college what I was preaching in court, so I had double the time to reflect on what was right and what was wrong. However, the system won, and the *desembargador* (the appeal court judge) disregarded my petition—*recurso*, for reasons that the three of us attorneys never understood.

I remember being at the court that day when the system announced the decision had been made. I stopped by the clerk and asked for the case number. He brought me a massive amount of papers, in which the decision was announced in the final three pages. My hands went straight to those last pages, and as my eyes started to read, I shook. I felt chills, and I couldn't believe the final declaration of the last line: "For these reasons, I reject the appeal and maintain the status quo."

My gaze lingered on the name of the ruling judge, and I imagined the corrupted system playing a part in that decision.

At that very moment, it was clear to me it was time for change.

My anger and disappointment remained stuck inside me until one day, as I was driving by the court, I purged. It was a bright sunny day. I was wearing blue jeans, a pink top, black high heels, and my signature sunglasses.

I approached the white building, and as it got closer, I followed the curve in the road to the side corner. As I slowed down, I continued to look at the immensely tall white glass building. It made me feel nauseous, so I parked my Mercedes-Benz that I'd bought with the contract money from my client who had received the infamous decision, and I opened my car door.

I looked up to the last floor where the sun was sparkling through the glass windows, and I said out loud to myself: "*Vocês juízes vão todos para a puta que pariu. Criei um ódio de trabalhar com este sistema. Vocês não serão mais parte da minha vida.*" (You bunch of judges all fucked up. Go to hell. I hate working with this system in which you are involved. You won't be part of my life.) With that, I spat on the ground a few times from the window of my car and drove away.

Materialism, false relationships, duplicity—was this my life?

All of it made me want to find another one; I just didn't know how to leave the web I had created around me.

···15···

THE FALL OF THE FATHER

MEANWHILE, MOM AND Dad relocated to the farm. Dad had started to slow down in quiet, unspoken ways, and the pull toward a simpler life among animals and open fields became stronger. The city had always agitated something in him, but the farm—the smells, the sounds, the memory of his father—offered peace he couldn't find elsewhere. He found solace in the company of animals: cows, pigs, horses, chickens, dogs, cats, and especially red bulls, which he admired for their strength and spirit.

Mom, as always, followed. She didn't question the move; she rarely questioned any of it. Her life had become a series of quiet adjustments to match the contours of his. When he needed something, whether it was a dream to chase or a place to rest, she was already there, waiting, blending into his story.

Plus, all the kids were grown-ups and taking care of themselves. Fernando was married and working as a *holic;* Fer is still a workaholic today. His job has always come first, even though he loves his family as much as he loves his work. Fabio was also married and devoted to a local transportation company whose owners adored him and trusted him to handle the human resources department. His talent for working with people was a gift. Fabiano lived in Australia for a while, trying out a new life, before he moved to New Zealand and then Miami, Florida. It was all for the same purpose: living his best life. After years, he decided to leave the banking and corporate environment, realizing that freedom meant nothing if he was chained to a desk. And that left me, Maria Christina, dealing with a heavy schedule, a heavy heart, and a heavy mind while trying to make the best of it on my terms at the right time.

While we, the children, built our lives in the city, Mom, Dad, and the animals enjoyed the farm life and seemed to be happy. I had concerns about Mom, but she appeared to be quietly enjoying the new reality. Fabiano was the only one living in the apartment; my other siblings already had their own places. Mom and Dad frequently traveled between the country and Curitiba because Dad began to experience pain in his knees. The pain was so severe that he was unable to play his favorite sport: tennis. He became frustrated and fearful of the unknown.

Dad became obsessed with his new physical reality. "Why this pain now when I have always been so healthy in my life?" Dad asked Mom.

"We must get some exams done, Rogerio." Mom was clear on what to do. She may have had an inkling that something was wrong.

Not being able to walk well and unable to play tennis, life for Dad became difficult. He decided to go to his knee doctor, the one in town he trusted the most. Dad had already had two knee surgeries in the past, so the doctor was aware of his history.

His advice to Dad was, "Go and find an oncologist. This does not look good."

So, he did.

Dad was diagnosed with multiple myeloma, a cancer that attacks the bones. That's why it began with pain in the knees at first, then moved to the legs, and eventually the joints. In quick succession, his body lost mobility, and he was unable to play tennis. Work at the farm eventually became impossible, as well. Ever loyal, my mom stayed with him as his body slowly broke down.

I didn't know the extent of his suffering until I received a call from Mom on a Sunday afternoon. I was walking in downtown Curitiba, coming back from the movies on a beautiful sunny day. Mom had been away with Dad for a few days after coming to Curitiba for the doctor's visit, but nothing had been shared with us, the children, about Dad's ailment.

I answered the phone while approaching my parked car: "Hi, Mom! I miss you so much," I said in a voice as fast as my pace.

Mom was sobbing. "*Filha, filha*! You won't believe what's happening!"

I stopped walking and sat down on the curb. "Mom, please, what's happening?"

With difficulty in her voice and short of breath, she told me that Dad had been diagnosed with a severe type of cancer in his bones that might eventually invade his blood.

"Mom, I can't believe this," I said, remaining seated on the curb under the sunny skies as Mom and I cried together, trying to find a way to console each other.

There was nothing left to say when she said, "*Filha*, I will be coming home with your dad next week, and we can see each other."

I sat on the curb, gazing up at the bright sky as tears streamed down my face. Memories of my dad flooded my mind—moments both painful and tender—playing like a reel I couldn't stop. *Why?* I whispered to God. *Why him? He's only sixty-two, too young,* I thought, *for an illness like this—too young to face an ending.*

The next day was Monday. Heavy-hearted from the news of Dad's health, I continued with my life. I spoke with my brothers the night before, and I called my Grandma Theresa and Uncle Tets, who were living in Porto Alegre. We were all in shock; it was the first cancer diagnosis amongst a close family member. We saw cancer as a relentless and unpredictable disease—one that comes and goes, yet lingers far too long, seemingly beyond human control despite the efforts of doctors and scientists to uncover its cause and cure.

On that same Monday, I taught with the heaviness of a broken heart. I didn't share the news with anyone at Unibrasil. It was too soon to be shared.

As I drove to the law firm for another week of commitments, my thoughts were consumed by Mom and Dad. I found myself counting the days until I could see them again.

Tears blurred my vision as memories of Dad's life surfaced—images of a little boy, orphaned by his mother and abandoned by his father. For the first time, I truly saw him not just as the man who hurt me but as someone shaped by his pain. He had been a man at odds with life, never able to achieve his dream of becoming a wealthy farmer or the successful attorney Mom had hoped for. Socially, his world had grown smaller over time, with strained relationships at work, tension with his sister, and even arguments with club members over tennis matches. His circle had shrunk to nearly nothing, a stark contrast to Mom's vibrant social life.

Emotionally, Dad had always seemed lost, burdened by thoughts that kept his mind heavy and restless. He never seemed to know how to steer his way through life with ease or joy.

As tears streamed down my face, I instinctively wiped them away, licking the salty streaks to save my morning makeup and lipstick. However, my mind drifted far from that moment, all the way back to the farm where Dad was born. I found myself wondering what had happened to that sweet little boy, the one who had once been innocent and who was now facing a battle with cancer.

···16···

CLINGING BECOMES A SYNDROME

SHIT. HEAVY MONDAY morning, I told myself as I started walking toward the office building at Rua XV de Novembro, 551, the street where thousands of people walk every day in Curitiba. I walked with eyes cast on the ground, trying to recover from the moment I'd just processed in the car, flashing back through Dad's life.

Today, I want to have a quiet day, I said to myself as I got in the elevator. But that was not to be. I pressed the fourth-floor button and checked the mirror to see if I looked okay to start the day. *Proper, strong, and ready to fight*. From the outside, I looked the part. However, on the inside, everything was as messy as mud.

As I stepped out of the elevator, I looked at the brown plaque on the white wall right beside the entrance to the firm. I noticed that a few letters from my name were scratched out of the nameplate. The letters a, r, c, t, h, and s were all missing. In their place, I could see scraped lines, the sign of a violent and intentional act. I moved to the right of the nameplate to greet Marcia, the firm receptionist, with a hug, my morning habit, and I stepped back and inspected the damage.

I looked over to Marcia and whispered to her, "What happened here?"

Another white wall, another shameful representation of my reputation. The first had been years earlier in high school; now, as a professional, in my law firm.

"Marcia, what happened here?" I repeated softly.

Marcia was our front desk mediator, always ready to settle small differences between lawyers, interns, clients, and staff. She was an expert in wall conversations, rumors, and frustrations; the law world was a heavy circus of constant tension and bickering. She stood up immediately and came over to give me the hug that only she could deliver.

"Dr. Maria Christina, when I opened the office this morning, this was already done. The letters were on the floor, and the scratches were there. I don't know who did this."

Having been the front desk young lady for quite a while, Marcia knew a little bit about everyone's life: the morning moods, who calls whom, the stress vibes, and the festive days. She just observed, always keeping the discreet information to herself.

As she hugged me, she whispered in my ear, "I think I know who did this to you. That lady who hates you was here early this morning before I arrived."

I moved gently away from her arms and looked her straight in the eyes. "Are you talking about Dr. Rubens's mistress?" I asked.

She broke eye contact and lowered her head, a sign of *yes*.

"She left as soon as I got here today, and she seemed furious. The plaque was already damaged when I saw it. I think she did this."

The woman was a stalker. The story began years earlier, when Dr. Rubens—one of the firm's senior partners—occasionally offered me rides home. I was his closest junior attorney at the time, often assisting with his most important cases. Though he was married, he was also involved with a woman who grew increasingly obsessive, not just with him, but with me. In her eyes, I became a threat, a symbol of potential betrayal, perhaps even another mistress.

That idea had never occurred to me. Not only was Dr. Rubens not my type, but I also had a firm personal boundary: never get involved with anyone in the workplace. Still, the optics might have suggested something else. Everyone at the firm knew about the affair, but no one talked about it. There seemed to be an unspoken code among the men: *What happens in the office, stays in the office.*

Her fixation with me grew more disturbing over time. It began with prolonged stares during my brief visits to Dr. Rubens's office to deliver files. She was often there, seated like a client, silent, watching.

I didn't grasp how intense her obsession had become until one day, during casual chatter among the women in the office, someone said quietly, "Dr. Maria Christina, that's his mistress. She's here early in the mornings, late in the evenings, sometimes even during lunch. He locks his office door and tells us not to disturb him."

That was when I understood. I hadn't just stumbled into a situation; I had unknowingly become part of it. And it would take a toll on me, both mentally and physically.

The administrative department was made up of women, Lourdes and her staff. As women, we sense things. Although I wasn't concerned about his personal situation, I believed it was inappropriate for one of the main partners to discuss his private life in the workspace. Her antics were becoming disturbing, and it seemed as though none of the men in the firm were capable of saying anything about it.

From a feeling of unease, the situation escalated quickly. Soon, her stalking became an obsession.

On one of the days following the news of my dad's cancer, I was walking to a client meeting, not far from our firm. I heard someone talking about me from a few feet behind, making inappropriate comments and using threatening language. If it were serious, I wouldn't have been able to run. I was wearing high heels and holding a stack of papers with my right arm. I turned around, and there she was, accompanied by a friend, both laughing at me.

Oh, my goddess, this woman is following me, I realized as my heartbeat increased. I kept walking briskly, thinking that I would be safe when I got to the client's office.

She continued with the insults and giggling.

I was now starting to panic, but never imagined what she was about to do. Feeling the anxiety boiling up in my system, I walked faster as I approached my destination in the hope that I would be safe.

She walked faster, too, seeming to sense my fear.

In front of my client's building, I panicked and ran up the stairs, unaware that she and her friend had gained on me.

In an act of intimate brutality, Dr. Rubens's mistress grabbed my pearl necklace from behind, a gift from my grandmother, and yanked me down the concrete stairs.

There, she started to beat me, screaming words of hate and jealousy. I was on the ground, she and her friend on top of me, my necklace broken, and all the pearls running around my head. It was as though I were drowning in a river of terror, each drop of water represented by the rolling pearls.

I screamed for help while trying to protect my face with my hands. Thankfully, my clients heard the noise and ran outside to rescue me.

The two ladies quickly escaped, leaving me on the ground crying, suffocating from the attack, and one more time ashamed for being insulted by someone who had created an imaginary war against me. It was high school all over again.

I could barely face my client, the weight of the situation pressing down on me. My heart raced as I dialed the number of a criminal attorney I trusted, someone who could protect me from the chaos in which I was drowning. I had to bow out of my client meeting, hailed a taxi, and went home.

When I walked through the door, there was Mom. At that moment, all I needed were her arms around me, her skin against mine, her presence offering the safety and love I desperately craved.

However, the nightmare didn't end there. It dragged on for months. I had to involve the police and hire attorneys to ensure my protection. In court, I came face to face with the woman who tore my life apart. The judge issued a restraining order, barring her from coming within a certain distance of me or my office. I was legally declared a victim of both physical and emotional assault. But the fear lingered. For years, I flinched at the feeling of someone behind me, a constant shadow haunting my every step. The trauma was deep, not just in my body but in my mind, too.

At the firm, nothing changed. No one stood up for me, not even Dr. Rubens's colleagues. I overheard one partner mutter, "We understand how serious this is. We'll talk to Dr. Rubens."

And just like that, the whole ordeal was buried, as if I had never been hurt at all.

That Monday morning, when the letters of my name were scratched off the wall plaque, was the morning that Dr. Rubens ended the relationship with his mistress. He never told me, or anyone in the firm, but one more time, the walls talked, and the ladies of the office were aware, always protecting one another. As I got to my desk, sat down on my white chair, and closed my eyes after taking a deep breath, Lourdes and Marcia, the administrative team, came to my office.

"Dr. Maria Christina," Lourdes started, "I was here early this morning, and they were screaming at each other. I could hear him telling her to stop coming here, to stay away from him. 'I am going to get the police involved. It's over,' he said. And she smashed the door, crying. He didn't know I was already in the office. I believe that, in anger, she went over to your name and scratched off the letters."

That was my Monday: news of Dad's cancer first, then my reputation, once again, painted in shame.

Those past few years of life were difficult, despite the victories, successes, and money. Sitting on my chair, I asked the ladies to leave my office, and I locked my door. I told Marcia to let everyone know that I wanted to be alone and needed some quiet time to digest all that had occurred. I asked her to have one of the partners fix my name on the plaque. And then I sat. I closed my eyes and cried nonstop. I could feel my heart compress internally from so much emotional and mental pain.

As I turned my chair in the opposite direction, gazing out the windows into the horizon, I asked myself the same question I had when I was a teen:

What could be out there that will deliver a better quality of life? This all feels like an incarceration. I've built a prison for myself: here, at home, at the university, in my heart. I feel suffocated by every single place, circumstance, and the people that make up my life.

I arranged a meeting with my partners for the next day. Monday was a write-off, so I turned my computer off, turned the lights down, and left the office. I didn't bother to talk with anyone else that day.

••• 17 •••

ESCAPING BEFORE EXILING

I DROVE TO yoga. It was the only place, at that moment, I wanted to be. On my mat, in silence, I was ready to remove the toxins of sadness, anger, and destruction in which I was entangled. Dad's health and his life played like a movie in my head, and the scene of the missing letters added to the drama. Flashbacks of my Dad's life story came and went, along with images of the high-school white-wall graffiti. I felt overwhelmed by the weight of my life—a tangled mess of emotions, choices, and circumstances, some of my making, others seemingly woven by the Universe itself. It was as if I were standing at the edge of a vast, uncertain path with no way around it. Yet, amid the heaviness, one thought surfaced, a quiet reminder of an old truth: *The only way is through.*

My yoga clothes were now always in my car. The mat, the pause, and the practice were now part of my weekly habits. I changed clothes and attended a lunchtime class, which was a new experience for me. Xico was teaching that Monday and was surprised when he saw me lying down on the mat, waiting for the class; in general, I was usually late, or almost late, for practice. "Always on the run," he'd frequently say to me.

But not that day. That day, I chose to run toward myself—toward my body, my mind, and my heart. I had learned, through all the chaos and anguish, that only yoga could offer me the sense of calm, the stability, and the focus I so desperately needed. Only through the calmness of clarity would I stand a chance of facing my adversities.

During the session, there were moments when I crumbled, overcome by pain, discomfort, and relentless tears. Yet Xico remained steady, gently guiding me through each pose as he sensed my anguish rising to the surface. In those vulnerable moments, something shifted. I knew it was time—time to release the toxic reality I had been carrying for far too long, to cleanse myself of the emotional scars that had once felt impossible to heal.

The next morning, I had a meeting at the office. The letters were back in the brown frame on the white wall. All was looking clean and bright, as if nothing had ever happened. Even the scratches were touched up. It was now just a memory.

In the meeting, I was surrounded by the four senior partners, the men who had welcomed me as an intern back in 1993 and offered countless opportunities to grow my career. They trusted me, respected me, and genuinely wanted the best for me. To me, they were like father figures. One of them, Dr. Conrad, felt more like an older brother. He wasn't old enough to be a paternal figure, but he remained a trusted advisor and steady presence in my professional life.

Dr. Rubens, the source of the previous day's drama and emotional toll, was also at the table. He said nothing of his involvement in the situation. His only comment was a flat reassurance: "Everything is fine."

"I need to be honest with you," I began, my voice unsteady as I faced the partners in the room. "I'm exhausted, and I'm not sure how much longer I can keep going.

"My dad was diagnosed with cancer last week, and my family is still reeling from the news. On top of that, I've been working nonstop for the past nine years. I've pushed myself hard, achieved meaningful progress in my career, and I'm grateful for this space and for your support. But yesterday was the hardest day I've faced in this firm. I've been the female partner here, but I've always performed at the same level as any man—and I know that's what you've come to expect from me. Maybe it's because you know I can deliver. I can show up, push through, and deliver results. But right now, I'm not sure how much more I have left to give."

I paused before continuing: "But my health is now in jeopardy. I can't sleep due to the anxiety over recent events and my dad's recent diagnosis. The pain in my body is constant. I need a break. I know that I'm not due any vacation time at the moment, and the cases I'm handling in the family law department are at crucial stages, but I am exhausted. I need a break."

Years ago, when I decided to go to Paris to study for three months, all four of the partners were the first to embrace the idea; Dr. Gilberto even paid for my ticket to fly to Paris. I remember the surprise greeting: "Good Morning, Dr. Spicy! Here are your tickets to fly to Paris. Enjoy your adventure!"

Dr. William had written a message for me and read it in front of the whole office in one of our monthly meetings, applauding my courage to go to another country alone, pursue another language, and use it as a source for my master's dissertation research.

They were those kinds of men: generous and supportive. Even Dr. Rubens had a unique way of being kind: When I needed a loan to support my extra expenses, he was always there to extend me credit. And Dr. Conrad was always generous in sharing his cases with me. "Let's work together on this case, Tina," he'd say. "And this client needs some assistance with his company, as well as his marriage." We had that kind of partnership. I still have enormous gratitude for these four men, who, at one time, were the foundation of my professional life. For ten years, we worked and lived side by side.

When they heard, "I need a break," and saw the tears covering my face, the oldest one, Dr. Gilberto, said: "Tina, you have been going through a lot, pulled in different directions. You've achieved many things but suffered in many ways. We are here to support you. But before you fall apart, you must take a break. I take constant breaks in my life; I feel they are necessary. You are much younger than I am, but you do much more than I do. Yes, go and take a break, and you have our word that we will take care of your clients while you are gone."

Dr. William, the father figure who offered me my first car, said calmly, "You should go to the beach. You love the sun."

And Dr. Conrad suggested without hesitation, "Go to Cancun. It's summertime there, and you can move away from the cold that's on its way to us. I know of a very nice hotel there. Go and stay at the Casa Magna Marriott. You will love it."

Dr. Rubens just smiled—quiet—still embarrassed about the stress from the day before. But he said, "If you need extra cash, just let me know." One after the other hugged me and asked about Dad's health, offering their support.

Dr. Gilberto ended our discussion with, "Now go and book your trip, and let us know when you leave."

My trip was booked for July 24, 2004, the only weekend that was available at the recommended Casa Magna Marriott. Andi, my colleague who had helped me land the job at the firm years earlier, had also recently visited Cancun, and when I shared with him that I was heading to the beach for a week, he was enthusiastic.

"You will love Cancun. The water and the sand are the most incredible I have ever seen. Just be careful because Cancun is the American man's playground!"

I replied to him, laughing at his worry: "I won't have anything to do with American guys, Andi."

Famous last words.

In the month leading up to my trip to Cancun, I found myself navigating the usual chaos, yet something had shifted. The anxiety I had struggled to suppress now felt exposed, but strangely, that awareness brought a sense of ease. I moved through my days more freely, almost as if acknowledging my limits had loosened their grip.

My workplace was remarkable, yet relentless. The pressure was constant, the expectations high. On top of that, my role as a college instructor demanded time and energy, and my monthly trips across the country to give speeches and lectures, once a passion, had become yet another checkbox on my endless to-do list. The demand was great, the money even better, but chasing both had taken a toll on my health—a slow, quiet erosion I couldn't ignore any longer.

Then there was Leonardo, a chapter in my life that no longer fit the story I was trying to write. We'd been together for three years, and while I once believed I loved him, the relationship had grown heavy with tension. He was younger, driven, and carried a self-importance I didn't yet have the language to call narcissism. My family had never approved. Mom, Dad, and my brothers had all voiced concerns early on, but I hadn't been ready to hear them.

Underneath it all, my insecurities lingered, clouding my judgment. My intuition had been whispering for some time what I wasn't ready to admit: He had likely been unfaithful.

The break I needed from work felt deeper than professional burnout. It extended into my personal life, into the growing realization that my relationship with Leonardo had run its course. As much as I dreaded the confrontation, I knew in my heart that whatever lay ahead, he wouldn't be part of it.

••• 18 •••

INTERRUPTION AS GRACE

DAD'S HEALTH QUICKLY became our main concern. Cancer was something new to our family. With the doctor's treatment plan in place, Mom and Dad made arrangements to split their time between Curitiba and the farm in Santa Catarina, a little south of Paraná, our home state.

Dad didn't want to burden us with his illness, so when we all gathered for lunch, he was very clear and straightforward: "This is something I'll handle on my own, with your mom. You four should go on with your lives, focus on your jobs, and help your mom with her expenses. I don't want to have to worry about you. I'll keep playing tennis as long as I can, and I'll take care of my animals on the farm. Your mom will move with me to the countryside, and Bano can stay here in the apartment to look after it while we're gone. We'll come back home once a month for my treatments."

I accepted it just as Dad wanted, quietly, without protest. The boys did, too, though Fabio, true to form, carried the weight a little heavier than the rest of us. That was always his way: deeply protective, especially when it came to Mom and Dad. There was something about the way he took on their burdens, as if he believed it was his job to absorb what the rest of us couldn't. Looking back, I can see the quiet ache behind his concern. Some people carry more than their share, and somehow, they know, on some level, that their time may not stretch as far.

Plans in place, July 2004 came quickly, and it was high time for me to hit the pause button. I needed it.

It was a cold day in Curitiba, yet there I was, packing for summer. New bikinis—this time chosen without fear or the sting of criticism. No harsh remarks about my body, my nails, my hair, or my clothes. Just freedom. Mexico—*ulalala!* Here I come.

It would be my first time in the Caribbean, and I remembered what Dr. Conrad and Andi had told me: "The water there looks unreal; the blue is magical." Magic—that's exactly what I was hoping for, something pure and healing, wrapped in white sand, turquoise waves, and golden sunshine. I had no idea what awaited me, but I knew one thing: I was finally stepping into a space that was mine to claim. Another dot on my journey, the lines between them beginning to reveal themselves.

My luggage was packed, and I had layered on winter clothes: boots, scarf, and jacket. As I stepped outside into the cold, rain-slicked streets, the wind whipped against my face. Just as I reached the taxi, a neighbor rolled down his car window and called out, "Heading to Cascavel to see your boyfriend?"

I froze for a moment, caught off guard. Leonardo—he was already gone, erased from my mind and my life. With a sharp breath, I smiled and shouted back, "No! I'm going to Mexico, Cancun!"

I slid into the taxi, his question still echoing in my head. But this time, I didn't dwell on it. Instead, I claimed my truth: *Forget Cascavel. Forget Leonardo. That chapter's closed.*

I leaned forward, grinning at the driver.

"*¡Arriba, amigo! Vamos a México!*"

And with that, we drove off toward warmth, toward freedom, toward whatever came next.

ACT III
THE CONNECTIONS

"Depois do medo, vem o mundo."
Clarice Lispector

••• 1 •••

THE OTHER SIDE OF FEAR

AFTER YEARS OF battling burnout in law, you'd think a trip to Cancun would be easy—but somehow, trading stress for sunshine felt like a bold move.

First, it was a momentous occasion because I decided to make my health and well-being a priority. The trip would provide a pause and some distance from my reality. Sure, I had traveled before: Paris, France, in 1999 and 2001, and Punta del Este, Uruguay, in 2003. However, this time, the tone and the adventure would be different. Traveling would be the most effective way for me to detach from reality and regenerate a stressed body and mind. I would eventually come to understand that solitude means time to think and rest without distraction. I would be able to focus on myself, which included my internal needs and insights.

These days, I elevate moments of solitude, recognizing them as the highest means of repairing stress and exhaustion. Solitude is the richness of self, as the mind gains strength and learns to lean upon itself.

Second, I was leaving a heavy reality behind in the name of self-love and self-care. It was a difficult thing to do as my parents dealt with Dad's cancer treatment, which was taking its toll on Dad and forcing Mom into becoming a farmer. Poor Mom took on the responsibilities of primary caregiver to Dad, along with the role of head honcho at the farm, taking care of the property and its many animals.

Meanwhile, my brothers were living their lives: Fabiano was adventuring in other parts of the world, moving and trying out different cultures in Australia, the United States, and Indonesia. He tried his hand at various jobs, surfing, and meeting girls. Fernando and Fabio, already married, were starting lives with their wives and working hard. They seemed to be following the path that Dad had set up for them: school, college, a job, a wife, and a family—nothing eccentric. Fabio was selling life insurance at Prudential, while Fernando was selling electrical wires at Pirelli. Seemingly happy with their modest lifestyles, they each married young ladies, but both relationships ended rather prematurely in divorce. I suppose Fabiano was the only one living a life by design.

Third, I was leaving two anchors in my life: my prestigious role at the law firm and the reputation accorded to me as a college professor. Those two appointments were my identity. They put me squarely in the spotlight, cementing my reputation and my legacy while, at the same time, drowning me in their pools of stress and incessant need to perform.

Wearing all black that cold Saturday morning, with winter boots, leggings, a heavy jacket, scarf, and a full suitcase, I hadn't learned the art of traveling light (let alone being the light). As the taxi driver took the route to the airport, I felt as though I was leaving behind a reality that didn't belong to me anymore, or perhaps one that I was ready to move away from. It didn't take long to realize that my sixth sense was shouting: *Christina, stop chasing. Pick a runway and see what happens.* The runway I chose left Brazil on a cold Saturday—destination: free will.

The check-in line at the airport was an interesting start. I noticed different Brazilian women's styles: Some looked like my business self with high heels; some had kids; some travelled with friends or partners. Quietly, I contemplated. I appeared to be the only one traveling without someone else; everybody had someone to talk with, except me. After all, it was a vacation destination; who would go alone?

Alone—what an interesting concept. I'd spent most of my adult life working with people. The concept of being alone for such an extended period was foreign to me, and it probably is to most people. But I found myself alone. For how long? Only time would tell.

The first leg of the trip took me through São Paulo and then onto Cancun. The estimated travel time was supposed to be about eight hours, but for the first time in years, I wasn't in a hurry. Not knowing anything about what to expect on a Caribbean beach, I stayed calm and enjoyed the ride. I was in the moment for the first time since I could remember. Getting there quickly didn't occupy any part of my mind the entire way there—another first!

I arrived at the Cancun Casa Magna Marriott Hotel around seven o'clock in the evening. It was raining, but in a beautiful tropical way. I checked in, opened my suitcase, and then headed to the porch through the glass doors. I was greeted by the magnificent ocean and a fresh summer breeze, as the trees dripped fresh rain after their shower. I changed into something summery and went to explore. I was hungry and ready for a beer. *It's hot and humid here*, I thought, *the perfect time for pizza and beer on a Saturday night*. Off I went hunting, but I was also tracing. *You're not in a hurry*, I reminded myself.

Casa Magna was gigantic; it still is today, twenty-plus years later. It's a typical Cancun destination adapted to American desires: Everything is large and expensive. The main building was white with a pool at its center, surrounded by over three hundred white chairs for basking and a thirty-step staircase linking the beach to the hotel. I was impressed with the abundance of space in the lobby: three restaurants with varying cuisine, a creative store with vibrant windows attracting the wanting eyes of its patrons, and a welcoming spa. I hadn't seen anything quite like it in my life. Eventually, I found a way to connect with my family and the law firm in Brazil using the telephone. I had a cell phone, but it didn't have an international roaming feature. Public phones were my lifeline, especially to let Mom know I was safe and having fun.

My trip was scheduled for seven days. *I am going to have the best time of my life here*, I said to myself. I figured no one knows me, and I don't need to say hi or answer any questions or be anywhere at a certain time. All I wanted to do was eat, sleep, and get tanned while exploring such a magical place. Ironically, with my newfound freedom, one of the first things I did was call Mom. With that out of the way, I went to the spa and made an appointment for a massage the next day, got a nail fixed in the salon downstairs, and went for dinner. It was already close to nine o'clock in the evening.

Between the three restaurants, I chose the most casual one: a sporty bar-type location with doors facing the ocean and pool area. That night, Brazil was playing soccer, and the TVs were showing the game. The Brazilians were facing off against the Mexicans. It was going to make for an entertaining night; that's for sure. As a result, there were lots of Brazilians at the bar that evening. Enjoying the first signs of solitude, I got a tall table for myself and ordered a pizza and a cold glass of beer. New and liberated is how I felt. Sipping the beer and tasting the hot cheese and sausage pizza made in the fire oven—the best way—I kicked off my trip in a peaceful style, until a gentleman approached my table.

"*Ola! Sozinha? Vi você no avião e depois pegando a mala. Meu nome é Joca, sou de São Paulo. E você, como se chama?*"

Darn, a Brazilian guy approaching me right at the beginning of the trip. I didn't even notice him in the bar, I said to myself, seconds before thinking what to answer. He introduced himself as a Brazilian from São Paulo, named Joca, and he said he had seen me on the airplane and at the baggage claim. Now he wanted to know my name.

As I ate and drank, he asked if he could sit at my table. I said yes, and we started to share why we were there, along with little tidbits about ourselves. He was a widower, traveling with his two teenage kids. I didn't ignite the conversation, thinking he'd catch on to the "I want to be alone" vibe, but he didn't. He remained at the table as I requested the check. Bill paid, I was ready to leave the conversation.

"Christina, would you like to take a walk around the pool area?" he asked. *Unrelenting.*

Despite any misgivings, I felt it was a good opportunity to explore in preparation for the next day. The rain had just stopped, and a gentle breeze kissed the air, a typical Caribbean breeze that makes you feel light.

"Yes, let's go," I responded. We walked out through the doors that accessed the pool and beach area, a little awkwardly, but I was content to let the moment live. There was nothing to share with Joca, only a few candid comments about the view. We walked around the wet deck. I had bare feet, feeling the recent rain on the concrete and the warm ocean air of the summer season. To this day, the smell of the ocean is one of the most inspiring scents that helps me decompress. We kept walking in circles as the talk started to die. Suddenly, he lunged for my face and tried to kiss my lips. I moved, faster than normal, away from him, grabbed his arms, and said straight to his face, "Joca, no. I just arrived at this magical beach to have a full week of rest. I didn't come to find a man, a boyfriend, or even to kiss someone on the first night. Please, stay away with respect." He apologized, after which we separated, and I went to my room. I couldn't help but think, *Why do Brazilian men need to be so aggressive in their approaches?*

The next morning was Sunday. It was raining again, and the ocean was agitated as the waves crashed high and loud. July is hurricane season in the Caribbean, but I hadn't been warned. I only discovered that later. I opened the glass doors to the porch and said, *"Bom dia, Senhor, bom dia vida, bom dia mundo,"* as I still love to do today. (I receive your blessings, and I'm thankful.) I may well have said, "Where the heck's the sun? I want to get a little tanning in," but I didn't. Instead, I changed my clothes and got ready for breakfast. I was starving.

Have you ever had breakfast in a hotel in Cancun? It's not only a time for eating, but it's also a time for celebration. It's a feast, with mariachi band music, decorated tables, and delicious homemade tortillas, sauces, and quesos. It's an invigorating way to start the day, and

I dove in headfirst. As I ate and listened to the music, I started to feel completely detached from my Brazilian reality. *This is so different. I am in love,* I thought.

At the spa, I dipped myself into the jacuzzi first. There was a window next to it, and like those Sundays at my parents' house where I gazed through the windows of my bedroom and contemplated the mysteries of what's out there, I did the same while in the jacuzzi. It was still rainy, windy, and cloudy outside. I focused my gaze on the brave ocean, where the waves broke loudly and ferociously. I wondered about what this trip would show me. Little did I know it, but a rainy day at the spa was the perfect way to start a seven-day retreat.

Monday morning arrived with skies painted in brilliant gold, the sun casting its warmth over the landscape. The beach stretched before me: endless, pristine, with soft, white sands that shimmered in the light, and the sea was a vast expanse of turquoise that beckoned me with its hypnotic pull. I stood there for a moment, caught in the spell of its color, mesmerized by the way it seemed to shift with the light as if alive. It was the most mesmerizing shade of blue I had ever seen, a hue that only nature could create. I felt an irresistible urge to plunge into it, to be enveloped in its magic. As my feet met the water, I marveled at its warmth, the sensation of being both weightless and held.

I stepped onto the soft, powdery sand next, and it embraced my feet with a lightness I hadn't expected. Each step left an imprint as if the earth itself was welcoming me, the delicate grains teasing the spaces between my toes. The sand was so fine; it felt like a caress and seemed to weave together with the water in a seamless dance—two elements that, though distinct, were bound together in perfect harmony. The tactile sensations, the warmth of the sun, and the rhythm of the waves all melded into something profound and sensual, a reminder of nature's quiet, unspoken beauty.

That's how my week started—plus a dive with the dolphins. As they say in Mexico, "Let the dolphins hold your feelings while you open your heart for a new beginning," which is exactly what I did. From the initial discomfort, all of it slowly disappeared as I let the creatures guide me in a sacred swim of trust. It culminated when the dolphins took my whole body out of the water, and the guides instructed me to "open your arms and let your heart feel the freedom and the joy." The dolphins in Cancun were a pure experience of love and bravery, which allowed me to shatter the defensiveness that has been permeating my behavior for years. I finally trusted, and I let it be.

Sunny and hot days became my routine. There was no more rain. I achieved my lofty ambition of doing nothing except eating, sleeping, and tanning. Occasionally, I made phone calls to the office and Mom, checking in on Dad's health. Mom was so supportive. "*Filha querida, você trabalha muito meu amor. Você não pára um minuto. A mamãe se preocupa com você. Pense que dinheiro não é tudo. Se de algumas férias*". That was Mom's constant message: that I had been working nonstop and that money wasn't everything—that I should give myself some vacation time.

"Mom, one day I want to be here with you," I said on one of our calls. It was a plan we would keep for the rest of our lives.

At the office, Juliane, my assistant, was taking care of the cases and implored me to rest. "All is under control here," she said.

Dr. Conrad, who had suggested the hotel to me, wanted to know if I found it as special as he had. He was the kind of guy who wanted to be sure that what he had told me was the truth.

Since college was on winter break, there were no assignments to mark and no lectures to prepare. For now, it was time to do nothing, and that's what I did.

I found the perfect spot for my daily ritual, a quiet place where I could bask in the sun with my books, a hat, and sunglasses. My favorite routine began with a leisurely breakfast, followed by a stroll along the beach, and then hours spent lounging in my white beach chair.

When I wasn't reading or drifting off to sleep, I found myself watching the families around me, mostly American families of four or five, with parents and their children laughing and playing in the soft white sand. There was something comforting about it: a picture of safety and love.

As I watched those families, I felt an unexpected warmth, a quiet kind of happiness just knowing those moments existed. I couldn't help but think back to my childhood, to summers at the beach in Itapema with Mom, Dad, and my brothers. *I was that little girl once, I realized, the one playing in the sand without a care in the world. And now, here I am, a grown woman, watching scenes that mirror my past and feeling their quiet beauty.*

There was something about it, a gentle pull toward that kind of life, yet it was fleeting. Just as quickly as those thoughts came, they faded. I turned back to my book, returning to my solitude—my life as it was, for now.

Joca appeared now and then to say hello, his approach much more relaxed than the night before. There were no more attempts at kisses, just friendly conversations on the beach, casual and easy. I met his kids—two bright-eyed children who seemed to be navigating life without their mother. Joca spoke of the challenges he faced as a single parent, sharing his struggles with a tenderness that revealed just how deeply he cared for his children. As I listened, I couldn't help but feel a quiet understanding grow inside me.

That's when I realized, with peaceful clarity, why I had held back the night before: Parenting, especially under those circumstances, was no small feat. It wasn't something I was ready to take on, not yet—not when I still had so much work to do on myself. I had come to Cancun to finally carve out a space of solitude, to let my mind and body breathe after months of pressure. The thought of stepping into a relationship that involved children, with all the complexities that came with it, felt like too much for me right now.

I wasn't ready to carry that responsibility, especially not in someone else's life. I knew that if I were to ever embrace the idea of parenting, it would need to be my own, and only when I had healed enough to give it the care and attention it deserved. For now, I needed to focus on myself, on finding my balance before I could even think about becoming part of someone else's family. And that was perfectly okay.

I continued to explore the restaurants at the hotel, tasting red meat and Italian pasta, and falling in love with the Mexican cuisine and culture, after bright days at the beach.

So far, so good.

For the first time in my life, I felt like I was exactly where I needed to be, doing what was right, and truly listening to myself. After so much turmoil, it felt as though things were finally falling into place. That moment marked more than just a change of scenery; it was the beginning of a new life unfolding in ways I couldn't have imagined, more perfect than anything I could have asked for.

It took me years to understand the quiet power of timing, how the right moments seem to arrive when the stars align, even when you can't see it happening at first. Now, whenever life grows complicated and I find myself asking *why*, I return to that truth: Timing is everything.

The week was going by quickly. As I lamented that it was already Thursday, I wasn't aware of what would be coming next. Yet I was slowly getting to the bottom of my physical and mental exhaustion, almost ready to see a new path.

Until one is ready, one can't see it.

••• 2 •••

FLAVORING NEW FEELINGS

IT WAS JULY 29, 2004. After the festive Mexican breakfast that became a sacred morning routine, I had a fleeting glimpse of my life in Brazil: Back home, I rarely had time for breakfast. For me, breakfast had always been a ten-minute affair, represented by grabbing a coffee and rushing out the door.

I went back to my room and dressed myself in my favorite turquoise bikini, the one I had chosen without any retaliation or disapproval from Dad, revealing my dark skin and fine curves. "I like what I see," I said to myself, looking in the bathroom mirror. "I see a body and a face covered in light, rested, and bathed in solitude and a slow pace." It was a new feeling for me. The past, while not forgotten, wasn't attached to the present moment.

Carrying books, sunscreen, a hat, and water, I picked a white chair for the day in my favorite area between the staircase and the turquoise water.

Here—this is perfect.

My ideal beach spot had to be just right: peaceful and pristine, not too crowded, yet not completely isolated, and close enough to the ocean to hear the rhythmic crash of the waves but far enough back that the tide wouldn't creep too close. The air carried only the soft hush of water meeting sand, with no chatter or commotion to break the calm. It was a delicate balance, a quiet refuge where the world seemed to pause, leaving only the sound of the sea.

I walked along the shoreline, my steps slow and deliberate. It was a morning ritual I'd inherited from Mom after all those years of visiting the beach during Christmas break. The rhythm of the waves seemed to sync with my breath, washing away the tension I'd carried for so long. Afterward, I waded into the crystal-clear water, letting the cool salt embrace my skin, a quiet baptism that seemed to cleanse more than just my body.

Back in my chair, I settled in, hat on, book in hand. For the first time in what felt like forever, I whispered to myself, *I couldn't be happier.* In that moment, I felt as though no other life existed beyond this one: the life I had been given, or perhaps gifted.

There's something about the sea. Maybe science explains it, but to me, it felt like magic. My mind seemed to quiet at this level, my thoughts no longer racing.

I dug my toes into the warm sand, absently carving a small hole, a habit I'd picked up from Dad. It was such a simple movement, yet it seemed to ground me, releasing the restless energy that had kept me so tightly wound.

It struck me then, even here, away from everything familiar, I was carrying pieces of them with me, their quiet rituals: Mom's morning walks, Dad's way of playing with the earth. They had become my own. In those moments, I felt their presence, not as burdens of the past but as quiet reminders that healing had been with me all along.

The books I brought to the beach that morning were an adult cartoon series called, *Mulheres Alteradas,* written by the Argentinian author Maitena Burundarena. I chose them without knowing much about the content, but one of the book covers beautifully expressed my state of mind: *Me tirem daqui!* (Get me out of here!) Those words represented my life and my mind at the time. *Mulheres Alteradas* means women in transformation, variation, or change. All the stories in those books related to that theme. Maitena maintains that "...a woman in transformation is not a crazy woman, changing something that she can't support to carry on anymore. The only ones that can't reinvent themselves are the stupid ones, or the dead ones." Her short stories provided a sip of laughter and reflected the transformation I was enduring on a solo vacation. They were insightful in a sarcastic way, perfect reading content for a woman longing for a new life.

Getting too warm under the sun, I closed my book and stood up to place it inside my Adidas beach bag. As I set my book aside and lifted my head, still shaded beneath my hat and sunglasses, a man with silver hair and sun-kissed skin walked past my chair. He was heading from the hotel toward the ocean when he paused, glancing my way.

"How's your book?" he asked in English.

His voice was warm and casual, the kind that lingers a moment longer than expected.

I understood him. Years of English classes in Brazil had prepared me for that. But speaking it—that was another story. Unsure how to respond, I smiled politely and said, "I'm sorry. I don't speak English. I'm from Brazil."

He smiled back, an easy expression that seemed to say, *That's okay*. Without another word, he continued toward the water.

A few moments later, I found myself at the water's edge—not intentionally, not deliberately, yet somehow, following fate.

Immersing my body in the turquoise paradise, I saw a man with gray hair talking in English with a group of men and women. *They must be friends on vacation together*, I thought. I stood in between two worlds, observing their way of talking and laughing, everyone with a white drink in their hand. They sounded happy and enjoyed each other's company. They looked like best friends, the kind that made a habit of traveling together.

Back at my chair with my book, the happy image I had just framed for a few seconds faded like a week-old tan. Eventually, I turned my attention to real beach business: tanning, reading, snacking, and repeating. After such hard work (ha!), I found a chair close to the beach bar where I could rest and sleep. It was already afternoon, and I had been in the sun for a few hours. I closed my eyes as I felt the sea breeze kiss my skin. It felt amazing to be alive.

I woke from my nap and went back to the sun. I'd resolved to go to downtown Cancun that evening to find some goodies I could bring back for family and friends since it was only two days away from my return to Brazil. Back on the chair, the same man with gray hair, brown shorts, and an incredible six pack and chest, walked by me a few times, going back and forth from the white hotel staircase to the white sand, always carrying orange drinks. Every time he passed by, he looked at me. With sunglasses and a hat on, I pretended not to notice his conspicuous glances. His group was now on the sand and near me; I could hear them laughing and talking in a language that was impossible to understand. Studying English is one thing; speaking English is another.

Mr. Six-pack approached me, accompanied by another man, a much shorter one. "Hi", he said.

"Hi," I said back.

"What's your name?"

"Maria Christina," I replied. He seemed confused, but he smiled nonetheless.

"My name is Mark, and this is my best friend, Gabriel. He is from Argentina, and I am from Texas."

Remaining in surprise mode, but also a bit embarrassed due to the language barrier, I didn't quite understand why Argentina was being brought into the conversation.

Mark, the man with gray hair, continued, "Did you say you're from Brazil? Before you went to take a nap by the beach bar, remember?"

"Yes, you are right," I said.

"My friend Gabriel speaks Spanish," he said, at which point Gabriel introduced himself and invited me to join their group at the beach.

I left my things in the chair and joined the group. I was met with an incredibly happy energy. There were five couples, two single ladies, and one single guy: Mark. Most of them spoke only English, and a few were able to communicate with me using a mixture of Spanish, English, and Portuguese. Over the course of a few exchanges, I began to piece together their story: Gabriel was engaged to Beatrice. They both lived in Houston, Texas, which was a new city to me. She was from Spain and had lived in Mexico for a few years. He was from Buenos Aires and had moved to Texas as a young boy. They were getting married in two weeks in Houston. To celebrate their marriage, they were in Cancun with their best friends. It was, what they told me was called, a "bachelor and bachelorette party." Mark came alone, Beatrice explained, clarifying that Mark was divorced and lived in Dallas, with no kids.

For a moment, my heart skipped. It marked the first unmistakable sign that I found him attractive. And when I learned he didn't have kids, well, that felt like a bonus.

The couples at the table were close friends, and the two single women—Beatrice's best friends—were both divorced. It was obvious Mark wasn't with either of them; Beatrice had made that clear as she painted the picture of their group.

Between my limited English, their Spanish, and my Portuguese, I managed to follow the conversation enough to understand their stories and share a little of my own. I told them I was a single woman from Brazil, escaping burnout and hoping that a solo trip to Cancun might ease some of the heaviness I'd been carrying.

For the first time in a long while, as I sat amongst strangers who felt oddly familiar, I felt lighter, like maybe this place and these people were exactly what I needed.

The chemistry developed between the ladies in the group and me. I hung around, traveling back and forth between the turquoise water and the white sand, while the men drank and supplied us with a steady stream of refreshments from the pool bar.

With a booming voice, Gabriel shouted, "Hey, Maria Christina! Join us tomorrow night for a dance party at Coco Bongo, the most famous nightclub in Cancun. We will have a special table for our bachelor and bachelorette celebration, and we would love to have you with us."

When not making trips to the pool bar, Mark spent all his time next to me. I noticed the little holes he was making in the sand, just like I was doing earlier, and just like Dad used to do. I also spied Mark's feet and hands, the first parts of a body I like to notice on a man. Mark had beautiful hands and feet: strong, defined, and toned with a beautiful olive color. Mark was mostly quiet, except when using Gabriel as his translator. We were communicating through a whole new language, affectionately known as *portunhol*–a blend of *Portuguese* and *Espanhol*, as we say in Brazil (the only country in Latin America that speaks Portuguese, not Spanish). Mark was a listener, Gabriel the translator, and Beatrice a warm new friend. Life was off to a surprise start.

They had plans for that evening, and I had mine. We said our goodbyes and went our separate ways. Later, as I savored my steak, my body still warm from a full day under the sun, I found myself replaying those moments on the beach. Meeting the man with the silver hair stirred something familiar, a memory from summers long ago in Itapema, Brazil. Back then, there had been another boy, one who made my heart race in that same unexpected way. But like most summer flings, it had faded with the season.

In Brazil, they say, *"Amor de verão não sobe serra."* (Summer love doesn't climb mountains.) I knew that meeting Mark would likely be no different. Cancun would hold this memory, and that's where it would stay. The distance between us, in miles and in lives, felt too great to imagine anything lasting.

Yet despite the odds, the air that day had been light and joyful. The group's laughter still rang in my ears, their carefree jokes, their easy connection. They were simply basking in the sun, sipping their drinks, and sharing pieces of their lives without pretense or pressure.

I want this for my life, too, a quiet thought whispered.

However, just as quickly, reality crept in—a hollow vision of my life flashing before me. I brushed it away, willing myself to stay in the warmth of the moment just a little longer.

••• 3 •••

FROM DOTS TO THREADS

FRIDAY WAS MY last day in Cancun. *I'd better enjoy this day fully*, I thought. *Bikini for the day—orange! Bright orange, dark skin, breakfast, and one more full day at the beach.* I was thinking about pictures. I could see it all.

I met Joca while I was tanning. He was walking on the beach with his two kids and stopped by my chair. As Joca and I were exchanging our impressions of the trip, Mark and Gabriel walked down the staircase toward the beach. A gentle hi was said between us, and I kept talking with Joca, mentioning the Americans and their invitation to Coco Bongo.

"Oh yes, my kids also want to go there tonight," said Joca.

Feeling slightly insecure, I invited them to join me. I felt that being with a Brazilian man would protect me from the unknown, mostly my fear of the language barrier and our cultural differences.

"Cancun is the playground of the American guys, Tina," Andi had warned me in Brazil.

Beware of the Americans is how I interpreted it.

I saw the group at the pool as I was ending my day at the beach, and Beatrice came to remind me about the night plans.

"Hi, Christina! We will meet you at the lobby at seven-thirty in the evening. You can join us for dinner, and then we'll go to the club. Can we wait for you?"

"Yes," was my simple response.

I became a little insecure about the plans, since I was still largely in solitude mode. Being around a large group of aliens suddenly didn't sound so attractive. But I was determined to keep my word, on my terms.

I traveled back to Cancun for some more shopping and dinner, and then returned to the hotel around seven-thirty, exactly the time I was supposed to meet the group for dinner. I did that on purpose, creating a scene in which I could insist on skipping dinner and meeting them at Coco Bongo, with Joca; they just didn't know it yet. As soon as I stepped into the lobby, wearing my white shorts, tank top, and tennis shoes, Mark saw me and rushed over, grabbing me by the hands, and looking directly into my eyes.

"Christina, you're coming with us, *right?*"

I could feel the expectation from his tone of voice and how hard he squeezed my hands. "Please, say yes," he said.

"Yes, Mark. I will meet you all at Coco Bongo," I said. "I will grab a taxi and be there at ten-thirty." And with an unspoken confidence in destiny, he let me go, and I went upstairs to shower and put on an outfit to enjoy the hottest club in Cancun.

I chose a jean mini skirt, an open-back dark-green top, and platform sandals—simple, fun, and jovial. I wore my glasses for distance as a safety measure, and I met Joca in the lobby at ten o'clock. His kids had already left for the club, and he kindly offered to take me to meet the Americans. He was a gentleman that evening. There was no spontaneous kissing this time; he was more of a kind-hearted bodyguard. The casual conversations we had with each other at the beach that afternoon continued as we took off to Coco Bongo. When we arrived, there was a long line in front of the club entrance, with about a hundred people.

"What should we do?" he asked me as we got out of the cab.

"Let's just get in line, and we'll meet them inside," I said.

I wasn't worried about finding the group, or even Mark. Sure, there was something intriguing about Mark, but a fun night wasn't contingent on meeting up with anyone, even an attractive grey-haired American. It felt good not to have an agenda. After all, I was on the trip to find myself. But still, I wondered what the American playground was going to be like.

In line, Joca and I continued our soft talking, feeling the melodic spirit of the night. It was dark outside, and the thunderous sounds of Latin music escaped from the club's entrance.

As we continued to chat, someone with strong arms came up from behind and hugged me fiercely. It felt pretty good. I hadn't felt someone grab me with such a gentle force in a long time. It was a good surprise kind of hug, and as I turned around, I saw Mark right behind me.

"No lines with me, Christina," said Mark. He grabbed me by the hand, guiding me out of the line, but had no idea Joca was with me.

"Mark, this is Joca, my friend. He's also Brazilian. I invited him to join the party with your group tonight."

"Hi, Joca, nice to meet you." I was pleased to see how gentlemanly Mark was acting. "Yes, join us. Come on, both of you. Follow me." With no clue where we were going, Joca and I looked at each other and laughed silently.

There was a private VIP entrance, where Mark's group was waiting to go in. Mark was in a festive mood as he introduced me to the group and, right away, introduced Joca as my Brazilian friend. Joca and I felt a warm energy from the Americans. It probably didn't hurt that the rhythmic beats were pumping at that point, and we could see lots of blinking lights through the doors—a festive mood, for sure. It sounded like a real party beyond those doors. And that's what we did: party. Well, I did—Joca, not so much.

I danced. I drank. I felt like a free bird. *I haven't felt this way in a long time, perhaps never in my thirty-one years of life*, I kept telling myself. As the music pierced my soul, I could feel the pain I'd bottled up pour out of my body. Anger, frustration, resentment—they all spilled onto the dance floor. Everything felt new: the people, the music, the ambience, and the free drinks—lots of drinks. My body let loose as I mirrored the American women dancing on the floor, and the ones who had the courage to climb the stairs and dance in the rafters. What a party!

I may still have been close in proximity to Joca, but we were in different worlds.

"Maria Christina, I think you found a new boyfriend," Joca shouted over the crowd and the music.

"Yes, Joca. I think I like this guy," I said, as the intensity of the rhythm continued to penetrate my body.

Mark was all dressed up that evening, and he smelled divine, wearing a cologne carefully selected to seduce me, I would learn later. The cologne was Gabriel's favorite, a famous Versace one. Gabe had been lucky with girls in Cancun before, including a Brazilian one, and now he was sharing his secret weapon with Mark, his best friend. Mark and Gabe had been best friends since high school, and Mark had only taken the trip because Gabe made it possible. Mark was a broken man in Dallas, in many ways.

However, the figure next to me that evening was whole. Nothing I saw was broken. He was a gentleman who orbited me the entire night, simply observing my joy of being around the group, and he was free. I liked his approach, the opposite of Joca's from my first night in Cancun. As the music invited me to approach Mark a little closer, I began to let the moment exist, free of expectations and fear. Questions like, *Should I? But what if? When will I or he?* evaporated from my mind. I danced, inching the back of my body into Mark's body as he met my intentions. Hands around my waist, my naked back touching his chest through his half-unbuttoned shirt, we moved exquisitely together. It felt good. It felt like a real man was embracing me, perhaps one I had been hoping to meet one day. Until then, I'd only met players who were never available to love me.

It felt safe and exciting to be around Mark. He had a way. No words were needed, the sensual physicality speaking as loudly as the percussive Latin beats. Rather quickly, our body language spoke of mutual attraction, two adults finding each other, unexpectedly.

Be careful, Tina. Cancun is the playground of the American guys, Andi's mantra slashed through my mind as I laughed in silence.

Yes, Andi. I like this playground. It feels liberating.

We moved closer and closer to each other, linked by the sweat of our skin on that humid summer night in Cancun. Warm from the sunny day and softened by the alcohol, it was obvious to me: *I like this man; I like this feeling. It feels safe, fun, and good. Is he going to kiss me at some point?* I wondered.

The music rang, the rhythm pulsated, and though we couldn't have danced any closer, we did. The divide between skin and sweat disappeared. The primal bass and thumping drums united us in a pool of passion, and I said to myself, *I'm not going to wait anymore.* I turned, and feeling the inevitability of oneness, I kissed Mark.

We woke together in my hotel room the next morning, sunlight spilling through the curtains like a quiet promise. The air felt different, charged with something new and tender. As I opened my eyes and looked over at Mark, a sense of calm washed over me. We made love again, slowly, sweetly. There was no rush, no pressure. Just warmth, connection, and the feeling that something extraordinary had begun.

It feels safe to be with him, I thought, surprised by how natural it all felt. My body responded to him with ease, but it wasn't just physical. It was as if something deep inside me had been waiting for this kind of closeness. As we lay tangled in sheets, giggling and trying to piece together the wild night before, I found myself fascinated by this kind, attentive American man next to me. There was a tenderness in him I hadn't known I needed. It existed in his kiss, in the way he touched me, in the quiet way he asked, *What comes next?*

Next.

I turned to him, heart caught between awe and reality. "Mark, I'm flying back to Brazil tonight," I said softly. The laughter paused. A silence settled between us, his arms still wrapped around me, our bare skin warm against each other in that quiet, sacred moment, Saturday morning, July 31, 2004.

There was no panic in his voice, no plea for more. Just Mark being Mark: steady, grounded, holding space for whatever *this* was becoming. He leaned in close and whispered with that matter-of-fact calm, "First, let's have breakfast. Let's enjoy the beach. What time is your flight?"

And just like that, he made the impossible feel simple.

We met downstairs where his group was slowly recuperating from the bachelor and bachelorette festivities of the night before. I joined them for the delicious morning *déjeuner*, and I noticed how the Texans loved their Mexican-style food. After a long party night, the only thing my body could handle was a cup of coffee, toast and butter, and some fruit—nothing heavy, no tortillas, queso, guacamole, beans, or pico de gallo. Them? They ravaged the kitchen, mopping up every pastry, cheese, and spicy salsa in the resort. I would come to learn, from the pros, that anything Mexican is a hangover cure.

There were some language barriers during our breakfast. However, the welcoming vibe and kindness from the group were so immense that I never felt unable to integrate myself into the dynamic. I did a little more listening than talking, but after breakfast, I joined the Americans at the pool in honor of my last day at the beautiful Casa Magna. I also took a few long walks down the beach with Mark. In those moments, he and I did our best to communicate and provide information about our lives and what had just happened overnight. Despite only having met Mark the previous day, I felt safe. Mark's presence, voice, touch, and approach to me came from a place of respect. He seemed to be curious and anxious to know who I was and why I was still single at the age of thirty-one. He told me about his divorce and added that there were no kids in his previous marriage. *Yes, he has a chance*, I thought.

After another beautiful day in the sun, it was time to get ready to depart. It was a bummer to have to leave Mark and the group, but an interesting occurrence in the early hours of the morning provided a glimmer of hope.

As we came back from Coco Bongo at six that morning, still high from the rhythm of the night, an invitation was dropped out loud by Beatrice, the bride-to-be: "Tina, come to the wedding in Houston!" We were at the entrance of the hotel after the driver dropped us off. Everyone looked exhausted, but we were all still buzzing. She grabbed a piece of paper and a pen from the valet stand and wrote, "Beatrice and Gabriel's wedding: August 14, Houston, Texas," and added her phone number. "Here, for you. This is our wedding invitation. Please, come!" she implored.

With that little paper in hand, plus the one Mark wrote for me with his email and phone number, I packed my suitcase, took a shower, made love with Mark one more time, and received a back massage with the Brazilian passion fruit body lotion that Mark had fallen in love with. Clothes on, we took our last picture together, and he took me to the lobby to meet everyone. The gang was at the bar preparing for their last dinner in Cancun. A bus was at the entrance of Casa Magna waiting for the Brazilian group to be taken to the airport. Joca was there with his kids. We exchanged eye contact, but no words were spoken.

As I walked toward the bus, suitcase rolling behind me, my body still humming from the long hours of dancing, drinking, and making love, I didn't dare look back. Mark was somewhere behind me, maybe watching, maybe not, but I couldn't bring myself to turn around. I wanted to hold the magic without unraveling it. There was something sacred about leaving it intact.

I passed through the doors of the resort, that enchanted bubble where something inside me had awakened, and for the first time in a long while, I felt real peace. *What just happened to me felt so good,* I thought, letting the memory settle quietly in my chest. I didn't obsess over the past or mourn the ending. I didn't beg the Universe for more time. I simply carried the experience, like a seashell tucked gently in my pocket, soft, shining, and complete in its own way.

I let out a breath and leaned my head back, closing my eyes for a moment. When I opened them, there he was—Mark—just below my window. I hadn't seen him approach, but he was looking up at me with that steady gaze I already knew too well. His mouth moved: "Please, come to the wedding." I couldn't hear his voice, but the words were clear. I nodded slightly, mouthing, "I'll try, Mark." Then his lips shaped more words: "I love you. I'll miss you, Tina."

The bus lurched forward. I closed my eyes, sealing the image of him in my mind, tucking it into the folds of my heart like a prayer.

I watched the resort slowly disappear behind me: the bright colors, the palm trees, the laughter of strangers who felt like old friends, all of it fading. But the joy stayed. Gratitude, too. No sorrow. No regrets. I had lived exactly what I needed to live. I had met a man in a playground made for Americans, and we found something real in a place that wasn't supposed to promise anything more than fun.

Later, on the plane, I spotted Joca with his kids. I stepped toward their row and offered a quiet thank you. "Joca, thank you for Coco Bongo last night. Here's my number in Curitiba, in case you ever want to connect." He nodded but said nothing.

That was the last time I saw Joca.

But not the last time I saw Mark.

Flying from Cancun to São Paulo was smooth. It was an overnight flight, and I fell asleep pretty quickly.

The sleep was peaceful. But before my brain shut down, I connected with my feelings as I closed my eyes. The colors of turquoise and white swirled through my mind and around my heart, reminding me of the peace and clarity I found on my trip. There was only one word that could aptly describe my time: magic.

Something had touched me.

I arrived in Curitiba, and the feelings of overload and stress embraced me like a familiar stranger. After such a relaxing time, the feeling of my vitality being sucked away consumed me. I wanted nothing more than to withdraw from all my personal and professional commitments in Brazil.

I now recognize that state as "burnout," but that was twenty-one years ago. Most thirty-one-year-olds would consider that feeling to be "normal." *Work hard, play hard, live hard.* That's what they say people in their thirties are supposed to do. But what if that pace isn't sustainable? What if that mantra, instead of empowering you, slowly breaks you down?

When I returned to my hometown, the noise of it all—the emails, the meetings, the deadlines, the expectations—hit me like a wave I wasn't ready to surf. But I was lucky. My partners at the firm had seen the cracks forming. They saw my unraveling, the exhaustion behind my smiles, the sadness tucked beneath my success. It was the reason they'd all recommended the vacation.

However, I know how rare that is. Many women don't get the chance to unplug. And just as many men won't allow themselves the pause. We're conditioned to believe that breaks are for the weak, that slowing down means giving up, that rest is indulgent or even shameful. That was me in 2004: convinced that strength meant busyness, and stillness meant failure.

I don't believe that anymore. Now, I know better: Stopping isn't quitting. It's surviving. It's healing. And sometimes, it's the only way forward.

I'd stepped into my courage to take a few days off in Mexico, and it had been delightful. My mantra had been *seven days of nothing*. I ate, slept, and got tanned. That was my plan, but as is so often the case, the Universe had a different one: love as a souvenir.

Back at home, I inventoried the events of the previous seven days, the last two standing out the most. For the first time since I could remember, I felt a lightness to life. Another Maria Christina inhabited my body. I could sense her presence internally. *Did this really happen to me?* I wondered. It felt as though I was breaking an old shell and creating a new one. Part of that new shell was flavored with Mark's calm and sincere energy. But notably, none of those thoughts brought me any anxiety or sense of worry about what the near future would hold for me—*or for Mark.*

My new Texan friends were on their way back to the Lone Star State, where their foreign lifestyle existed, one I could only dream of.

I had no clue about that culture. The United States of America had never, ever been on my radar. Until that moment, I'd never had any intention to learn about American culture, lifestyle, or tradition. The only preconceived notion that existed in my mind was the familiar story of capitalism and consumer addiction, so typically attributed to American culture.

"Be careful in Cancun," Andi's words echoed through my mind once again. "It's the backyard of the American people."

"American people?" I'd said. "Are you crazy? I have no interest in meeting an American guy. Never!"

"Never say never" is a saying that comes to mind. After my trip, not only was there an American man in my head, but I had developed a modicum of interest and curiosity about the country known for its stars and stripes.

On my way back, when I was at the São Paulo Airport, waiting for my flight to Curitiba, I called my best friend Viviane, who lived in São Paulo. Vivi and I had been friends for about ten years. We were two attorneys who loved self-development, movie theaters, and Carnaval. We'd created a sistership that remains strong today.

"Vivi, I discovered America," I said, covering my mouth with my hand, the subconscious signal of a real secret.

"Tina, what happened?" she asked.

I told her I'd met a guy in Cancun and that I thought I liked him. Vivi's the kind of girlfriend/sister-type who cheers for her best friend, so I could envision her jumping up and down upon hearing the news. And although she was going through a divorce herself—I was her attorney—she screamed pretty loudly.

"*Menina, pelo amor de Deus me conte todos os detalhes disso assim que você chegar em Curitiba,*" she said, asking me to tell her all the details as soon as I arrived in Curitiba.

Mom and Fabiano were waiting for me at the airport. She had come to town with Dad for another round of chemo that week, and Fabiano had taken the wheel, as always. I slid into the backseat, the weight of the trip still clinging to my skin like sea salt.

"Mom," I said, already smiling, "I met someone in Cancun. He's American, from Texas."

She twisted in her seat to look at me, her eyes narrowing with curiosity. After a pause, she tilted her head and said, half-teasing, half-stunned, "You went all the way to Mexico to find another farmer like your father?"

She and Fabiano burst into laughter. "Please, Tina," she continued, wiping her eye, "one farmer-husband is enough for this family. Don't tell me you fell for a guy who loves cows and wears cowboy boots."

Fabiano glanced at me in the rearview mirror and gave me a knowing wink, a soft smile tugging at his lips.

"Mom, he's not a cowboy. He's in real estate; he's a builder. And he's very handsome. Gray hair, sun-kissed skin..." I trailed off, realizing the resemblance. "Okay, maybe a little like Dad."

Mom just shook her head, grinning. "Let's hope he's the kind of builder who sees your strengths."

Mom had prepared an early dinner at her house to welcome me back, but it also provided a moment to see Dad and check on his well-being. As it turned out, Dad wasn't doing well. His pain had increased significantly, and he had to stop all physical activity. Even work at the farm had become a challenge. The MM cancer had spread, creating metastases, which meant that any form of movement caused him pain.

"How are you feeling, Dad?" I asked softly as he lifted a spoonful of *canjica*—Mom's warm corn and milk soup, made the way only she could, as if each bowl was a whisper of love.

He swallowed slowly, carefully, and before he could answer, Mom spoke for him, her voice a mix of worry and quiet strength. "He doesn't want to give up, Tina."

We were sitting around the table, where everything felt strangely ordinary: fresh evening coffee, soft bread, slices of cheese and ham, and my favorite strawberry jelly. The smells, the warmth—it all wrapped around us like a memory I didn't know I still wanted.

Dad finally spoke, his voice low and worn. "It's just been difficult, my daughter."

Fabiano and I exchanged a glance. We could both feel it: the weight of his words, the ache behind his eyes. "Not giving up" wasn't about pride or ego anymore. It meant he didn't want to die. And yet, there he was, smaller somehow—not just thinner but diminished, quieter, as though the fight had taken not only his strength but also the parts of him that once loomed large in every room.

I wondered if he ever sat with the question, "Why me?"

He'd never been reckless with his health. He didn't drink alcohol and smoked a little back in the day but quit. He exercised, slept well, had friends, and a life outside. Maybe that was what hurt the most. He'd done all the "right" things, and still, cancer came.

Dad had always been an outdoor man, his soul stitched to sunlight and open air. Court or field, tennis racket or shovel, cow or horse, he needed motion, space, and purpose. He was never meant for a desk or courtroom. Law had always felt like someone else's dream forced onto him.

His farm was his sanctuary, his animals, his companions. Chanel—his favorite horse—was silver-gray and graceful, with long legs and an elegant gait. He named her after his days selling shoes, during a short but oddly glamorous chapter of his life. Everything with Dad had meaning, even the land. He named it *Negrinho do Pastoreio*, after the folkloric shepherd boy saved by the grace of Nossa Senhora Aparecida, Brazil's patron saint.

Even in his pain, even in his undoing, the poetry of his life remained. And sitting there with him, I realized I was no longer looking at my tormentor, but at a man who had loved in the only ways he knew how and who now just didn't want to be forgotten.

Back at the dining room table, Mom mentioned to Dad that I had met a cowboy in Cancun. Dad laughed and asked, "What is a cowboy doing in Mexico?"

"He was looking for Tina," said Fabiano, which made us all laugh as we continued dinner. The cowboy in Cancun ended up being a sigh of relief in the heavy atmosphere that enveloped us that Sunday night.

Eventually, it was time to go, so I bid Dad an emotional goodbye as I kissed his forehead, bringing his face close to my chest. His hair was thin. And so was he. I could feel his skin and his bones.

In my apartment, it was time to unpack and get back to reality.

Sunday nights were normally reserved for freaking out and stressing about the week to come. However, that Sunday evening was lighter. Mark was in my head, and as I unfolded my clothes, I kept flashing back to the night and day we spent together. I looked at the piece of paper on which he'd written his phone number. That piece of paper was a treasure to me, held precious in my purse.

I held the small piece of paper in my hand like it was something sacred and fragile, but full of possibility. I walked to the solitude chair, the one that had witnessed so many quiet moments of longing, where I had often sat alone wondering, *Will I ever meet someone who truly sees me and loves me?*

This time felt different.

I still wore the clothes from the day I said goodbye to Mark, as if some part of me had been suspended in that moment. Reclining back into the familiar curve of the chair, I stared at the number, the line that stretched from my world to his. The irony wasn't lost on me, the one who always said *no* to America, now trying to figure out how to call it.

My fingers trembled as I dialed, not from fear but from the weight of change in the air. That call—simple, quiet, full of hope—was the beginning of everything. Maybe, just maybe, I had met *the one*.

The phone rang.

No answer. *What should I do?* I wondered, *leave a message or hang up?*

The call went to his voicemail, which produced a complete electrical discharge from my body as I heard his voice.

"Fuck! His voice—it's magnetic," I said aloud. "His feet, his hands, his sex, his kiss, his hugs—I miss all of it," I continued.

I squeezed the back of my chair, upset that he hadn't answered. But I summoned my best English and left him a message: "Hi Mark, it's Maria Christina. I am back in Brazil, and I would like to talk with you. Call me back."

He's never going to call me back, I figured. *This is insane, Tina. Go back to your fucking life!*

With that, I went back to my room and continued to unpack. I burned incense, put on some music, and organized my "back to reality" game plan.

"Tomorrow, I will teach," I said. "Then I go back to the office and work on the family case I'm leading. Ugh, what a life."

But just as soon as I'd uttered those words, Dad's face appeared in my mind as I was complaining. *Who am I to complain?* I asked. I shed a tear as I closed my eyes, placed my hands on my face, and surrendered into the bed, feeling the soft support of my pillow. I lay curled up, wrapped in white sheets that felt too soft for the weight I was carrying. The only image I could see behind closed eyes was Dad—fading, suffering, unraveling in a way I never imagined life could allow. My chest tightened as I whispered into the silence, "Why, Dad?" The words broke apart in hiccupped sobs, and I pressed my face deeper into the pillow, trying to hide from a grief too big to hold.

Just as the sadness began to pull me under, the phone rang.

The sound startled me—sharp and unexpected in the hush of a late Sunday night. *Who would be calling now?* I thought, lifting my head slightly. The memory of the phone call I had made to Mark earlier that day had already melted into the fabric of my sadness. For a moment, I wasn't sure if this ring was real or part of a dream, an echo reaching through the sorrow, offering me something I wasn't sure I could hold.

"Alo?" I said.

On the other end of the line, I heard an American voice. "Maria Christina, hey! It's Mark. I got your message. I'm happy you called me."

I turned my body over, took a deep breath, and summoned my English-speaking skills. But as everything was unfolding, I kept thinking to myself, *This isn't happening.*

After a beautiful conversation on August 1, 2004, I made a decision: I was going to see Mark again. I was going to that wedding.

• • • 4 • • •

BRAZIL, TEXAS, AND EVERYTHING IN BETWEEN

MONDAY WAS A cold day in Curitiba. I put on my black suit, boots, and warm scarf, making my way back to college to teach. My words weren't precise and lacked the enthusiasm that marked my teaching style. Looking at my students' faces, all I could think was, *I wanna get out of here.* Though it was a Monday full of commitments, I wondered, *Where am I?*

The answer was only too obvious: I was still making love with Mark and tanning at the beach. But there were more important matters to attend to. I was planning another trip that was supposed to happen in only twelve days.

I had no visa.

I had no extra money to pay for another international trip.

I had no excuse to take more time off.

But I had courage and desire—and I was in love.

I want to see that man again.

I made a phone call as soon as I got into the office. I called Leo, who had been my longstanding travel agent. In fact, she'd recently prepared my Cancun itinerary.

"Leo! Please, don't ask me why. I'll explain later. I need an email from you with a list of all the documents necessary for an American visa."

With the email in my inbox that afternoon, I checked off everything on the list. *I have it all. It's easy,* I said to myself.

I made another call closer to the end of the day. "Leo, I need an appointment for a tourist visa. I met a guy in Cancun, and he invited me to join a wedding party. The wedding is in eleven days—in America."

After 9/11, entry visas had become a necessity for Brazilians wishing to visit the US. And even worse, I would have to travel to São Paolo to get the visa, which was not a simple process, but it didn't discourage me. I kept going.

"Tina, this will be difficult," said Leo. "The schedule for interviews is tight, but I'll check for you."

True to her word, she checked and got back to me pretty quickly. "The soonest spot for a personal interview is August 18," she said.

"Leo, the wedding is on the 14th. Are there any other options?" I pleaded.

"No, Tina, the consulate is very strict, and this is the only day."

Deflated, I asked her to make the appointment anyway. *Worst case*, I figured, *I'll miss the wedding, but not the trip. I am going to see this man again. Period.*

That was on Monday, August 2, 2004. All at once, as I was trying to focus on my reality despite the emotions, the setbacks to my trip, and my emerging dreams.

Meanwhile, all the partners were asking how my trip had gone, and I was trying to escape answering. It was too good to be shared and too early to reveal my developing plan. The real story remained a secret. And it would remain a secret until it was time to outline the plot.

… 5 …

LEGACY IN LIVING

THAT WEEK WAS an important week at the law firm. We would be celebrating fifty years of existence, and we were all set to have a party on Thursday, August 5, in the afternoon with speeches, cake, and champagne. Everyone was excited for the upcoming party, except for me. My mind was in Texas.

The first days of August also marked a decision that had to be made regarding my college career as a professor. The owner of the institution had formally invited me to become the director of the law department—the first woman ever to be offered the position. The invitation had been presented weeks before my Cancun trip. At the time, I was burnt out, which only added more anxiety rather than feelings of pride and accomplishment. As I struggled with the decision that had to be made, I thought, *Maybe shifting gears at thirty-one years old, retiring from the court scene, and dedicating my career to academia would be a healthier path for my life.* But I hadn't responded to him, and crunch time was fast approaching.

I continued to mull it over. *What should I do?* I wondered. A part of me wanted to return their faith in me by accepting the position and stepping into a leadership position. However, my mind had already crossed the equator and journeyed to the Northern Hemisphere.

I couldn't wait to finish my day, go home, and call Mark.

"I wasn't able to get an interview, which is a necessary step in getting a travel visa," I said to Mark that evening. "I won't be able to get there in time for the wedding."

Hearing his voice allowed my heart to breathe a sigh of relief. I was dealing with a ton: Dad's health, frustration with the legal system, exhaustion, two jobs, plus weekend traveling. But all that heaviness disappeared when I heard his voice at the end of each day.

Mark's response was simple and beautiful, "I miss you so much. Please, let's see each other again soon."

In a matter of days, Mark had become someone I trusted and a man I desired—not in a crazy or passionate way, but in a safe and comfortable way. His voice, the memory of his touch, and his way of talking to me in another language were a new experience for me. My previous relationships with men had been hard, fraught with lies, jealousy, drugs, cheating, and boatloads of anxiety. This time around, with an American man, it was different, and I felt good. I felt safe.

Eventually, the conversation shifted to logistics. "What do you mean you can't get an interview before the wedding?" Mark asked.

I explained the bureaucracy around tourist visas after 9/11. "Mark, I have to travel to São Paulo for an interview that has to be scheduled in advance. Then I have to provide proof that I have property, stability, and reasons to come back to Brazil. They're also going to need to know why I want to visit the United States. It's really not that simple! Maybe it's better if I visit next month during one of our Brazilian holiday breaks. I'm also dealing with a ton over here, including my dad's health." It was a mouthful.

On the other end of the line, Mark's compassion was evident. But there was something else that intrigued me—a decisiveness that felt caring and supportive.

"I'm going to call the American consulate in the morning and see what I can do," he said.

"What? Call the consulate?" I asked in awe. "Do you know someone there?"

Maybe he didn't want to get my hopes up, but he didn't elaborate on whether he had a connection at the consulate. So instead, we spent the rest of our conversation dreaming about the next time we'd make love, kiss, and be together. Eventually, I fell asleep relishing the possibilities we were creating. I put my head on my pillow, feeling a deep sense of protection and love. It was the first time in my life that I felt so unconditionally loved by a man.

Tuesday arrived unceremoniously, marked by another day of heaviness. My housekeeper, Martinha, showed up and started to prepare my coffee. It was a morning routine that she and I created. While I showered and got ready for work, she would arrive silently and prepare my coffee, so that when I got out of the shower in my white robe, I would be greeted by the smell of fresh coffee made specially for me. She was there that Tuesday, always so loving and ready to hug me. Housekeepers and manicurists in Brazil are known as confidants. We, women, treat them as family, sharing our life stories as though they are our therapists.

"Martinha!" I screamed as I saw her, then took a deep breath, savoring the delicious aroma in the air. I hugged her and squeezed her chest to mine. "Martinha! I met the love of my life in Cancun! I think my whole life is going to change!"

She laughed and said, "Tina! Are you crazy?" I may well have been, but it didn't stop me from sharing the whole story with her as we sipped our coffees together, seated by the kitchen table.

She cried as she listened to all the details. Martinha had been part of my family for more than twenty years by that time, working for my parents at their house, my brother Fabio, and now for me. She was a devoted Catholic woman who knew everything about our family dynamics. A close confidant of my mom's, Martinha, knew how much we were struggling at that moment. After hearing my story full of adventures and surprises, she told me, "If you feel that this man is the one, go for it. Tina, you have done it all. You are successful, and you have everything you need. But you deserve more than to live alone; you deserve someone to love and someone who loves you. All your other boyfriends were no good for you."

I hugged her one more time, cried with her, and expressed my gratitude for her words. "I need to get ready to work."

Mark called me around lunch.

"Tina, I got your name on an emergency travel visa list. But you must be in São Paulo tomorrow. Your appointment is tomorrow at eleven in the morning."

"How did you do this, Mark?" I asked.

"I called the consulate, and someone named Roberto listened to me on the phone as I explained who you are, your situation in Brazil, and your desire to come to my best friend's wedding. He said, 'Yes, let's bring Maria Christina to the wedding,' and he told me your name will be on a special list for tomorrow's schedule. But you have to be there in the morning."

Things just got real! I thought.

My heart said, *Fuck everything, fly to São Paulo, Vivi can help. My best friend will understand the craziness: consulate, visa, wedding, Mark. It seems doable.*

My mind, on the other hand, said, *There are a lot of demands that require me here. I can't travel due to court, the office party, the college offer, and Dad's treatment. It's too crazy to risk it all for a man I've only known for a few days. I just got back from a trip; I can't take another one.*

I decided to listen to my heart.

That night, I flew to São Paulo. I had all the necessary documents in hand and, according to Mark, a man by the name of Roberto had placed my name on the emergency travel list. *I'm good*, I figured. *I'm confident that I'm doing the right thing.*

Vivi seemed happier and more excited than I, if that was even possible. Despite the duality of the respective moments in our lives—her divorcing and me falling in love—she was able to be there for me at the airport with open arms, quite literally. She met me at the airport in São Paulo with the warmest hug a friend could receive.

"Tina, I am so happy for you," she said. "Let's get this visa done, and you will embark on a new life, my friend!"

She and I were each other's alibis through life's winding chapters—partners in curiosity, seekers of truth. Together, we dissected heartaches and celebrated triumphs, always returning to the mirror of self-reflection, asking life's hardest questions, and daring to hear the answers. Our bond was stitched with laughter, vulnerability, and the kind of loyalty that doesn't flinch when the going gets tough. The depth of our complicity remains one of the greatest treasures of my life. And to this day, I am profoundly grateful, blessed, to still have her by my side.

I arrived right on time at the São Paulo consulate. It was August 4 at 11:00 a.m. I was right at the emergency line entrance while Vivi waited for me across the street in a cafe.

"Your name?" the American woman at the desk asked me.

"Maria Christina de Almeida," I replied.

"Your name is not here," she said after double-checking what seemed like a long list.

I had no choice but to surrender. Officers at the consulate don't take well to arguments. What they tell you is the *law. Don't argue, don't start an argument. You will always lose.* These were the thoughts screaming through my mind.

My only option was to turn around and tell Vivi my name wasn't on the list.

"Call Mark," Vivi said without hesitation.

I got through to Mark quickly. "Tina, Roberto said he couldn't put your name on the list today, but he will do it for Friday. You have to go back on Friday. Can you?"

There was no reason to second-guess Mark—not for a second did I believe he was playing or lying to me. "Yes, I can. I will be back Friday," I said.

What I didn't share with Mark was the type of mess I would encounter upon my return to Curitiba. I'd missed an important court date back home, and my partners were becoming less tolerant of my needs. This would only be amplified with every subsequent absence I would take. But I was on a mission.

"Friday at noon. Go back there, and your name will be on the list," said Mark.

I bid goodbye to Vivi and travelled back to Curitiba that evening. Another plane ticket was issued for Thursday night, and I knew I couldn't be late for Friday's appointment.

I made it back in time to celebrate the law firm's fifth anniversary. I justified my previous day's disappearance by maintaining that I was working on Vivi's divorce, which was kind of true.

After only three days back from Cancun, I felt like I had lived three years of emotions, dreams, and difficulties. Interestingly, the hardships in obtaining the visa didn't discourage me; they actually inspired more desire to turn the idea of a trip into a reality. But while my heart was shifting gears and beginning to feel the pull of the unknown, the hard reality of my current life became a lot heavier.

A sign would have been perfect. And as it turns out, I wouldn't have to wait long for one.

My flight to São Paulo wasn't until seven, but the firm's celebration had begun at four. It was a golden-hour gathering meant to honor the people who built the foundation of our success. Dr. Gilberto, our founder, stood at the microphone delivering a rousing speech—a retrospective on the firm's history, its trials, and its triumphs. Then came the naming of names, each colleague called out in a proud, declarative tone, accompanied by flattering remarks about their work and character. I stood there with a polite smile, waiting for mine.

But it never came.

He skipped me. My name vanished into the space between two others—one colleague above me, one below. Maria Christina, the attorney, erased, a ghost in the lineup.

A sharp silence wrapped around me like a noose. I smiled faintly, but I was crumbling inside. *Had it been a mistake? A slip of memory? Or something more telling?* Either way, the omission landed like a punch in the gut. People around me shifted uncomfortably.

A few whispered, "He forgot you," and I tilted my head slightly, answering only with a hushed, "I don't know."

The speech stumbled forward. And then—too late—Dr. C interjected, "Dr. Gilberto, we can't forget about Tina!"

Gilberto's response was a rushed afterthought. "Ah, yes, of course—Tina! Our Dr. Spicy."

A nickname. A shortcut. An awkward chuckle followed.

I felt like curling into myself, folding into invisibility. The damage had already landed—public, personal, and too familiar. Once again, I had become the woman almost seen, almost remembered, almost respected.

However, in that shameful moment, a strange clarity surfaced: *This is not where I thrive anymore.* I had just returned from a week that stirred my soul, where love had touched me like a breeze across the ocean. And here, I was dragging myself through days heavy with work, expectations, and the invisible weight of being overlooked.

That night, something shifted. Whatever doubt I'd harbored about Mark, about making a radical change, about following the pull of my life was gone. That speech was my answer. I had outgrown this space. It was time to write a new chapter.

I boarded the plane that evening and arrived in São Paulo. Vivi was there for me, again, with her arms wide open.

"What time's your appointment at the consulate?" she asked.

"Tomorrow at noon," I replied. "But maybe we can get on the list before noon."

"Yes, vamos, Maria Christina."

We were there at 9:00 a.m. the next morning. Vivi left for work, and I spent the time with Mark on a call.

"Please, Tina, let me know as soon as you get the visa today," he said.

I waited until noon in the nearby cafe. It was cold and raining.

Though it felt like forever, noon finally arrived. I was greeted (and I use that term loosely) by the woman who saw me on Wednesday. "Roberto put my name on the emergency travel list. I'm Maria Christina de Almeida."

"Who is Roberto?" she replied curtly.

"I don't know, but my friend in Texas mentioned his name to me," I said.

She remained quiet, no eye contact, exercising diligence on being a hard ass. She checked her list, made a phone call, and came back. "Your name is not here."

That's the answer. Don't question. Accept it and leave. That's how it works. I felt like there was no other choice. So, I called Mark back.

"Mark, again, my name is not here!"

"It's impossible!" he said. "Roberto guaranteed me your name would be there. Stay tight. I will call him again."

And he did. Roberto told Mark to "tell her to come back on Monday."

I was back at the airport by one o'clock. Vivi dropped me off, and I told her I would be back on Sunday night. "Vivi, I will give this guy, Mark, one more chance," I said. "I believe him."

She agreed.

Back in Curitiba, I stopped by the office to check my desk. I called the Unibrasil founder and told him I needed a few more days to reflect on the offer. I was confused; too many decisions had to be made in such a short time. But the excitement of the unknown and the obstacles in my path provided the fuel I needed to continue.

I flew back on Sunday night. Once again, my beloved Vivi was there.

Monday at 11:00 was supposed to be the new appointment time. Roberto had promised it to Mark; Mark had promised it to me. And I had promised myself that this was the last chance. *It must work, or I am out*, I said to myself.

It was cold that August morning and raining in São Paulo. Vivi drove me to the consulate. This time, she stayed with me. "I am going to be here with you until you get the visa in your hands," she said.

With trepidation, I went back to the same front desk.

This time, there was a man on duty. "Your name?" he asked, void of any emotion.

"Maria Christina de Almeida."

"Apologies, your name is not in the list," he said.

"What?" I asked, incredulously. "Roberto told my friend in Dallas that my name would be here today for sure!" Almost in despair, I asked the guy, "Can you please check with Roberto?"

"Sorry, we can't communicate with the employees inside the building," he replied.

I ran to Vivi, who was waiting for me near the desk, holding her umbrella and anxiously awaiting a better outcome.

"Vivi, you won't believe it. My name isn't there *again*! I'm going to call Mark right now and tell him I'm not doing this anymore. This is ridiculous!"

So, I called Mark. And Mark called Roberto. All the while, I waited across the street with Vivi under the umbrella. Neither of us spoke, but her presence transcended words.

"Maria Christina de Almeida!" a consulate police officer called from across the street and waved to me. I ran over, and he said, "I have an order to let you in for the interview."

At that moment, I figured one of three things: 1. Roberto must exist. 2. Roberto must be an angel. 3. Angels exist. Thinking back, after all these years, I think at least two of those statements are true. Maybe even all three of them.

In the end, I got through the interview, and they told me it would be ready on August 10.

"I am sorry," I said. "My visa is not being given to me now?"

Coldly, the clerk said, "Your passport remains here for your visa processing, and it will be ready for you on Wednesday."

Oh no, I thought. *Another trip back and forth?*

But it was my only way.

I hugged Vivi, and we cried together. It worked.

Mark celebrated over the phone when I called him.

My next call was to Leo to purchase my ticket to Dallas, Texas, on August 12.

It was Monday, August 9. I would be flying out on Thursday, August 12, be in Dallas on Friday, and then Houston, where the wedding was happening on Saturday, August 14. It would be a long week of tasks before I stepped on that plane, but something inside of me was on fire. I had zero doubts and zero ifs. Just a *do it* mentality.

So, I did it.

I flew to São Paulo, yet again, on Wednesday to pick up my passport—another court day missed; college classes, missed; replacements for me here, there, and everywhere. Ever the perfect alibi, Vivi provided my cover under the auspices of settling her divorce.

Thursday morning, August 12. Office. Desk.

I created an email to be sent around lunchtime letting everyone know that I would be gone for a week, this time to the United States.

Mom and Dad were back on the farm, and I had told my brothers that I was going to meet the guy I met in Cancun. I gave my brothers Mark's phone number and Beatrice's contact info, as well. At the office, my assistant Juliane was the only one who knew the real story. As for my college duties, another teacher would replace me in class. And Martinha, my housekeeper, was praying hard for my new adventure.

The plans were finally all arranged. My brothers were in shock, but they knew me well. "Tina always has something unusual planned," I'd heard them say a million times.

Juliane and Viviane were the only friends who knew about the real reason for my trip, and they were cheering me on. "Go for it, Tina. It's time for love."

I sent out an email to the partners while everyone was gone for lunch.

I left the office and took a taxi to the airport.

American Airlines flight 962 was set to leave São Paulo at 10:30 that evening.

As I left everything on pause, my reality shook. But I knew in my heart this would be an incredible experience.

Mark would be waiting for me at the airport in Houston the next morning.

I closed my eyes, sipped some wine, and fell asleep. Twelve hours and I would see Mark again. My dreams were literally in flight. I felt proud of myself and of my journey. The reinvention had just begun.

··· 6 ···

LIVING, IN COURSE

AT THIRTY-FIVE THOUSAND feet, I allowed myself a little peace, a little time to feel the moment.

I landed in Dallas the next morning. Walking around the gigantic Dallas-Fort Worth Airport felt different. *The United States felt big*, I thought. In the past, the US had never spoken to me, had never called. And yet there I was. I took it all in as I walked between terminals, observing the landscape outside of the white windows. *Everything is so different here*, I thought as I contemplated the journey.

My next flight was to Houston, in southern Texas. I had no idea where that was, but I was confident Mark would be waiting for me with flowers, a smile, and a hug. And I'd decided that during the hug, I would smell Mark's skin again, and I would be reassured that I'd made the right choice to come here. I also entertained the idea that if it didn't happen, at least it would be a long weekend of fun, and nothing else. I was allowing my heart to play the game and show me which direction I should take.

I landed in Houston around lunchtime, and even just looking out of the plane windows, I could feel the heat. August is the hottest month in Texas, and by the middle of the month, the city's a furnace.

The summer heat hit me as soon as I got out of the plane. That wave of warm air boosted my energy, and I began to like Texas. Summer is my favorite season, and the temperature created optimism in Brazil on American soil.

At the baggage claim, there was no suitcase. It was an open area where people were expecting passengers. I looked over, and even worse: There was no Mark. *Hmm, what's happening here? My bag didn't make it, and Mark isn't here.* I remained peaceful and looked for a phone. At that time, my cell phone wouldn't work outside of Brazil, so I had to find a public phone. *Who should I call?* I wondered. After a few seconds of reflection, I called Beatrice, the bride. *A woman supports a woman. Not sure why Mark isn't here*, was my thought, but I stayed calm.

The gentleman at the desk near the baggage claim saw me and smiled, asking, "Do you need any help?"

"Yes, sir. I need to call a friend. May I use this phone?" I asked.

He kindly handed it to me, and I called Beatrice. A small act of kindness—but a clear reminder that I had just arrived in Texas, the friendliest state in the country.

The words, "Hi, Beatrice. It's Christina," were barely out of my mouth, and she went into nonstop mode immediately:

"Tina! Mark is on his way! He and Gabe went to a different airport. You are at Hobby Airport, and Mark thought that you were flying to Intercontinental. Stay there, please! I am so happy you are here!"

As I was ending my conversation with her, I heard someone whistling. I looked to the left and saw Mark. "He is here, Bea!" I exclaimed excitedly. "I'll see you tonight!"

I hung up and ran into Mark's arms. We stayed glued for a few minutes, and as I mentally prepared myself, I smelled him again and again. We kissed, and he said, "Welcome to America, Maria Christina."

His voice, his smell, his arms, his body—all felt so good, safe, and masculine. *Yes, I like this man. Let this adventure begin.* My analytical mind took note of the flip-flops and blue jeans he was wearing, paired with a nice shirt. This style was new to me and challenged my concept of masculinity. I digested the difference and let him hug me hard on the way to the airport entrance, where Gabriel was waiting for us.

My luggage had stayed in Dallas, but it would be delivered that evening to my hotel, which was just fine. I didn't need anything at that moment, except a margarita, some conversation, more hugs, and sex—all on repeat.

As Gabriel sped down Highway 45 in his convertible BMW, headed toward the hotel where lunch and drinks awaited, Mark reached from the front seat and gently rested his left hand on my right leg. A quiet gesture, but one that said, *I'm here.*

I sat in the back seat, watching the Houston skyline blur past, letting the wind move through my hair and my thoughts. *I hope nothing happens to me on this highway,* I thought. *My parents have no idea I'm even here.* But instead of letting fear take over, I stayed present, soaking in the strangeness and newness of it all.

And somewhere in that moment, I made a decision.

It wasn't impulsive or dramatic. It was calm, grounded, and clear. I knew exactly why I was here, what I wanted, and how I would move forward. I was going to try—truly try. I was going to give this relationship with Mark an honest chance.

From the outside, maybe it looked reckless. But from the inside, it felt like clarity, like choosing something with my whole heart, like the beginning of something real.

I had promised my brothers to call them as soon as I saw Mark and give them the hotel phone number. We were staying at The Houstonian Hotel, where the wedding was happening. After a quick stop for a few margaritas and tacos and an ice-breaking reconnection, we arrived at the hotel.

It was a beautiful, hot, and sunny Friday in Houston. We got in the room, and I called my brothers. "Fer! I made it safely. I am with Mark. This is the hotel where I am for the weekend. You have

Mark's phone number in case you need to reach out to me. And don't say anything to Mom and Dad. I will be back next week."

My brothers and I built a quiet channel of secrets between us, a way to survive the storm of Dad's behavior. It became our unspoken method of support, of complicity without judgment, a bond that still holds strong today. That sense of harmony and unconditional loyalty among us has been one of the greatest sources of happiness in my life.

Fortunately, my luggage arrived late Friday night, which means I had a dress for the wedding.

The wedding was beautiful, and it felt wonderful to reconnect with the Cancun tribe. I could confidently say that these were my American friends from the playground days. Being with them again gave me an even deeper sense of safety and belonging.

Mark introduced me to his mom, Mrs. Betty Jene Siepiela, who was at the wedding. I sat down next to her at the table and tried to communicate. It was difficult, but I enjoyed the challenges and differences, and I did my best despite my limited English skills. I knew that smiles are always helpful, so I kept using that as a way to make connections and become more familiar with this new world. Mark's dad, Mr. John Frank Siepiela, had passed away years ago from emphysema. I was piecing together Mark's life: an older sister, Janet, who lived in Houston and was married to George, with kids; and an older brother, Jim, who lived in Dallas and was married to Marina, with kids. Mark was the youngest, his mom's third child, the one who came late in her life and became her eternally protected young one. "Mark is a special man," she confided in me.

As the party was ending, and we were saying goodbye to the group at the hotel lobby before going back to the room, one of Gabriel's friends, Matt, looked at me directly and said, "Marry him, please, marry him," pointing to Mark, who was entertaining another group near me. I looked at him, and then I bowed my head as a sign of acceptance.

The whole weekend shimmered like a hidden world I hadn't known I was searching for. It was nothing like the one I used to imagine on quiet afternoons, forehead resting against the windowpane of my childhood bedroom, watching the wind stir the trees and wondering what lay beyond the borders of my small, familiar life. Back then, the view was a question. Later, it became a longing. Now, as I stood on the edge of something entirely new, it felt like an answer. The structures I had once clung to, so carefully built from duty and expectation, began to feel distant, like shadows cast by a house I was ready to leave behind. Ahead of me, through this new window, life stretched out, wide open and waiting.

Mark and I left Houston on Sunday evening to go to Dallas, where he'd built his life. He grew up in Houston, where he met Gabriel while playing tennis in high school and where they became friends for life. Mark moved to Dallas to work with his brother's company in the late eighties and owned a Ford F250 truck, something my Mom would reject as the surefire sign of a cowboy. But in Texas, everyone drives a truck. In my mind, it was just one more detail to be digested in addition to the jeans and the flip-flops.

The trip to Dallas, however, was a real opportunity to evaluate Mark's everyday reality.

I met him in Cancun; that's one kind of experience, away from reality. Then we connected in Houston, surrounded by family and friends. But what I really wanted to learn was who Mark was in real life, where he lived, and where he worked. I wanted to see his house and routines. I wanted to soak it all in—the essence of his life. I wanted to know if the safety I felt was justified. And I only had two more days to find out.

I liked what I saw. Mark proved to be an uncomplicated person, trying his best to make life work.

He lived in a small house in a family-oriented neighborhood. But I learned that Mark was in the process of recovering his life. He was going through a divorce from a woman he had been married to for ten years. I could see that it was a balancing act to keep his finances stable. Working for his brother's company provided stability after losing a lot of his business during the divorce and in the final years of his turbulent marriage.

He was indeed a simple man with a simple life—a man with talent and character, which was evident after meeting his family and friends. In Dallas, I had the opportunity to meet his brother and his brother's wife during my visit. I also met several of his colleagues at the office. Mark presented as a middle-class, hard-working man, similar to my dad.

Was I replacing Dad for Mark? Was I considering swapping my life in Brazil for a similar one in the US?

None of those questions crossed my mind. Though in hindsight, it's interesting to evaluate the decisions one makes.

All things considered (and some not), the moment brought me positive and calming feelings, an excitement that started to build inside me.

My heart beat with a new rhythm, and my mind started to conceive of a new, fresh reality.

But soon, I would have to share the truth with everyone back in Brazil.

The Monday after the wedding, Mark went back to work, leaving me alone in his home—a place still humming with the remnants of celebration and something sweeter I couldn't quite name. I wandered through the quiet rooms, breathing in the scent of him, of wood floors and laundry detergent, of a life lived simply. Susie, the yellow Lab, and Sammy, the golden retriever, padded alongside me like old companions. We strolled through the front yard, then the back, where the green spilled out without fences, without fear. The neighborhood felt impossibly still, like the world had paused just for me to notice its ease.

There were no sirens, no looming sense of danger, no sharp edges—just the soft thump of paws on grass and a slow-burning question that had started to bloom in my chest: *Could this be my life?* I didn't need much—just this kind of peace. This kind of safety.

However, five thousand miles away, my real life waited. In Brazil, emails piled up. Responsibilities tightened like a noose. No one even knew where I was that morning, walking two dogs through a sleepy neighborhood in Texas, asking the sky, *What if I didn't go back?*

I found a bookstore near Mark's house where they had public phones.

That afternoon, I called Juliane, my assistant, who was the only person other than my housekeeper, Vivi, and my brothers who knew where I was.

"*Ju, como estão as coisas por aí?*" I asked her how things were over there, and she answered with panic in her voice.

"Tina, everyone here is furious about your email and your disappearance," she said. "They keep asking me where you went, and I keep telling them I have no idea. But they don't believe me. They're saying I'm protecting you. Anyway, how are you feeling there?"

"Happy and safe," I replied. "I like what I see here, Ju."

Our conversation continued for a few minutes, but it was clear to me that whatever decisions I was about to make all carried an element of risk.

So, on Tuesday night, I flew back to Brazil.

Meanwhile, Mark and I made plans for him to come to Brazil in September to see my reality and meet my family and friends.

By August 18, I was back at the office, pretending that I'd been away for a personal reason, which wasn't untrue.

No one asked any questions, but the words were short, eye contact disapproving, and a sense of mystery loomed in the air. However, before anyone had the chance to interrogate me, I had to leave again, this time to São Paulo for a speech. Yes, I missed work again, and an email went out to the partners indicating that I would be back on Friday.

Mom and Dad also questioned my absence, but I used Vivi's divorce as my alibi. That day in São Paulo, I met Vivi, and I told her that I was about to change the course of my life. With zero hesitation, she said, "Tina, just do it."

••• 7 •••
FORGIVENESS IN TRANSLATION

BACK IN THE office that Friday, the silence spoke louder than any reprimand. My partners didn't ask where I'd been, though their pointed glances and clipped greetings made it clear they noticed. I returned a missed call from the president of Unibrasil, the one who had offered me the role of director of the law department, a position that once would've thrilled me. And my parents were on their way from the farm again, bracing for yet another round in my father's battle with cancer.

Reality had returned like a sharp wind, cold and insistent. Yet, my thoughts kept slipping back to Texas, to the slow, golden mornings and the quiet certainty I'd begun to feel. I missed Mark more than I expected. It wasn't just longing for a man; it was the recognition that something had shifted.

Meeting him had drawn a quiet but powerful line between who I had been and who I might now become. The way I'd been treated by men before—sometimes adored, sometimes ignored, sometimes bruised—had shaped me, but it no longer defined what I desired. With Mark, I had glimpsed something gentler, truer.

And I knew, deep down, that life as I knew it was about to change. And it did.

Friday morning at the office was quiet.

I had lunch with Juliane, where I was able to confide in her about my recent experiences.

However, that afternoon, Dr. Conrad indicated that the four main partners wanted to meet with me in the library at two o'clock: "Tina, we want to talk with you about what's been going on over the past two weeks."

It was one of the most defining moments of my life, standing before the four partners, knowing I was about to be questioned, maybe even condemned, for following my heart. And yet, I wasn't afraid. There was something powerful about being able to speak openly, to own my choices without shame or apology.

When we truly trust our desires, when our intentions are aligned with the quiet, steady truth of our hearts, courage rises naturally. The heart speaks, and the mind translates it into words. And when those words are rooted in truth, we don't falter. We act.

Sitting around the table, right in front of me, was Dr. Gilberto, the founder. On his left was Dr. Conrad, the youngest of the partners and the one who had always supported me professionally and personally. To my left was Dr. William, my mentor and a father figure who sold me my first car. Finally, there was Dr. Rubens, whose mistress had beaten me a few years ago.

Then there was me, in a black skirt, a light rose top, black high heels, and a heart full of truth that was ready to be shared.

"Tina," Dr. Gilberto started, "you must know how much we value you and the work you have been doing for the firm over the past ten years. You started here as an intern eleven years ago, and since the beginning, we've seen your ambition and trusted your dedication. However, over the past two weeks, since you returned from Cancun, you have exhibited a behavior that we cannot read or understand. You've never neglected your clients before, but recently, you've been disappearing and asking others to do your work. There has to be a reason for your behavior, and we would like to hear from you and understand what's going on."

As I calmly listened to Dr. Gilberto, my mind could see the answers. Though the confrontation was unexpected, the consequences were my responsibility. The onus was on me to defend myself, but also to honor my choices. Unlike a well-crafted legal argument, my words were aching to emerge from somewhere else—somewhere outside the realm of craftiness and cunning. As a defining moment in my life, I was ready to be completely honest with the four men who had taught me so much and for whom I was deeply grateful. In that instant, I realized that honesty would be the best way to give back to the founders of our firm.

So, the truth emerged.

"There are two reasons for my recent behavior," I began, steadying my voice. "You're right; I haven't been the same these past two weeks."

Taking a deep breath, I continued, "The first reason has to do with my work. After years of litigation, years of stepping into courtrooms ready to defend and fight for justice, I've come to a painful realization: The system I believed in, the system I poured my time, energy, and integrity into, is broken—or worse, corrupt.

"Over the past decade, I've committed myself to studying the law, continuing my education, and mastering every case I was given. But what I've seen—what I can no longer ignore—is that knowledge and preparation aren't always what wins. Influence does. Politics do—connections behind closed doors. I've witnessed solid cases unravel in the hands of biased judges or morally compromised attorneys. I've lost not because I wasn't prepared, but because the rules were never followed in the first place.

"Carrying that truth has become unbearable. The weight of my disillusionment is no longer something I can hide behind a suit or silence in a courtroom. I don't trust the system anymore—and I can't keep pretending I do. For me, this marks the end of the road as an attorney. And that's the first truth I needed to say out loud."

Then I paused. They were quiet, absorbing my answer.

No one reacted.

As though they knew there was more to the story, they waited.

I obliged.

"But there's more," I said, the words catching slightly in my throat.

I paused. My eyes dropped to my hands resting in my lap, and in that stillness, a single tear slipped free. I didn't wipe it away. I let it fall, let it speak for me, before I found the courage to speak for myself.

The silence stretched, but no one interrupted. They waited, the founding partners of this place I'd given so much to, sitting in stillness, giving me space to find my voice.

"When I was in Cancun," I began slowly, "something happened to me."

Another pause. I could hear my heartbeat in my ears.

"I met someone, a man from the United States. He was staying at the same hotel—the one you recommended. And I fell in love with him."

I said it with a soft, steady conviction—like a truth I'd been carrying in my chest, warming it quietly until this very moment. The words weren't rehearsed, but they were real. They came not from logic or strategy, but from somewhere deeper—the quiet knowing of the heart.

"I'm thinking of moving to the United States," I continued, "to see where this might go. That's not his plan, at least, not yet. It's mine. And maybe it's a little crazy. But right now, it feels like the most honest thing I've felt in a long time."

I let the words settle into the room, my mind echoing them back at me: *I hope this really is the plan.*

Then I took a breath and opened myself further.

"I need to be honest with all of you, the people I admire deeply, the people who have given me so much: I'm tired of always performing, always carrying the weight, at court, at the university, for the clients, for the firm. I'm tired of being the one who always holds it all together, of going home at night and having no one to share it with. And now, my body is beginning to show signs of wear, of stress that's become too familiar."

I looked up, my voice steadier now.

"This place has been everything to me. But I've reached a point where I need to live differently. I want to give myself permission to step into a new rhythm—one where peace, love, and breath are not luxuries, but essentials, one where I don't have to earn rest. I think I've had enough of the life I've known. And I'm ready—truly ready—for what comes next."

As I scanned the room, I could see teardrops coming from every face. What began as a hostile meeting with an investigative tone turned into a group healing session, full of understanding, support, and love.

Dr. Gilberto spoke first, "This is a beautiful story, Tina. I am in shock at what you've just told us, but I believe in God, and I know that we all have a plan in life. If this is your decision, I want to say just one thing to you: Hold onto God's hand and move."

Dr. C. was the next. Crying more than the others, he said, "I can't believe I was the one responsible for all of this! I told you to stay at the hotel where you met this man, and now, you're in love." Everyone erupted into laughter. He continued with a smile, "Tina, I think you have created an enormous amount of professional relationships, success, and money, but now, it's time to pay attention to your personal life. Yes, it's time. We will miss you here, but I am also very happy for you."

The other two partners, who were quieter and more subdued, smiled nonetheless, a sure indication of their understanding and support.

At the end of the meeting, we gave each other hugs, and the question was, "When can we meet the lucky American?"

That weekend, Mom and Dad also received the news, and I explained where I had been for the past few weeks. "I went to São

Paulo first, for the visa, and then to the United States to meet Mark, the man that I told you about, the guy from Texas."

They were both surprised but took the news with interest and warmth. "Tina, you always have a way of shaking our realities," said Mom.

"Does he have a ranch in Texas?" was Dad's reply.

••• 8 •••

LOOSENING THE GRIP

FROM THAT AUGUST weekend in 2004, the shape of my life began to shift—quietly at first, then unmistakably.

Soon, I became the story everyone was whispering about—in the office corridors, around family tables, within my closest circles. "Tina's in love with an American," they said. "She's moving to the United States. She's leaving everything behind for a man she barely knows."

I heard it often—sometimes with concern, sometimes with disbelief. But I let the words pass through me. They weren't mine to carry. I had accomplished everything I once set out to do. I had built an identity that fit the life I'd lived until then. However, now, it was time to listen inward. I needed to listen to my soul, my heart, my deeper needs. That meant stepping away from the world of achievement, even if just for a while. I wasn't entirely sure if choosing this new path with Mark was the "right" decision, but I knew it was mine. This choice wasn't about proving anything to anyone, not to a judge, not to a partner at the firm, not even to my father. It was about honoring my truth. I hadn't yet written the story I wanted for my life, but I was finally ready to start tracing the lines. And for that, I needed to be brave enough to take the risk.

There was still one final place I needed to show up with honesty: Unibrasil. The president's offer still stood—his invitation to lead the law department, a role many would have seen as the pinnacle of their career.

In our meeting, I sat across from him and shared a version of the truth, one that gave me room to leap without burning the bridge behind me. I told him I had plans to spend 2005 in the United States, pursuing a post-doctorate program. It wasn't exactly the truth. But in my mind, if things didn't work out with Mark, returning to Brazil to step into that role would still be possible, and I knew I would return to it with love.

With grace, he accepted my decision. I asked that my teaching contract be put on hold, and he agreed without hesitation.

He smiled warmly, wished me well, and sent me off with a blessing: "Go have a beautiful adventure."

And so I did.

September came. Mark landed in Brazil.

It was a particularly sunny and warm day in Curitiba. I was waiting for Mark at the airport, and this time, there was no misunderstanding regarding airport locations. There's only one of them in Curitiba!

I was carrying my little dog, Yanick, though by then, he had become more Dad's dog than mine. Years earlier, overwhelmed by my schedule and the demands of city life, I had handed Yanick over to Dad at the farm. But something unexpected happened: Dad, who had often been such a challenging presence in my life, grew attached to him. "This way, I can feel you closer to me, Tina," he once said, cradling Yanick like a keepsake. Now, with Mom and Dad visiting Curitiba to meet Mark, I took the chance to bring Yanick with me. But I'll admit, it wasn't only about the reunion. Mark is a dog lover, and part of me hoped that walking in with Yanick in my arms would soften the moment, maybe even speak for me in a language Mark understood best: trust, warmth, connection.

He saw me at the waiting area, and once again, smell played a significant role in my attraction to Mark. We hugged each other, and I could feel Mark's tension and anxiety. I could also tell he was ready for a cigarette. My heart beat faster now that the next phase of our adventure was beginning. Cigarette smoked, a quick stop at my apartment for sex, wine, and a bag drop, and then we were off to see my parents.

Mom awaited the cowboy from Texas with a family favorite meal: pasta and Mom's handmade sauce with onions, tomatoes, garlic, and peppers, red meat—fresh from the farm—salad, and the most popular dessert in Brazil: *pudim de leite* (milk flan). Still anxious and a little tense, Mark was genuinely happy to be in Curitiba. We felt like it had been years since we met. However, in reality, it had only been a month and a half since we saw each other for the first time.

The sincerity of our connection meant that I was able to be myself for the first time. *I don't need to pretend to be anyone other than myself,* I reflected. It was a different way of seeing my reflection in a relationship, and it felt healthy. There was no walking on eggshells and measuring my thoughts or words; things just developed naturally between us. Was there any apprehension? Yes, but it was more about the excitement of the unknown. There was no fear. It felt refreshing to express my feelings to someone I loved. And I felt loved and desired in return.

When in Dallas, Mark didn't make up anything about his life. He was truthful about all the pain and uncertainty he faced. That truth between us became a seed that was growing into something special.

As we stepped out of the elevator, the apartment door was decorated with two flags: one Brazilian and the other American. In between them was written, "Welcome, Mark!" My brothers were always surprising me.

I could tell Mark was already loving the spirit of our Brazilian family. As soon as we entered the door, I yelled, *"Chegamos!"* (We have arrived.) My whole family—Mom, Dad, brothers, and sisters-in-law started to chant loudly: "Mark! Mark! Mark! Mark! Mark!" This was probably the moment he discovered what it means to be part of a Brazilian family: lots of hugs and everyone talking at the same time (and loudly), laughing, and asking tons of questions.

It only took an hour for Mom and Dad to realize that Mark was not a cowboy but a regular man from Texas who builds houses, plays guitar, smokes, and loves to drink wine. My brother Fabiano, who has the most accurate English, made an early connection with Mark. Sitting next to each other at the lunch table, Fabiano kept looking at me and blinking his eyes, a sure sign indicating that "you found the right guy for you." Mark enjoyed the meal Mom had prepared with such love and joy for her daughter that it quickly became *the* dish she insisted on making every time she knew he was coming.

After a few hours around the table, Mom and Mark moved to the window to enjoy a cigarette as Dad played with Yanick on the floor. My brothers left for work. With the party over, a quieter atmosphere developed, and I got closer to Dad on the floor. We hugged each other, and I could feel Dad's bones. He still had his hair, but not on his legs, arms, and chest. Yanick was his little angel, his companion. As we looked at Mom and Mark by the window, Dad said to me, "I think you found a good guy. I am going to invite him to play tennis tomorrow. Do you think he would join me?"

Dad was hesitant to stop his activities, especially tennis. "Yes, Dad. I think he would love it," I said.

The integration between my family and Mark happened quite naturally and quickly.

In the office, the feeling was the same amongst my partners and the entire firm. By that point, they were all aware that in a few months, I would be saying goodbye, and the family law department would be led by someone else, or possibly closed.

Mark's days in Brazil were lighthearted and full of playful flirting. However, beneath the laughter, our conversations were deepening. Reality set in: We were no longer just a vacation romance; we were navigating the beginning of a long-distance relationship.

I had met his family and friends in Texas, and now, he had met mine.

The spirit between our two worlds—north and south—found an easy rhythm, evolving with a natural grace neither of us tried to force.

We slipped away for a few days to the beach, then returned for an important lunch with Dr. William, my senior partner at the firm and a quiet father figure in my life. It was he who had arranged the meeting, a gesture less formal than it appeared, but one weighted with meaning. Dr. William needed to see for himself that I was in good hands.

Over lunch, with Wiilliam's unpracticed English and Mark's attentive conversation, they managed to build a bridge of understanding between them. It wasn't about words so much as it was about presence and sincerity.

That meeting, brief as it was, offered something close to a silent blessing.

William never voiced his opinion aloud, but he didn't need to.

This was the same man who, years earlier, on the day of my engagement to Fasano, had quietly pulled me aside and asked, "Are you sure you want to marry this guy?"

Sometimes, the absence of protest speaks louder than any advice.

Sometimes, silence is agreement.

At Florianopolis beach in southern Brazil, Mark fell in love with Brazilian cuisine. I introduced him to *muqueca na moranga*, a traditional Brazilian dish made with shrimp and local spices, designed to be enjoyed by the ocean. He also loved Brazilian coffee and cappuccinos.

Mark fell in love with Brazil almost instantly, a passion that set him apart from the cautious voices of his friends and colleagues back in Dallas. They had told him, "Be careful, Mark. Brazil is dangerous. Women there date Americans for green cards and then leave them."

But that wasn't the story written in Mark's heart.

During our romantic trip, as the air between us thickened with unspoken truths, I chose to be the one to cross the bridge first. I looked at him, my heart steady, my voice clear, and said, "I love you.

I want to be with you. I'm ready to change my life to be with you in the United States."

Mark held my hands and smiled—softly, warmly—without rushing to fill the silence.

I pressed on, needing to be fully honest. "Long-distance dating is too expensive for us—emotionally, financially, in every way. If you don't feel the same, we should part ways when you return home."

There was no fear in me as I spoke, only a raw, empowering honesty that felt both terrifying and beautiful. It was the same force that had moved me in Cancun, the same pull that made me kiss him without hesitation, that led me to invite him into my world without second-guessing myself.

With Mark, there were no calculations, no shrinking. I didn't need to measure my words or hold back my feelings. For the first time in my life, I acted exactly as my heart urged me to act: without shame, without fear.

I had never known a love that allowed me to be so fully myself.

Holding my hands and looking straight into my eyes, Mark told me he was feeling the same, and he would love me to move to the United States. "But I can't get married now," he said. "I'm still dealing with my divorce. We should try it and see if you like living in America first."

I felt a togetherness on this new journey. We were about to redesign our destiny and our lives together. I feel as though the alignment in the sky the day we met was intentional. We were two souls escaping their pain, having suffered from the deceptions of previous relationships. However, now, these two souls were united, craving pure love and commitment without any pretension.

"No rush in life, Maria Christina. Just wait." I still remember those words, spoken by a German man named Rolf in 1999 while I was visiting a friend in Switzerland. We were sitting at her kitchen table, the scent of dinner filling the air as we sipped beer and talked about love. I had confessed how much I longed to meet someone, to marry, to find the right man to share my life with.

Rolf smiled and said, "Tina, stop searching for him. Just wait. When the time is right, he will come—and you'll know."

So, I waited. Five years passed between that summer evening in 1999 and the summer of 2004. And when he came—when Mark walked into my life—it was when I least expected it, when I wasn't even thinking about love at all.

The Universe, I've learned, is always at work, quietly placing dots along our paths: moments, encounters, shifts we cannot yet understand. It is up to us to trace the lines between them, to connect these points with the thread of our choices, our courage. Sometimes, we step backward; sometimes, the path winds away from where we thought we were headed. However, every dot matters. Every line we draw shapes the story of who we are becoming.

After an incredible week together, Mark flew back to the United States, and we made a plan: I would move to Dallas in December, and we would live together. I told Mark, "Find me a yoga studio, a church, and a school to study English at. That's all I need for now."

We visited each other two more times, and on December 28, I left Brazil behind: my family, my career, my friends, and the life I had built over thirty-two years. I departed with four suitcases full of clothes, shoes, and essentials I needed to make Mark's house our new home.

My family was happy and excited for me. The love Mark and I shared, along with the trust we were building, was real. My housekeeper, Martinha, told me that the first day she saw me after the Cancun trip, there was a different light in my face.

"That trip has changed you, Tina," she said. "You found light again."

That December, before I left, I invited Mom, Dad, my brothers, and their wives to come to my apartment to celebrate Christmas. Grandma Teresa and Uncle Tets stayed in Porto Alegre for the first time in many years, which meant we didn't all spend the holidays together as was our tradition. It would be the last Christmas my immediate family sat together around the same table. Grandma Teresa died four months later at the age of ninety-two, but until her death, I called her weekly from Dallas. I even brought a few keepsakes to the US that she had given me the year before her death. One was a complete silverware set in gold and silver that was from her wedding. The others were a Bible and a bell. All of them are still with me today.

Although Grandma suffered from cardiovascular disease in her last year, she held on for a long time, but the true gift was that Mom and I inherited her fighting nature. Her death, however, was most difficult on Tets, who had been her caregiver for as long as anyone could remember. I even recall suggesting that the two of them move closer to us so we could help with the caregiving, but Mom's hands were full with Dad at that time, and she'd told me that it was better if things just stayed as they were.

When I departed Brazil, my friends were divided: Some celebrated my happiness while others warned me of being overly optimistic. "You are brave, but crazy," I heard several times. Although "I hope everything goes well" was the most common response. Regardless, I was listening to my heart and flying with my wings.

Farewell. "Farewell" to my family and friends. And a simple "goodbye and good luck" to the law firm.

As it turns out, the family law department was never resurrected after I departed, and in some way, I suspect they knew that would be the case. The success story created there has left a lasting impression on me, and it's now part of my memories.

··· 9 ···

THE MARRIAGE I MISTOOK FOR FREEDOM

AFTER AN EMOTIONAL Christmas dinner filled with tears, laughter, and whispered blessings of "I hope all goes well with your dream," I boarded a plane and landed in Dallas, Texas, on December 29, 2004. As we hugged at the airport, Mom's parting words echoed in my mind: "Go, enjoy, and make lots of babies. Children are an important part of life." Dad could barely find his voice through the tightness in his throat, but his embrace said everything.

Thirty-five thousand feet above the earth, I flew toward a life unwritten—no expectations, no promises. It felt less like a move and more like a sabbatical from everything I had ever known, a long vacation without a set return date, a crossing into a land where the language, the culture, and even the air would be unfamiliar. There was no drama in my leaving, only the quiet certainty that one chapter had closed.

In Brazil, I had traced the lines of a life shaped by duty, by the silent scars of abuse, by years of my voice being censored. For thirty-two years, that little girl inside me had been sketching an invisible map to freedom, and now, at last, she had found a door she could walk through.

What I didn't yet realize was that this new chapter wouldn't be a clean escape, but another layer of discovery. One that would test my understanding of love, safety, and what it truly meant to be free.

Still, standing at the edge of the unknown, I was ready to let life draw its next constellation of dots, ready to trace new lines with my hand, no matter where they would lead.

I landed in Dallas, Texas, on a dark winter morning. It was 6:30 a.m. Mark was expecting me at the airport, and this time, there were no mistakes. He was waiting with arms open and a genuine smile on his face. His body was warm, just the way I remembered it, and one of the things that attracted me to him.

"Welcome home, Tina," Mark said to me as we arrived at his home. It was a beautiful sight: Christmas presents were under the tree, and Mark's dogs, Sammy and Suzie, were there to greet me with their wagging tails. Mark carried all four of my suitcases into the house.

Now what's going to happen? I wondered.

We celebrated our first New Year's Eve together, promising to always spend birthdays, Christmases, and New Year's by each other's side. It was a new way of turning the page: cold, quiet, and far from the Brazilian traditions I had known, like wearing white, eating grapes, and jumping waves for good luck. Slowly, I began to mold myself to a new culture.

My days settled into a simple rhythm: morning yoga, walking the dogs, studying English in the afternoons. Mark bought me a bicycle so I could get around the neighborhood for groceries and errands, a lifestyle that amused the locals, who thought it was "European." I kept my laugh to myself, thinking, *No, just Brazilian—and living simply.*

I discovered Starbucks chai tea lattes, learned to cook for the two of us, and fell into long, peaceful walks with the dogs. Mornings were especially sweet: Mark would bring me coffee in bed, greeting me with, "Good morning, Sunshine," and he often left love notes hidden between the bathroom and the kitchen.

We lived in a small, two-bedroom, one-bathroom cottage-style house, much more modest than the sprawling American homes around us. While Mark went off to work each day, I built a quiet life: yoga, dogs, school, cooking, making love, and starting over.

I spoke to Grandma Teresa every Wednesday and Sunday, and her first question was always the same: "How is he treating you?" Meanwhile, Mom stayed busy caring for Dad as he continued his cancer treatment. Life was different now: quieter, simpler, and just beginning to unfold.

Four months passed. For the first time in my life, I wasn't chasing, planning, or hunting the next move. I was simply living, often barefoot, perceiving life as it unfolded, one breath, one moment at a time.

Mark lived simply. There was no money for extravagance, but once a week, we would treat ourselves to dinner at Hillstone, a cozy bar where we would sit side by side, drink red wine, and talk about everything and nothing. A hundred dollars for a dinner out—that's what Mark's modest budget could stretch to, and it was enough.

Back in Brazil, I still had a few lingering financial obligations, but here, I allowed myself to flow with the present—no grasping, no forcing, just being.

Each day, each week, each month, I felt myself softening. Peace and love settled into the spaces where anxiety used to live. Commitment and support became our quiet rhythm. I had left behind a Mercedes-Benz in my garage in Brazil, but it was on an old bicycle, pedaling through sleepy neighborhood streets, that I felt true happiness and a freedom I had never known.

It was a shift in perspective I couldn't have imagined before. I had spent years clinging to the pursuit of success, building an identity of power, achievement, and material wealth. I believed it was what would make me whole. However, here, in the simplicity, I was discovering something far more precious: my essence, my spirit, my truth.

The earlier chapters of my life had taught me about survival, performance, and ego. First, because I had to survive the prison of my mind and the silence and shame of childhood. Later, because even after I found my wings through education and hard work, I was still flying with the mindset of a prisoner, seeking approval and settling for less than I was worth.

The best way out is through.
I didn't know that until I had already crossed the threshold.

Sometimes, the first step toward transformation is simply removing ourselves from people, circumstances, and the familiar habits that keep us small. The Universe plays a hand in moving the dots around, but it is up to us to be willing to step into the unknown and trust that the lines will trace themselves if only we allow them.

It was Wednesday night, April 15, 2005. I was in the bathroom, drying my hair, getting ready for a small celebration for the completion of my first quarter of English as a Second Language classes. We were planning to eat at Gloria's restaurant, a simple gathering to mark the beginning of a new chapter.

As I stood in front of the mirror, caught between the old and the new versions of myself, Mark appeared in the doorway. He said nothing at first. Then, slowly, he dropped to one knee on the bathroom floor, right there between the hum of the hairdryer and the ordinary clutter of our life together.

"Tina," he said, his voice steady but full of something deeper, something trembling underneath. "Will you marry me?"

I froze. My heart stuttered in my chest. I hadn't seen it coming—not tonight, not in this way, not in the middle of our everyday life. And yet, it felt exactly right.

With my hands trembling and tears filling my eyes, I bent down to him, wrapped my arms around his shoulders, and whispered into his ear, "Yes! Of course, I want to marry you!"

He slid a delicate, princess-style diamond ring onto my finger, a small circle of light, a promise made tangible. In that quiet, unglamorous room, surrounded by nothing special, everything changed. It was not the grand gesture that mattered. It was the simplicity, the sincerity, the way life had drawn another dot on the map of my story—one I would gladly trace for the rest of my days.

Without forcing anything, life seemed to be working out well. I started to exercise and began to understand that being less worried and less planned would bring me a more authentic way of enjoying the rhythms of life.

The next step was to travel to Brazil and formally announce the engagement to my family and friends. After a simple celebration with Mom, Dad, my brothers, and their wives, I returned to America as a formal bride-to-be. I also took the next step of making plans to obtain a green card. Despite the speed at which we were moving, we began to discuss the idea of starting a family.

But what about the fear?

•••10•••
DOTS CREATING FIGURES

BACK FROM BRAZIL with a ring on my left hand, the sabbatical I'd convinced myself I was taking began to fit the shape of reality. I ended up selling my apartment and my car in Brazil, closing my bank accounts, announcing my retirement from the college job, and formally registering as a legal resident of the United States. My temporary tourist and student visas were expiring, and as a former attorney, I respected the letter of the law. I never wanted to abuse the warm welcome the country had shown me, and following the legal process of obtaining residence and citizenship became a priority.

Routines became quite important to me, allowing time to acclimate to the new country and learn skills that would set me up for success. As my routines became my new way of life, I was slowly moving away from the thought that my decision to move to Texas was temporary or a trial.

Now engaged to Mark, I found myself not just redesigning my life in America, a country I had long resisted even visiting, but also reshaping who I was within it. The old Maria Christina de Almeida belonged to another chapter, one that had served its purpose. In her place, Christina Siepiela was beginning to take form. She was a woman stepping into a new story, learning how to exist within the rhythms and expectations of a different culture and within the intimate universe she was building alongside Mark. It wasn't just a move across continents. It was the quiet birth of a new identity.

What I didn't yet realize was that I was still seeking safety in something outside of myself. Mark had given me room to breathe—more space than I'd ever known—but I hadn't yet learned how to breathe for myself. I was trading one kind of structure for another, no longer bound by fear or dominance but by roles I didn't fully question at the time: wife, mother, newcomer, country club member. While deeply loved, I was still defining myself in relation to someone else. Though this chapter was softer and more beautiful than the ones before it, I hadn't yet asked the most important question: *Who am I when I stop performing for the world around me?*

Time has a quiet power not only to reveal what we need to see but also to guide us toward who we're meant to become. It carries us through the necessary seasons of growth, transformation, and becoming. I once read a quote that stayed with me: "Your life right now is a result of what you did a year ago. Your life a year from now will be a result of what you do right now. Act accordingly." —Anonymous

On July 1, 2005, Mark and I tied the knot at a beautiful private ceremony in his brother's backyard. At sunset, the priest declared us husband and wife, and we exchanged necklaces in the name of our commitment. I was still living a form of sabbatical life in Dallas while Mark worked hard to recreate his business. Watching it all unfold, Mark remained steadfast in providing a safe and nurturing environment. Every step he took was in the name of happiness, our future, and love. Words of reinforcement were always exchanged, and his actions always mirrored his supporting words.

Meanwhile, we rented a new house with a pool. Mark came to understand how much sunshine and water meant to me, especially during the relentless Texas summers. One afternoon in 2005, we were sitting at a sushi bar, flipping through a calendar and dreaming aloud. We circled the date and sealed it with meaning. While I waited for my green card and couldn't travel internationally, I channeled my energy into planning the wedding I had always dreamed of. And I made it happen—every detail, every moment, just as I'd imagined.

According to tradition, a Brazilian wedding needed to be planned and paid for. I chose March 11, 2006, in honor of my mother; it was her birthday. She never had a wedding of her own, never wore a dress, or posed for photos. But now, through me, she would. My father was ill and struggling financially. My mother, too, was getting by with help from my brothers, now that I was no longer in Brazil to contribute. So, how could I afford my dream wedding?

I called Jocymara (JO) my architect and best friend, the same woman who once helped me choose two sinks instead of one. I told her, "Jo, I need to sell my apartment. I live in America now. I don't need property in Curitiba, and I want to celebrate this new life with the wedding of my dreams. I don't have the money yet, but once the apartment sells, I can pay."

As always, Jo didn't hesitate. "Tina, no worries. That magical place will sell fast." And it did.

It was bittersweet. Jo had designed every detail with love, elegance, and care. Letting go wasn't easy, but she understood why I was doing it. She said she had never seen a woman so radiant about what was to come. Perhaps the apartment had never truly been meant for me to live in forever. Maybe I was the one to dream it into existence, so someone else could live their dream inside it. Sometimes, we are the creators, not the keepers.

In just two months, the apartment was sold, furnished at full price. The money landed in my account, and just like that, I could make my dream real.

My wedding cost me my first property. Was there any pain in that? None. I had no regrets. My hard work and accomplishments were now funding a new dream.

My green card arrived on February 14, 2006. That was the day I formally became a legal resident in the United States.

I left for Brazil on February 16 while Mark stayed in Dallas to work. He and his family would land in Brazil a few days before the wedding.

Fabio, the oldest of my twin brothers, was going through a divorce and had requested some time with me to view his documents and organize files.

When I landed in Curitiba with my suitcase in one hand and my silk wedding gown in the other, Fabio, Dad, and Mom were there waiting for me. Their smiles were wide, their arms warm with welcome. It had been nearly a year since we'd last been together, and this time I was returning not just as Tina, but as a bride-to-be. True to form, Dad said, "Let's get a picture of this moment," and flagged down a passerby at the airport to snap one. We all rolled our eyes, as we always did, but stood close and smiled for him. It was one of those small, familiar rituals we didn't think twice about. That is, until life shifts, and suddenly, those ordinary snapshots carry the weight of everything.

On Sunday, Dad left to go back to the farm after welcoming his only daughter as the bride-to-be. Before he left, we shared a conversation about the wedding plans, and he updated me on his treatment. We were all set to see one another a few days before the big event.

I woke up that Sunday to a gray, cloudy sky. "Mom, no chance for a pool day today!" I joked. Instead, we went to Mass, then returned home for a quiet lunch, just the two of us. As we finished the meal she'd prepared, she asked, "What time does Fabio want to meet you to talk about the divorce?"

"He said he'd call around three-thirty," I replied.

After lunch, I stretched out for a nap while I waited. Just two nights before, Fabio and I had talked on the phone. He'd shared some of the challenges he was facing with his soon-to-be ex-wife. There were no children involved, but he faced the usual struggles over property and support. Despite it all, his voice was calm and gentle, as always. He mentioned how much he loved the hat Mark had sent him. At the time, I didn't realize how precious that conversation would become. I was distracted, caught up in wedding plans and the whirlwind around me. It was a quiet lesson I'd only fully grasp later: Sometimes, we don't know when a moment is the last one we'll have.

Three-thirty came, but Fabio didn't call. I gave it some time—four o'clock, still nothing. By five, I dialed his cell, and there was no answer. Then I called his house—nothing. "Mom, it's weird. Fabio's never like this," I said. "He's not answering, and he's late for our meeting."

"He probably went for a bike ride," she offered. "You know how he loves the park on Sundays."

We waited until seven, thinking maybe he'd gone to evening Mass. However, by 7:15, the silence was too loud to ignore. I called my other brothers, Fernando and Fabiano, and told them what was happening. "Mom and I are going to his house to check on him."

Fabiano picked us up, and Fernando met us there. It was dark. Rain was falling. The house was silent. The lights were off. Fabio's car was in the garage.

The curtains were drawn and the doors locked. My stomach dropped. I held Mom's hand tightly, heart racing.

"Could his ex-wife have done something?" I whispered. "Was there a break-in? Is he hurt?"

No one had a key. We were frozen—literally and emotionally—standing in front of the house, unable to move.

Fabiano acted. He climbed onto the garage cover and broke the glass of a small window, which was Fabio's bedroom window. We watched, holding our breath, as he crawled inside.

Mom, Fernando, and I stood motionless on the front step, our minds racing, our bodies numb.

Then we heard Fabiano's voice.

"He's here! He's here! I found him!"

A pause.

Then a scream, raw and shattering. "He's not alive!"

Mom collapsed into our arms. We caught her, shaking and speechless. Fabiano ran to unlock the front door, and we carried

Mom inside, where Fernando kept her seated in the living room, shielding her from what we knew she couldn't bear to see.

I stepped into Fabio's room.

He was lying face down on the bed, unmoving. His body had already darkened. His arms were tucked beneath him, the way he always liked to sleep. I stood there in disbelief, unable to touch him, unable to speak. My brother—my sweet, kind brother—was gone.

He had passed in his sleep sometime between Saturday night and Sunday morning. After having friends over, he'd gone to bed and never woken up.

The autopsy the next day confirmed what we never could have guessed: a brain aneurysm, not his heart, as I'd suspected, though heart issues ran in Mom's family. No, it was his brain. The very part of his body that had challenged him since birth. The quiet, hidden threat that had been with him all along.

Congenital conditions. Surgeries. Medications. Seizures. And now, finally, this.

At thirty-six years old, Fabio—our angel—was gone. The aneurysm, silent and swift, had taken him from us without warning.

"Mom," Sophia said softly, "you never talk much about your brother."

I closed my eyes for a moment. The memory of Fabio still lived just under my skin, never far, never fully gone.

"It's hard to talk about him," I admitted.

Helena tilted her head. "Was he older than you?"

"A little, but emotionally, he felt much older. He carried everything, everyone's pain, everyone's weight."

I paused. The silence around us thickened with the unsaid.

"His death broke something in me," I continued. "And for a long time, I didn't let myself feel it. I was a newlywed, far away, building a new life. It felt wrong to grieve while the rest of my family was drowning in sorrow. So, I pushed it down and told myself I had to be strong."

Sophia reached over and took my hand.

"Sometimes, I still dream about him," I said, "not the way he died, but the way he lived—his laugh, his kindness, his quiet strength. When he left, it was like a thread in me snapped, and I didn't know how to tie it back together."

"Is that why you're so open with us about feelings?" Helena asked.

I looked at her, my throat tightening.

"Yes," I said, "because grief shouldn't be carried alone. I did that for too many years, and I want you both to know that strength isn't about holding it in. It's about letting it move through you and then choosing to keep loving anyway."

"You know, Mom," Sophia said, "you couldn't have stopped what happened."

"I know that now. But back then, I was still clinging to the idea that I could protect everyone. I figured that if I loved enough, worked hard enough, stayed present enough, maybe I could keep the bad things from happening."

Helena laid her head on my shoulder. Sophia leaned in closer.

We sat in silence for a while—not to fix anything, just to *be*.

In our family, Fabio had always been our symbol of peace. He was the one who protected me and tried to stop Dad from being so physically and emotionally aggressive toward Mom, my brothers, or me. He was the one everyone loved, both at the workplace and in social settings. He was also Tets's favorite. For a few years, Fabio lived with Tets and Grandma when he wanted to spend more time in Curitiba to be closer to us. He was the guarantor when I signed my first apartment lease. "I want you to be able to create your life, Tina," he told me at the time.

It stung even more because during my last call with him, I rushed to hang up because I was too busy with my wedding plans. He wanted to talk more, but I said, "Okay, Binho [his nickname], we'll talk more on Sunday."

"All right, Tina, just tell Mark I am wearing the hat he gave me every day." Those were his last words to me.

After the ambulance took Fabio's body away, Mom, Fabiano, and I drove back to Mom's house while Fernando followed behind, alone. I held her—not just her hands but her entire body. "Who is going to call Dad at the farm to tell him about what happened?" I asked.

"Fernando will call Dad tomorrow morning," Fabiano replied.

We were in the middle of two opposite forces: life and death.

"Mom, would you like me to cancel the wedding?" I whispered in her ear as we both continued to wet our faces with the saddest tears we had ever experienced.

She held my hand hard, squeezing it, and told me: *"Minha filha, cada filho tem uma história de vida. A do seu irmão terminou hoje. O teu casamento vai acontecer. Você continue a tua história."*

I still hold on to those words and the lesson my mom shared that day: "My daughter, every child has their story. Your brother's day ended today. Your wedding will continue to happen, and you will continue your story."

The next day, Fernando went to pick up Dad at the farm. When Dad answered the door, Fernando was speechless, eyes soaked with tears.

"Who was it?" Dad asked, immediately registering the loss communicated by Fernando's face. Sometimes, more is said without words.

"Fabio."

And with that, the two men returned in silence to Curitiba.

Given Fabio's beautiful personality, his funeral attracted over four hundred guests, including friends and family.

The sight of my parents, broken and hollowed by grief, standing beside Fabio's casket that afternoon is something I will never forget. It tore through me like a blade to my soul. Numb to the weight of reality, I scanned the scene: my mother and father trembling in disbelief, my brothers, Fernando and Fabiano, standing frozen in pain, a sea of mourners shedding tears for a man who embodied peace, kindness, and quiet strength. I kept asking the same questions repeatedly: "Why did this have to happen?" and "Why, now, in the middle of this new chapter of my life?" I found myself caught between two truths: my heartbreak over the timing and a deeper sorrow for my family's loss. In that delicate balance between personal longing and collective mourning, I tried to hold onto grace. Maybe this, too, was one of the dots the universe planted—uninvited, cruel, and senseless as it seemed. And maybe, somehow, it belonged to the line I was meant to trace.

Flowers were sent from Mark's family, symbolizing their support and offering joy and optimism for the big wedding day.

All of us moved forward with the wedding plans, except that the pain became part of the process, not an ugly pain, more of a sorrowful acknowledgment of the beauty of marriage and the heartbreak that represented Fabio's passing.

Unfortunately, in the aftermath of Fabio's death, Dad's condition seemed to worsen, stripped of the last vestiges of his vitality. His mental state was precarious, and he became more aggressive, especially on the day I took him to try on his wedding suit. I remember him not talking to me, and that made me feel guilty. I felt as though I should have cancelled or postponed the wedding. While he never confirmed the reason for his behavior, his actions told the whole story.

Mom was numb. She was quiet for a few days, but when Mark's family arrived, her bright spirit emerged and made all of them feel like they were at home.

··· 11 ···
THE SHOW MUST GO ON

THE CEREMONY STARTED at 6:00 p.m. That day, I felt like the most beautiful woman in the world. As I finished getting ready in my hotel room, my hairdresser, Jose, who had done my hair for years, and Jane, the makeup artist with whom I also had a relationship, were the only two people in the room. As confidants, they were aware of the painful circumstances mixed with the joy and anticipation of my incredible life story about to culminate in marriage. I was their treasure that day, and all the energy and talent they had were directed to the spirit of love.

With hair and makeup done, they put the veil on my head and asked me to come closer to the bathroom mirror. "Open your eyes, Tininha," Jose said.

I did, upon which I saw the most beautiful young lady in front of me, ready to present herself as a bride to the man for whom she had completely changed her life. "I see you, and I love you," I told myself as I looked at the mirror.

Dad was waiting for me downstairs in the lobby.

He was emotional and, once again, couldn't articulate his words easily. "*Você está linda, filha*" (You look beautiful, daughter), he said, looking down, a tear dripping as he returned to his quietness.

Mom was dressed yellow to match my bouquet of calla lilies. To this day, they're still my favorite flowers. Dad and Tets looked dapper in their elegant suits. Fernando and Fabiano were handsome, too. The absence of Grandma Teresa and Binho was felt by us all.

Interestingly, a yellow butterfly was captured on film by a friend during the ceremony. Afterward, she came to me and said, "Your brother was here tonight in the form of a butterfly."

The photographer also captured it, and as Mark and I met him after the wedding to review the proof, he asked us, "Did you guys see the butterfly throughout your entire wedding ceremony? It was dancing around the mirrored disco ball the entire night, and it's in tons of your wedding pictures."

From that evening on, Fabio came to be symbolized by a butterfly—a gentle reminder that life doesn't end, it simply transforms. We are always changing, always becoming, which added a deeper meaning to what Mom once said to me with quiet wisdom, "Each child, each person, has their story. Follow yours."

Fabio was gone. My family was shattered. And yet, I had a new relationship to care for and a life to build. I felt like I was holding joy in one hand and sorrow in the other, not knowing how to carry both without dropping one.

What I didn't fully understand at the time was how tightly I was still clinging to the identity of the good daughter, the peacemaker, the bridge between worlds. *Clinging syndrome* showed up in my grief, too, convincing me I had to hold everything and everyone together. However, grief doesn't care about our roles. It demands presence, not performance. Eventually, I had to face the fact that letting go was an act of love, not betrayal.

...12...

THE ART OF TRACING

THE PAIN OF losing Fabio never disappeared from Mom and Dad's lives. Dad's cancer path became worse, and his mental stability was adversely affected.

Years later, Fernando was diagnosed with type two diabetes, the roots perhaps tied to the amount of pain he incurred on the night we found Fabio and the ensuing five-hour drive to deliver the news to Dad. Fabiano developed psoriasis, his skin a symbol of the stress that contaminated our family on that tragic night. Bano was the one who had found Fabio dead on his bed. I can't even imagine what Bano's system registered the moment he turned on the lights and found my brother dead, blackened, and in his pajamas. Those moments and scenes would have been forever recorded in my brother's brain and heart.

After a beautiful honeymoon on the beaches of Trancoso in northern Brazil, it was time to step fully into the new life I had chosen and to become Mrs. Christina Sicpicla. The woman I had been, Maria Christina de Almeida, was no longer. Her identity, her cocoon, her life in Brazil had been lovingly laid to rest. As a close friend, the one who spotted the butterfly on our wedding night, once told me, "Your life will never be the same. Maria Christina, the attorney, is gone. If I hadn't known her before, I'd never believe she existed." I used to call this friend "my witch." She, too, is no longer.

Christina Siepiela wasn't just a new name; it was the birth of a new me, a woman unbound from the past, rebuilt from love, loss, and everything in between. This was not just a change on paper; it was a declaration: *I am no longer who I was. I am who I choose to become.*

I returned to the United States, leaving behind a family shattered by loss. The joy of my recent marriage stood in stark contrast to the grief of losing Fabio. The emotional dissonance created a kind of numbness that allowed me to step into the new life I was building with Mark, even as part of my heart remained in Brazil.

Mom's words from that terrible night echoed quietly in my mind, words that gave me permission to keep moving forward. I knew she would mourn in her way, as would Dad and my other brothers. We each had our story to live, and mine was asking me to continue. So, hand in hand with Mark and carrying the weight of both love and sorrow, I flew back to Texas to begin shaping a new reality.

Back in the States, a new life lay ahead of me, just like a blank sheet of paper in front of a writer or a blank canvas for an artist. I went back to Dallas ready to restart the story of my life.

I didn't want to carry my family name anymore. I couldn't fully explain it at the time, but something deep inside me knew that the new Christina needed more than a fresh start. She needed a new name, a new identity to match the woman I was becoming. So, I removed "de Almeida" from my legal documents and officially became Maria Christina Siepiela.

To me, it felt like a quiet burial of the woman I used to be. The one who had achieved so much but at such a heavy emotional cost. I was finally ready to write a new story, to live from a place of freedom, not survival. However, what I didn't yet understand was that even with a new name, old patterns have a way of following us—unless we choose to face them.

Little by little, based on the foundation of communication, safety, and mutual admiration, I redesigned myself. I'd never imagined being married, much less living in America. Though I always dreamed of something different and big, I didn't know that leaving my homeland, my career, my family, and all that was familiar to me would be that big and that different.

Suddenly, financial dependence wasn't just a concept; it was my reality. I had cut all financial ties with Brazil—no more property, no job prospects waiting. I was officially on my own, and yet, I was not.

Now, I was stepping into a life that many women start with: relying on their husbands for financial support. With that step came a quiet unease. I was opening not just a new chapter but an entirely new book, one written in the ink of contradiction and surprise.

My mother had warned me gently but firmly, "Create your independence, my dear. I gave your father control of everything: my time, my choices, my voice, all in the name of love. I don't regret the love, but I wish I had kept more of myself. Try to do it differently."

And I did. As an attorney and professor, I built a life on my terms. I fought for it. However, in the name of love, I chose a different path, only to find myself arriving exactly where I once stood.

••• 13 •••

BREASTMILK AND MOURNING

ON NOVEMBER 11, Mark and I went out to celebrate my thirty-third birthday. Mark was forty-two years old. During dinner, I addressed the topic of having kids. We'd been married for about six months already, and aging was on our minds, particularly as it related to becoming parents.

"Can we start having kids soon?" I asked.

Mark, a little hesitant, answered, "I think we should wait a little bit. I need to be more financially ready for children."

Was it a precaution, or fear?

It had been the same hesitation a year earlier when I asked him about living together, "Yes, but let's not get married yet. I still have financials to take care of from my previous marriage." However, here I was, married. So maybe my fear was unfounded.

To put it into context, Mark had just launched his own home-building company. I stood by his side, committed, supportive, and stepping into the unfamiliar rhythm of what it meant to be a wife in a traditional American household: devotion, adaptation, a quiet reshaping of self to meet this new beginning.

Pangs of familiarity may have rippled through my body, seeing a past version of my mom. However, they didn't fully register.

We were busy building a life together, and we were in love, so we decided to have children. However, by July 2006, we'd been trying to have a baby for months without success. I hadn't used birth control in over a year, and we were regularly intimate, yet nothing was happening. Mark had once mentioned fertility issues in a previous relationship, so I decided to take action and found a highly recommended fertility doctor.

At our appointment, the doctor asked direct, open questions about our sex life and goals. He ordered tests for both of us, and by September, I underwent a procedure to clean my fallopian tubes—a painful, sensitive exam I faced alone. As he finished, the doctor said many women conceive within a week of that procedure.

He was right. I got pregnant.

Whether it was the medical intervention, our increased intimacy, divine timing—or all of it combined—it happened. A miracle arrived. It could also have been the fact that we had sex twice a day, or maybe it was me lying on the floor with my legs straight up against the wall like a fertility yogi on a mission. Whatever it was, it worked.

Being pregnant was one of the most beautiful times of my life. I felt pretty, sexy, and healthy. I also felt blessed, light, and happy. Amidst losing Fabio and Teresa, my pregnancy brought back joy and radiance to my life. It also served to unite our two families: the Almeidas and the Siepielas. The baby was expected and desired by everyone on both sides of the family.

When I found out I was pregnant, I called Mark and told him to come home because I wasn't feeling well. As he approached the house, I was already outside, in my yoga clothes, waiting for him with three pharmacy tests in hand: all of them positive. He parked, and I jumped up to the truck window, showing the three pregnancy tests. He got out of the truck, hugged me, pulled me into his arms, and we went inside to celebrate with our dogs, Sammy and Suzie. Our smiling faces, the dogs' exuberance, and our families' excitement told the whole story.

In Brazil, Mom started to make plans to come to Dallas for the delivery date, which was forecast for the summer of 2007. Dad was still dealing with constant travel between Curitiba, the farm, and the hospital. He had visibly weakened, mostly due to the heavy medications, as the cancer began to aggressively spread throughout his body.

During the holiday season, Mark and I flew to Brazil for Christmas. It was a way to show off my beautiful belly and share with my family and friends the beauty and blessings of expecting a baby. The woman who had once left Brazil chasing ambition and independence returned carrying a very different version of herself: married, pregnant, and on the cusp of motherhood. Five years earlier, when I was immersed in career hustle and financial success, no one would have guessed this was where my path would lead, not even me.

We celebrated Christmas at the beach that year. The crew included Mark, Mom, Dad, Tets, Fabiano, his girlfriend, Fernando, his wife, and me. It was a new routine for Mark, who had previously spent all his Christmases in the cold—and sometimes in the snow. For us Brazilians, summer is the season of lights, gifts, and family time. In our family, it also meant beach time. That's how we rang in 2007, even if there was a dark cloud hovering over us.

The trip revealed the painful and sad reality of Dad's situation as his mental well-being had deteriorated profoundly.

Bano and Fernando had warned me, "Dad isn't himself anymore." They'd seen flashes of the man we all remembered from the darkest days: angry, volatile, even physically aggressive with Mom. It was as if the cancer, and perhaps the medications, were pulling apart his mind and body, leaving him untethered from reality. Or maybe it was the lingering grief over Fabio, still raw and unresolved, compounding his bitterness with that old, unanswerable question: *Why me?*

Dad never learned how to talk about his feelings. No one ever showed him how. His only language was pain, anger, and silence. He was a survivor in the harshest sense, mentally, emotionally, and now physically. But he wasn't really living anymore. He was just enduring, stuck in a slow-motion collapse, trying to claw his way through to something that felt like control.

When he saw me pregnant, he couldn't summon a single word of support or joy. Instead, one morning at the beach house, as I prepared coffee and set the table, he stormed toward me and erupted, spitting venomous words at me, at Mom, at all of us. There was so much hate, frustration, and heartbreak in his voice that it hit me like a wave. My body stiffened, instinctively recoiling the way it used to when I was younger and afraid of what might come next.

I backed away and went straight to my room. "Dad's not the same anymore," I told Mark, my voice shaking. Even he could see it; Dad was slipping, falling into his own kind of hell, dragging pieces of us with him.

That holiday was the last time I saw Dad. I remember our last hug, more fearful than loving. And I remember thinking, *I don't recognize you anymore, Dad.*

Even Mom was afraid of being alone with Dad, but a deep sense of duty kept her at his side as he attempted to win against an undefeated opponent. Had the battle been waged at the tennis court, perhaps he'd have stood a chance, but this nemesis would be too much to handle, maybe for both of them.

···14···
FIGHTING FOR SOPHIA

MY PREGNANCY CAME to an end, and with it, a beautiful new life began—for me, for Mark, and for our families. Sophia was born on a sunny Wednesday afternoon, May 30, 2007, marking the start of an entirely new chapter.

Mom had dreamed of being there for the birth, but the Universe had other plans. The American consulate denied her tourist visa, and she was horrified by the way she was treated—by a pregnant woman, no less. The woman assumed Mom was going to the United States to leave her sick husband and tend to her daughter's new baby. She even said as much, which caused yet another huge pain for my mother to live with.

I had Sophia after fourteen hours in labor. I tried to have a natural delivery, but it didn't work. Again, the Universe had another plan for me. I ended up having an emergency C-section, but it turned out beautifully. Sophia arrived healthy, pretty, smiley, and ready to be loved. Our families in the US and Brazil were in party mode, and they couldn't wait to see the new life that had just been born into the world. For those first four days, she was all mine and Mark's. And she couldn't possibly have received more of our attention. All the words and kisses directed at her filled every ounce of my heart with pure love.

Perhaps the most powerful moment during my stay at the hospital was the first night after giving birth. Mark went home after twenty-four hours straight in the hospital. Meanwhile, I practiced the first steps of breastfeeding until the nurse took Sophia to the nursery so I could enjoy a couple of hours of nap time. Exhaustion was real!

At around three o'clock in the morning, the nurse came back with Sophia in her arms and said to me, "Mom, she's hungry again." I was in a deep sleep, exhausted from being awake for over twenty-four hours. The physical pain of motherhood had just started, but as soon as I felt her little body against mine, there was no more pain. It felt like everything had started again at that moment, and I reconnected with the emotions of being a mom and looked at my baby nestled on my chest. In silence, the nurse left, and I remained fixated on Sophia as she sucked hard on my nipple, making the most beautiful skin-to-skin connection with me.

I understood love at that moment—the kind of love that comes purely from the heart, the unconditional love that connects mothers to children, the one kind of love that nobody can teach you because only if you're a mom you can understand the deep connection of motherhood. Moms recognize the smell, the touch, and the feel of the creatures we are blessed to create. The birth of a child marks the first sign of an invisible force that unites mothers and daughters. I've come to learn that the connection between these two humans can appear in different ways, sometimes in physical cuddling, sometimes in deep confessions. Whatever the method, it occurred to me that the force I was feeling was the same one Mom had felt with her kids our entire lives.

In 2007, after decades of captivity—emotional, psychological, and spiritual—Mom's long imprisonment came to an end. Dad lost his battle with cancer that year, and though he fought until the very last breath, peace finally found him. Fernando was the last of us to see him at the hospital. Even in his final hours, Dad clung to control, insisting he would return to the farm as soon as his doctor allowed it. Fernando didn't argue. He let Dad speak his last hopes aloud and simply sat with him. That night, Dad passed away.

It's interesting to me that the very same year, a new life arrived, offering a quiet, radiant hope. What's doubly fascinating is that Dad's end was also a beginning for Mom.

Sophia's birth reminded us all that life goes on, even when life tries to break us. Somehow, against all odds, we endure. Sophia's birth became a symbol for my family—a reminder that even after unbearable loss, after the devastation of losing Fabio in the most heartbreaking way, life still finds a way to bring light. She was that light. A quiet promise that joy could return, even in the shadow of grief.

When Mom finally obtained a travel visa for Sophia's first birthday, we caught up (fittingly) by the pool.

"Mom, you were brave until the end," I told her as we hugged and laughed loudly about our shared fate.

"Poor Dad," I said as I sipped a cold beer and looked at Mom. "If he only knew how different his end could have been, he would have lived differently."

Mom looked into my eyes, pressed my arms with her hands, and whispered in my ear, "Yes, but he gave me you and your brothers, so for that reason, I am grateful for him."

Since I wasn't in Brazil when Dad passed away, she recounted many stories of his final days, eliciting tears and an open heart. She told me that his last few days were spent at the farm, the place where he grew up before he was dispatched to the boarding school in Porto Alegre. He craved the refuge of the farm after days of chemotherapy and dialysis. Unfortunately, he developed Hepatitis at the end of his life, making his last days more taxing.

··· 15 ···

THE LAST SLAP

MOM ALSO TOOK the opportunity to share a story she had never shared with anyone else. The episode occurred during a long, cold drive back to Curitiba. The story still sends ripples through my nervous system, but I'll try my best to recount the story exactly as Mom told it to me.

Dad's behind the wheel of the truck, and I'm sitting quietly beside him. It's late. Rain taps steadily on the windshield. The cabin is thick with silence—no eye contact, no words, no warmth.

Dad's clearly in the grips of despair. I'm emotionally exhausted, yet clinging onto something that's eluded me for over forty years: my freedom. For four decades, I tried to create love where there was only control, to cultivate admiration from a man who never learned how to love without conditions.

Then, without warning, I feel a sharp, blinding pain on the left side of my face.

For a moment, I think something's shattered the window—a rock, maybe. I instinctively bring my hands to shield my face, eyes closed, stunned. And then came the words—spat out like venom from the man I once believed could be my partner:

"You! You, Lígia, are the sole reason for my illness!"

The Last Slap

That was the moment he released every last shred of bitterness, frustration, and rage he had stored inside himself over a lifetime.

With my face still burning from the blow, I slowly lowered one hand to the door handle. And I gripped it tightly.

One click, one more centimeter, just a little more pressure, and I would be free—free from the years of bruises, gaslighting, and suffocating silence. In that split second, I thought, I could throw myself out of this truck right now. I can end this.

But I didn't.

I held the handle, then I let go.

I leaned back into my seat, my face aching, my heart shattered.

And in the echo of that silence, a single thought began to rise—small but fierce:

My children need me. I have to survive. One more time, I have to survive.

This is a story she kept hidden from the world. She only told me. Now, I am telling you—her children, our family, our friends, the world.

My mother went through hell in the name of love. But at what cost?

How many of us—women—still believe that staying married is the only option, no matter the damage? How hard is it to cut the knot when the price of staying is your soul?

I include myself in this reflection. I, too, have stayed when I should have left. I, too, have hoped when I should have healed. You've read my story up to this point. Tell me: Were you screaming at me to leave when I was doing cocaine with Fazano? Now turn the mirror around and see yourself. What doesn't serve you anymore?

That was my mom's story, written by someone else. There was a time when I wasn't the author of my story either. However, I defy that way of living and am authoring my story now. Coincidentally, that's what my mom started doing on the day of Dad's passing, a day I will never forget.

On July 29, 2007, as I was breastfeeding Sophia at a family birthday lunch, I received a call from my youngest brother, Fabiano: "Dad is gone."

He passed away at the hospital, a few days after he hit Mom in the face.

I had the chance to say goodbye to Dad over the phone the night before his death, when he requested prayers for his health.

"I'm feeling really sick, my daughter. Please, pray for me," he said.

"Dad, I love you. I will pray you don't suffer. Thank you for the life you gave me. I hope you can meet Sophia soon when we visit Brazil," I replied.

He never met her. The next morning, as my baby was gulping the life fluid from my breast, I cried in torrents over my daughter's face, all while the life fluid had finally left my father's body. My whole existence, struggles, pains, joy, and happiness, all came flooding back to my mind.

"Dad is gone," I told myself. "Mom is now, finally, free."

Emancipation occurred for my mom on July 29 when she visited Dad one last time at the hospital. As she approached his hospital bed, she saw a white blanket covering his whole body.

She shakes.

She stops.

She takes a deep breath and walks toward Dad's body. Before she can touch the blanket, she closes her eyes and looks back, quietly, on her entire life with Rogerio.

Forty years of incessant difficulties. There were some disparate sparks of joy, but mostly, the daily grind of struggles and challenges.

She approaches the body and lifts the white blanket. Slowly, she uncovers Dad's face and chest.

With eyes wide open, she inhales life and whispers to the dead body lying in front of her: "I am finally free. You will never, ever, hit me again. You are never going to tell me what to do. You are dead, for real."

She takes one final look, incapable of producing a single tear, and covers his face.

"It's over. I am going to live my life with my children and my grandchildren." She leaves the room.

···16···

THE DOOR HANDLE

OUR NEWBORN, SOPHIA, didn't have a passport, so I couldn't travel to Brazil for Dad's funeral. Instead, I buried Dad in silence, in my memory. Quietly, I released him, offering forgiveness for the pain he caused, for the words and actions that held me captive for so long. He hadn't known how to face his emotions, shaped as they were by deep, unhealed trauma. And I had been a prisoner of that inherited pain.

Forgiveness didn't arrive all at once. It wasn't a moment. It was a slow unraveling, like loosening the knots that had kept me bound to a story I didn't want to carry anymore. In the wake of Dad's death, I didn't feel closure, not yet. But I did feel something shift. For the first time, I could see him not just as the man who hurt us, but as a man shaped by his wounds, carrying legacies he never knew how to release. Forgiveness, I would come to learn, isn't the same as absolution. It doesn't erase the harm. It doesn't require forgetting. But it does offer something precious: freedom. I wasn't there yet, not fully, but I could feel the door begin to crack open. And that, I would come to understand, was its own kind of beginning.

"Trauma is for sick people," Dad would've said—would've believed. In his mind, he wasn't shaped by wounds or pain. He was just who he was—"a difficult man," as Mom often put it.

However, in time, I began to see the truth more clearly: He, too, was a product of his story. Like all of us, he carried the echoes of childhood, only his were filled with absence, an emotionally distant father, a mother he never knew, and a family where love was a foreign language.

As I laid my father to rest in my memory, I began to release the disappointment, sorrow, and painful stories of the past, marking the first step in healing the wounds of my childhood. I once heard Dr. Gabor Mate on a podcast say, "Trauma is not the events that happen to you—those are actions, episodes. Trauma is what we do with the feelings, emotions, and physical memories of traumatic episodes. And what we do with them is everything. It's how our lives, our relationships, and our self-awareness are shaped." That rang so true for me. I began to understand that I still had work to do.

Dad was gone. Fabio was gone. Teresa was gone.

What was once a family of eight became a family of five. With that loss came a heavy inheritance, a lineage of traumatic events that needed to be faced, untangled, and gently placed where they belonged. My healing had begun the moment my father's actions were buried with him. It was finally time to confront what remained of my story—the silence, the abuse, the shame—and begin the work of healing and rewriting it with truth, compassion, and strength.

••• 17 •••

MOTHERING BACKWARD AND FORWARD

BEING A MOTHER became my full-time job and a new window into unconditional love. Sophia's baby sister, Helena, arrived twenty-seven months later, and Mark and I embraced our new reality as parents after a remarkably short time since we'd met in Cancun. Within five years, I had transformed my life by rediscovering and reinventing myself in a new country, where I had to learn a second language and adapt to a different culture. We moved homes multiple times, Mark redefined his career as a home builder, and somewhere along the way, amid the chaos and learning curves, we found a rhythm. Now, we were raising two beautiful little girls, and in that everyday magic, we were building something whole.

If Sophia was a planned baby, Helena came as a total surprise for us.

On a beautiful November Sunday morning, while Sophia slept in her crib, Mark looked at me on the bed and said, "Let's make another baby." He continued, "I may want to have a boy this time."

I got pregnant that morning.

A few weeks later, and just before another holiday trip to Brazil to see the family I had left there, I found out I was expecting another baby.

Helena was born on August 19, 2009, and just like Sophia's birth, it was another beautiful, sunny Wednesday. I had a C-section, but this time, it was planned. And for Helena's birth, I had Mom at my side. I still wrestle with who was happier: me, as the mother, or her, as the grandmother. She stayed with us for two months and enjoyed every single day. Sophia and Mom developed a deep bond during the two months they were together, and I felt safe having two kids under the age of three with Mom at my side, as she visited us frequently—visa issues a thing of the past.

Though the children's births may have been golden moments in the story of our lives, what followed was anything but the golden years.

Shortly following Helena's birth, the United States real estate market crashed. Mark had just opened his new business and had five houses on spec, waiting to be sold.

Only one of them sold.

The bank took back four of them.

Mark lost everything: his company, his business partner, and his job.

He also lost his faith—and found alcohol.

We were asked to move out of the house where we were living with our two little girls. I left for Brazil to take a breath and be close to Mom. I lugged Sophia, who was nearly three years old, and Helena, who was just about to turn one, all the way to Curitiba. In desperation, the only place I wanted to be was back inside Mom's womb, or at least in her arms, and sheltered by her unconditional love, her home, and her food. The womb that once held me in secret over thirty years ago, a refuge when the world outside was unsteady, now held new meaning. Being near my mother, a woman who had endured and overcome so much, wrapped me in a familiar sense of safety. In her presence, I felt protected once again.

Mark agreed that the support system in Brazil would be a safe place for the kids and me, even if my return date hadn't been determined. The United States economy was in shambles, and Mark needed time to assess and develop a new plan. However, without a job, the kids, and me, alcohol became a crutch, allowing him to numb the pain, frustration, and disappointment.

He found us a new house, a small cottage, like the one I fell in love with when I first moved to the US. We downsized, we changed our lifestyle, and we became vulnerable.

I returned with the kids after a few months, determined to be supportive and continue our lives. I was able to contribute to our sustenance thanks to a small inheritance left by Dad. While in Brazil, my brothers, Mom, and I met and decided to sell the farm, which included the property, the animals, and all the land. This would ensure Mom's financial stability for years to come, while helping Fer, Bano, and me. Oddly, it represented a small level of remuneration for the emotional tolls we'd all endured at the apartment.

However, we incurred yet another loss while I was in Brazil. This time, it was Tets. He died suddenly of a heart attack. Tets was a man who had lived for his family, especially for his mother and for us, his nephews and niece, whom he used to say were "the children the devil gave him, since God hadn't sent any." Tets was a light in human form: a cold beer, a good TV show, laughter shared with close friends, and the quiet joy of a simple life. His savings were modest, but his happiness was abundant. He died content. His heart, full of celebration and love, had simply reached its final beat. So, he went to join Fabio, his favorite, and Teresa, the eternal goddess of his life.

By 2010, we were busy with the two girls, and money was still tight. Mark was trying desperately to find a way to mitigate the losses and redesign his career. He was talented, hardworking, and connected to his art of creating homes. However, the recession caused him to lose his faith, courage, and desire to continue. It was the second time Mark had taken a step back in his career, the first time due to his divorce.

With some money in our pockets from my inheritance, Mark and I kept things simple and used the extra money to pay our bills. The girls and Suzie, our yellow lab, were living safely—and, most importantly, they were all loved. Sammy had passed away years before, around the time Sophia was born.

By that time, I had a car with which to drive the girls around, and we decided to join a country club in Dallas. Though that may sound like an irresponsible use of limited funds, the reasons for doing so were pretty sound at the time: Maybe Mark could make some new business connections there while he reimagined his business. Plus, it would be a great place for Mark to blow off some steam and perhaps be a location where I could make some friends, too. The irony that one of the first moves my parents made when they relocated to Curitiba was to join an athletic club is not lost on me. It may be evidence to support the idea that we tend to repeat the patterns that are familiar to us.

As it turns out, Mark did indeed find a loyal companion at the club: his new coping pal, alcohol. Everyone knows that the longest hole in golf is the nineteenth hole, the place where camaraderie really gets cemented, and where drinks are plentiful.

That became the portrait of our lives: a couple brought together by fate, two souls who found each other in the turquoise waters of Cancún, married for love, aligned by the stars. After the wedding, the protagonist pours herself into the home and the children. Her partner works relentlessly to provide. She tries to carve out something for herself beyond school pickups and lunch prep, maybe a few tennis matches, post-game drinks, and idle gossip about who's backhanding whom, both on and off the court. He works twelve-hour days, five days a week, and still manages to squeeze in golf three or four times. They connect briefly when no one else needs them.

Sound familiar?

It should. It was the life my parents once lived in Brazil. My father was always busy with tennis, business trips, or working the farm, hundreds of miles from home. My mother, left behind with four children, watching the days blur together, tight on money, wondering quietly, *Is this all there is?*

And now, here I am, reenacting the same script in a different country with a different cast—but the same questions echoing in my mind.

Patterns are everywhere, woven into families like threads we don't even see. We live inside them, often mistaking them for truth. And unless something shakes us awake, we pass them on, wrapped in silence or survival, calling them tradition or responsibility.

Some people never get the chance to see the pattern clearly. Others see it but feel too bound to it to step away. And for the rare few who try to break it, the effort can take years—or lifetimes. Sometimes, it takes a new generation to finish what the last could only begin.

I believe my mother belongs to that quieter category, the ones who couldn't break free but who planted the seed for someone else to try. And in her way, that was a profound act of love because she gave me the most powerful inheritance of all: awareness.

With that awareness, I choose differently.

I choose to walk with open eyes and an open heart. I choose to teach my daughters how to think for themselves, how to feel deeply, how to listen to the quiet voice inside that says, *This is who I am.* I want them to see their choices not as obligations but as invitations to live curiously, courageously, and with conviction.

That is the gift my mother gave me. And now, I give it to them.

How long can a woman, who once tasted freedom, who once made bold choices and carved her own path, live cocooned in a private world where routine dulls her spirit, connection fades, and the days blur into sameness, softened only by wine and distraction?

This was the question I was now asking myself.

For about eight years of my adult life, throughout my late thirties and early forties, I lived numb in my marriage and numb within myself. All my energy was devoted to my children and their needs, and life as a couple was disappearing. Increasingly, Mark was creating attachments on the nineteenth hole, paying the bills, and using alcohol as a way of finding joy in our nuclear family. Life had become heavy: boring, demanding, and unforgiving. So, Mark began to slip deeper into the comfort of vodka, tequila, or both, using the burn of each drink to blur the mounting pressure of tight finances, a struggling business, and the relentless needs at home. It was easier to disappear into the glass than face the weight waiting for him at the end of each day.

Meanwhile, I was contributing to my loneliness. I got involved in tennis at the country club where I could vent my frustrations as a wife, mother, and as an immigrant who hadn't found an opportunity to work. I had tried, more than once, to carve out a path for myself. I pursued opportunities in law, both in colleges and firms, but nothing stuck. Then I gave sales a shot, only to realize I was far better at buying than selling. Nothing seemed to land. *Was it my accent, the lack of US credentials, or something deeper, some invisible wall I couldn't name?* Eventually, I stopped trying. I retreated into the cocoon of motherhood and marriage, grateful for the security of a provider but quietly aching with the sense that I was vanishing into a life that no longer felt like mine.

I adjusted myself in small, quiet ways: the meals I cooked, the tone of my voice, the way I showed up at the country club. I said yes more than I wanted to. I suppressed parts of myself without even realizing it. That's what clinging can look like: holding tight to the image of who you think you need to be to belong.

※※※

"Was it really that hard, Mom?" Helena asked, walking back to the couch from the kitchen. "Texas, I mean, at the beginning."

I let out a breath I hadn't realized I was holding. "Harder than I ever expected," I said, "not because of the country or the people, even though everything was new, but because I had left behind my entire identity. I had to learn how to belong all over again."

Sophia tilted her head, curious. "What do you mean, like culture shock?"

"More like *soul shock*," I said with a tired smile. "I went from being a respected lawyer in Brazil to Dad's wife in the suburbs. I couldn't work yet, couldn't drive by myself at first. I had no friends, no language fluency, and no familiar smells or sounds. It was like I'd stepped into someone else's life and forgotten where I'd put mine."

"Did you like it—the clubs, the house, the lifestyle?" asked Sophia.

"I thought I did. Or maybe—I wanted to. I wanted it to work so badly that I started clinging to it. I told myself this was the version of me that would be loved, accepted, safe."

"Like clinging syndrome again?" asked Helena.

I laughed softly, "Exactly like that. Even in a beautiful house, with love and security, I found myself shrinking—not because anyone told me to, but because I didn't know how to stop playing the part. I didn't know how to be fully me—not yet."

"But you got there—eventually," said Sophia.

"I did. But first, I had to admit I was pretending, that I'd traded pieces of myself for peace. It wasn't until I started listening to my heart that I knew who I was again."

"Why didn't you just leave?" Helena asked, not accusing, just wondering.

I met her eyes gently. "Because I had chosen that life. I had to at least try to make it work. And because I still believed in love, and in me. Somewhere under all that loneliness, I believed I could build something beautiful. But first, I had to survive the ache."

Sophia reached over and tucked a blanket around my legs. "So that's when you started changing again?"

I nodded. "Yes, slowly. I stopped pretending I was fine all the time. I gave myself permission to feel lost. That's what allowed me to find my way back to myself."

Helena whispered, "You're so strong, Mom."

"Maybe," I said softly, "but not because I did everything right. I was strong because I kept going, even when I wasn't sure who I was anymore—and because I let those hard seasons teach me how to grow."

We sat in the quiet glow of the lamp, the weight of those years behind me, and the gift of my daughters beside me.

Drinks became a habit of mine, as well, during and after tennis matches—margaritas and white wine—and at home, too. Bottles were part of the daily groceries, with my consumption growing to two and sometimes three glasses a day. Imagine that: a five-foot nothing woman, 111 pounds, and drinking all that alcohol in just a few hours. And occasionally, I'd drive with all of it in my system—a true recipe for disaster.

Mark and I had become detached from one another. The sweet love and kindness from our early years together began to dissolve. More sips, less sex. More golf, less communication. More going out, less bringing in.

The girls were well cared for, but as a couple, we'd fallen out of step. The synchronicity that drew us together in Cancun was long gone. It felt like we'd lost ourselves, our feelings, and our connection. The time we spent at home revolved entirely around the children. Then came school: carpools, sports practices, volunteer roles, parent meetings. The rhythm of responsibility marched on with bills to pay and daughters to raise. From the outside, it must have looked like we were moving through it all like a well-oiled machine. We may have been moving in place. We knew our roles, but we no longer truly moved *with* each other.

···18···
CRAFTING SELF

THE LIGHT TURNED red in 2014.

I was at a tennis retreat with some girlfriends. Helena was only five, and Sophia was seven. Because they were both in school, the routine was a bit easier. It was my first trip away from the family, and Mark was excited to see me go away with some friends, by myself. My previous trips had all been to Brazil or were short stays in the Dallas area. Money was still tight, and we had lots of responsibilities to take care of.

The retreat was in Key Biscayne, Florida—beach, tennis courts, women, and tennis coaches; most of them were foreigners. I soon discovered it was a destination paradise for housewives, divorcés, and single women. Away from home, kids, husbands, and duties, it was all about playing, drinking, dancing, and flirting—lots of flirting, on and off the tennis courts.

I have always been a good athlete. Tennis and swimming were my favorites. I enjoyed anything that involved muscle movement and vitality. Dad had taught me a few tennis lessons in my youth, but it was in the States that I discovered a passion for the game. It just so happened to come at a time in my life when the circumstances allowed me to pour a lot of energy into the sport.

Tennis players are fanatics, but female tennis players are dramatic and, often, crazy competitive. The competition isn't limited to the court. It spills into outfits and social status, too. I'd already experienced that dynamic in the country club bubble and learned to flow with it. But then there was the ocean breeze, the sun-drenched courts, the heat of the days, and, well, the coaches. Everything and everyone felt hotter in that setting.

And I wasn't immune to it.

Away from Dallas, home, and duties, I was able to detach my mind from the heavy reality of what life had become for Mark, our family, and me—a routine. It all harkened back to ten years earlier when I landed in Cancun and savored the freedom. This felt similar, but under vastly different circumstances.

A pattern, perhaps?

The dream continued: outfits, rackets, cute bags, girlfriends, no kids, no husbands, no dishes, and no groceries to do. There was no need to check in or cater to anyone's needs other than my own. It was all about me, playing tennis, and having fun. I was ready to play and compete.

It was the first dinner of the trip. I was seated across from a man I hadn't seen before. He was quiet, reserved, and seemingly younger than I. These events always mixed up the seating to encourage new connections, people from different states with different lives.

He looked like one of the coaches. Most of them were younger than the women attending. I noticed him. *Cute*, I thought, then immediately corrected myself. *You're married. This trip is a gift from Mark—a break, nothing more.* I told myself that and smiled politely, trying to focus on the wine and the conversation around me. But something in the air had already shifted.

He was one of the coaches from New Zealand. Michael was his name, and I was placed on his team according to the night's announcements. After dinner, a space to dance was created, and the drinks were flowing. Some women retreated to their rooms while others indulged their wild sides, laughing, talking, and dancing. With everyone engaged, the party was on.

I leaned into the fun. Michael approached, and we struck up a conversation. *Where do you live? How long have you been playing tennis? What brought you to the US?* I answered briefly, letting my wine do most of the talking, feeling its warmth loosen the weight I carried.

As we danced and talked, something inside me began to stir. The woman who once danced freely at beach parties with her brothers, who once laughed loudly under the strobe lights of CocoBongo, that woman started to come back to life. Buried beneath diapers, routines, and quiet desperation, my true self was stirring—light, joyful, untamed. I could feel her return with every beat of the music.

This is who I am, I kept telling myself, *happy, playful, free.*

In that liminal space between flirtation and reality, between Dallas and here, I let the moment exist. It felt real. And, more than anything, it felt good.

After the dance, everyone went back to the hotel, and some of them, including me, stayed at the bar for an extra drink. That's when things started to spice up. "It's time for me to disappear," I whispered to my friend as I watched a whole scene develop between a lady and a coach. "Good night, everyone. See you on the court," I said.

Michael was within earshot and simply said, "Goodbye, Christina."

Back in the hotel room, I felt a little *pulga atras da orelha*, as we say in Portuguese. It means, "I was feeling uneasy" or "I smell a rat." Feeling a little unsettled with my feelings based on what I'd witnessed that first evening, I took a shower, got in my pajamas, and fell asleep.

The next three days were filled with tennis practices, clinics, matches, lunches by the beach, dinners, and dances. I allowed myself to be invaded by freedom. I also played well, tanned well, and ate well. The late-night dances fueled the wild woman inside me. I remember taking it all in and thinking, *This is a pleasant surprise. Thank you, Universe. I thought I had lost myself and my light. But I can see it emerging, inside me.*

The trophy ceremony was on the last night. As captain of the championship team, I was the celebrated superstar. Michael's team won the tournament, and I was his captain. The forces and the momentum moved me, and at the end of the night, Michael and I found ourselves sitting together around the pool.

"How is your marriage?" Michael asked. "Does your husband treat you well?"

Is he a mind reader? I wondered.

With a little doubt and some hesitation, I responded, "Yes, my husband treats me well."

I let the moment breathe, allowing its warmth to linger between us until the air shifted. The desire came quietly at first, then unmistakably. He leaned in, and I found myself moving toward him, instinctively, almost helplessly.

But just before the space between us disappeared, I pulled back.

"No," I said, the word catching in my throat like a sob I refused to cry. I swallowed the longing, steadied my breath, and looked at him with a softness that held both apology and resolve. "This is becoming dangerous," I whispered, more to myself than to him.

Then I turned, my pulse racing, and walked away, back into the safety of the night, leaving temptation at the edge of the pool.

That trip marked a significant turning point in my life.

For the first time in years, I reunited with the woman within me, the one who allows herself to feel desire, not just of the body but of the soul. It wasn't simply about attraction; it was a spark of spirit, a quiet but powerful ignition of something long buried. That night, I felt the pilot light of my inner world flicker back to life.

In that warmth, I reconnected with Christina's essence, the joyful, free-spirited, celebratory soul I had once known so clearly—the one who danced at the beach with her brothers, who laughed without restraint, and who believed in possibility. She was always there, just lost beneath the layers of survival.

As I looked back, it was like tracing a constellation, like connecting the dots of my life to make sense of the shape they formed. First was my father, whose presence was both protective and harmful. Then was adulthood, a tangle of systems and men—lawyers, clients, the legal world—that violated my spirit in more subtle but equally damaging ways. Even earlier were the whispers of trauma from school, from other girls' stories, and from my misguided choices in love.

Each line drawn between these moments revealed something crucial, not just the pain but the resilience. And now, I could see them clearly for what they were, not just scars but signs, a map back to myself.

However, the map ran through various events of the past; one of them was the marriage to a man who was losing the connection to my feelings. Perhaps with Mark, I had unknowingly allowed a familiar pattern to take root in our love story, one that slowly dimmed the light and joy we once shared. What began with passion and promise was now buried beneath layers of obligation, frustration, fear, and quiet rejection.

Being desirable and feeling attracted to another man while in Key Biscayne was something that shocked me, but woke me up. In a certain way, I felt alive again. The fiery woman still existed, and now it was time to come clean and work on something worthwhile—my marriage.

Back in Dallas and facing reality, I felt compelled to share the details of my experience in Key Biscayne with Mark. The trip had been an artificial way for us to put our animosity and dissatisfactions aside, to be apart so we could slow down the tension that had been building for months.

I met Mark at one of his construction sites. Inside his car, we shared our feelings and views on our marriage, and how the nature of intimacy had changed since becoming parents. It was a first for us, attaching words to the feelings that swirled around our relationship. For months, maybe even years, we'd forgotten to communicate our innermost feelings. As committed as we were to keeping our family together despite losses, a recession, changes, and new beginnings, we forgot ourselves as a couple. We let the tasks become our preferred method of communication, losing sight of our connection.

It was a crucial moment for me as I strung together the clues as to why I could have had such a response to another man's presence at the tennis retreat.

So, I said, "I felt attracted to another man while I was away at the tennis retreat." My words came out plainly, without drama, but heavy with meaning. "I'm telling you because I want to be honest and because I respect you, our relationship, and what we've built together with our children. But something's shifted. We've changed. Life has pulled us into parallel routines, and somewhere along the way, we lost each other."

Mark, always a man of few words but deep thoughts, sat quietly. I could see the gears turning behind his eyes as he stared out the window, searching for something—anything—to anchor himself. He looked back at me a few times, his face unreadable, as if waiting for the right words to surface. I felt a strange sense of relief just saying it out loud. Years of buried emotion had finally been given a voice.

"What really happened there, Christina?" Mark asked.

Whenever Mark calls me "Christina," it means he's doing some serious thinking.

"Nothing really happened," I said. "But something happened inside me. I felt happy again—away from you and our reality." Despite how difficult it was to say aloud, I continued, "Being there, around people who noticed me, including men, made me feel alive."

We moved from a car conversation to couples therapy, where we freely shared how we saw one another in our marriage and how we'd like it to look.

"Christina's known me for a long time, and she knows who I am," Mark began. "I work hard, and I provide so she and the girls have a great life. But I also love my golf. That and alcohol allow me to cope." But he did make one startling admission, "I know I can be an asshole when I have more drinks than I should, but I can work on that—on my own."

I listened, and I realized that the man speaking was the Mark I'd known for years. He was being honest with the therapist, though I wasn't entirely sure if he was being honest with himself.

Changing on his own? I had my doubts.

The therapist made a few points, but Mark maintained his thoughts. I had the opportunity to address my feelings and the questions I had about us. Though Mark listened and seemed to be receptive, he didn't show any signs of wanting to change the *status quo* to make me feel better or loved.

"This is who I am, Christina," he said.

That was the only therapy session we attended as a couple. Mark was determined to make some tweaks on his own, though I couldn't figure out how he planned to do that. To his credit, he acknowledged that he would become more aware of us as a couple and examine the habits that were causing a degree of toxicity in our marriage.

In the end, the attraction I'd felt didn't hold much weight. It wasn't a turning point. Rather, it was a symptom. Later, Mark shared his thoughts with quiet honesty, "I get it. I've been distant for a while. The stress since the recession—it's been a lot. I've been focused on keeping everything afloat for you and the girls." Then, with a half-smile and a knowing tone, he added, "And let's be honest, those tennis coaches flirt with every attractive woman who shows up to those retreats. That was never going to go anywhere."

Even with these honest conversations, the tension and distress remained present in our marriage.

Mark continued to use the golf course and alcohol as coping mechanisms to lighten the weight of the responsibilities he carried. Our financial situation improved steadily, and we moved into a beautiful new place with more space and a swimming pool. Mark was an incredible provider, and I fulfilled the role of a dedicated housewife and mother. Without intending to do so, I'd unconsciously taken on the same reality my mom faced so many years before.

But was it really a coincidence?

Until we know better, there's a tendency in humans to repeat what we know, what was taught to us by example, and to do so without critical thinking.

So, for two more years, that was my reality. And, once again, I was facing a physical breakdown, just like the one I'd incurred as an attorney. I remember having chronic cold sores inside my mouth. This painful experience inhibited me from eating or drinking for days, as the inflammation caused such a high level of discomfort. This led to insomnia and depression. It wasn't uncommon to endure three sleepless nights in a row in those days. I would close my eyes, incapable of shutting down my brain and mind, only to fall asleep at 4:00 in the morning and have to wake up again at 6:00 to take care of the girls, the house, and everything else that comes with a housewife's routine.

I was physically spent, lonely, and isolated. Mark continued to worry about providing material riches for our family, and I acquiesced to a diagnosis of depression.

"That's crazy, Tina, you have everything you need," said Mark, about my depression. But all the suffering and sleep deprivation came to a breaking point. As my nervous system stretched to its limit, unstable and dysregulated, something broke.

•••19•••
LOST IN MY DOTS

IT WAS A typical Sunday afternoon at the country club pool. Mark had come off the golf course and had a few drinks, and his behavior, agitated and sharp, began to grate on me. I'd seen this pattern before: alcohol shifting him into a space of emotional frustration, where his irritation needed a target. Too often, that target was me. I quietly gathered our things, corralled the girls, and said to myself, *I've had enough of this.* We left without looking back.

Driving home from the club, I left Mark behind, along with the tension that had slowly built between us. He had his ways of showing up for our family, providing what we needed, but sometimes, that came with emotional distance or the weight of unspoken expectations. I was angry and tired. As I drove, tears slipped down my cheeks quietly, the kind that come when exhaustion meets heartbreak.

The girls, lulled by the sun and water, had dozed off in the back seat. I glanced at them, cheeks flushed, hair damp, swimsuits clinging to sleepy little bodies. Barefoot and peaceful, they looked like angels. I parked the car near our house and sat there for a while, just watching them, caught in the beauty and ache of motherhood.

I loved them so deeply. I loved what Mark and I had created together. However, there was a quiet longing, a sadness inside of me, too. A part of me felt confined, like this wasn't quite the life I imagined when I met him under the warm skies of Cancun. The moment echoed a memory of my mother, sitting in her apartment in Porto Alegre, gazing out the window with two babies in a stroller and one on the way, asking herself, *Is this it? Is this my life?*

Same feeling, different woman, different decade—but the question was still alive in me.

As the girls slept, I cried out loud, then called Mom. Ironically, it was the same phone call I made to her in the summer of 1999 when I landed in Paris to study and lived abroad as a life experience. Riddled with emotional pain and fear, at that time, I questioned myself: *Why did I do this? Why didn't I stay comfortable at Mom's house instead of seeking a new reality, trying to figure out what life is about?* In 1999, Mom had answered the phone and said: "*Filha querida*, you are so brave. Your choice is right, don't turn around. Let life show you why you are there. There is a reason. Coming home now would cut short an experience that can change your life." So, it wasn't out of character when I called her in the summer of 2016 in desperation.

"Mom! Mom!" I began. "What did I do with my life? I feel like I'm a prisoner of Mark's money and the reality and circumstances we created. I can't hold this pain anymore, Mom. I don't know what to do! Help me!"

Mom patiently listened to me on the other side of the line, five thousand miles away, and said, "*Filha querida*, don't turn around from what you created. You have now to experience this pain and recreate your reality. You need to find something to keep your brain engaged. You have always been phenomenal in your planning and dreaming; you have created a family, and Mark is a good man. But don't let your life become his. He has his interests, and together, you both have the girls. But where is Christina? What would she want to do about herself? That's what you need to pursue—your new reality as a woman. Maybe find a job and make a plan to go back to work."

"Mom, I wish you were here to hug me," I said as the girls woke up and saw me crying.

Sophia, always the sensitive one, stirred first. Rubbing her eyes, she looked over and saw the tears still on my cheeks. Without a word, she unbuckled her seatbelt, climbed into the front seat, and wrapped her small arms around my neck.

"Mom," she said softly, "I can hug you. *Vovó* [Portuguese for Grandma] is too far away."

In that moment, it was as if my mother, so far away, had reached through space and time to hold me. Through Sophia's tiny embrace, her kiss on my cheek, I felt not just my daughter's love, but my mother's comfort, too—a touch passed down through generations.

"Why are you crying, Mom?" she asked gently.

I couldn't answer just then. But in her arms, I found the strength I thought I'd lost.

I hung up, but not before thanking Mom for being the strongest soul I could ever have by my side. She always knew what to say during my most challenging times and how to celebrate and create joy during the good times. It wasn't despite being an abused housewife but *because* of being an abused housewife that Mom could share her integrity, passion, and insights with me. Having learned the art of nurturing from her mom, Grandma Theresa, there was a legacy of love and compassion. I like to say that mothers are light. Mothers are life.

I once heard the following saying that rings so true to me: "If we lose a dad, we lose the foundation of our home, but if we lose a mom, we lose the whole home."

By the summer of 2016, I was broken down and burned out.

However, just like before, I woke up again, the darkness illuminating my resilience. With optimism and resolve, I determined to find a new way to trace my story, connect the dots, and create an image of beauty. Staying in the darkness was not an option, but feeling and exercising through the pain would be necessary to claim my spot in the light.

That year, following Mom's advice, I decided to take a turn.

I registered for a yoga teacher training course. I hadn't stopped practicing, but I wanted more from it. Perhaps being a teacher could fulfill the emptiness I was feeling. My girls were growing, Mark was busy rebuilding his business, and things were looking prosperous. *What about me?* Tennis, country club, and retreats—none of those were my calling. Sure, all of it was fun, but I'd come to this world to be and to do more.

I used my own line of credit to pay for teacher training. Surprisingly, the credit card I'd received in the mail also came with a line of credit. I knew Mark wouldn't be happy if I asked for $3,500 for a yoga course. The fear of rejection caused me to explore a more creative route. But I could imagine Mark's voice in my ears, "A yoga teacher?" He would think I was stepping down in career paths, I figured. So, I did it on my own, like Mom had done in dire situations, enlisting the help of Tets, Grandma, and sometimes her children.

Would Mom's advice turn out to be right for me?

···20···

CONNECTING MY DOTS

THE HOLE WAS deep.

Juggling a new home, kids, and a reinvented career forced me to move even faster than before.

Mark eventually became supportive of my new idea, but he remained quiet due to his uncertainty about where it would take me.

The journey wasn't smooth. The dots I began to connect were jagged and often painful. There were hard truths, unexpected revelations, and countless lessons wrapped in failure and missteps. However, every single one was necessary. I wouldn't change it. That mess, the discomfort, the wrong turns, and the resistance marked the beginning of my evolution.

And the first obstacle I had to face wasn't money. It wasn't Mark. It was me.

Engaged in the busy routine between home and training, I experienced something foreign during a late morning meditation session. As I lay on the mat at the end of practice, my heart, instead of being stabilized by the position, accelerated spontaneously. *What's happening to me?* I wondered, suddenly fearful. Hoping to calm my heart, I kept quiet and still, waiting a few minutes to allow my body and heart to align with the end of the practice. However, that didn't happen. Instead, my heart continued to beat faster and faster, and my whole body started to shake as if electrical discharges were being released from my extremities: hands, feet, and head.

As a yoga practitioner, I was embarrassed. *This isn't supposed to happen to me,* I thought. So, I stood up and told the teacher that I wasn't feeling well and needed to step outside for a minute.

I couldn't go back to the floor. I wasn't aware that the experience that morning would be the first of many panic and anxiety attacks that would take hold suddenly. I'd wanted something new, but this certainly wasn't what I'd expected.

That first isolated episode turned into several more episodes. Often, especially when I was feeling physically and mentally taxed and surrounded by noise or people, my sympathetic nervous system would activate, and the parasympathetic would collapse. I began to sense when it was coming: accelerated heartbeat, sweaty hands and feet, dizziness, fainting, and freezing speech.

It happened while I was at church during Mass; I had to leave.

It happened in restaurants with friends. One time, I was unable to say a word, right after having sat at the table, looking at the margarita glass, incapable of taking a sip. "Can you take me home, please?"

And the worst, it happened as I was driving, while I was taking the girls to school.

They were isolated but frequent episodes.

Dr. Vijaya Mummadi, an internal doctor who still cares for me today, had a holistic approach to physical and mental health. She diagnosed me with chronic anxiety, aggravated by panic attacks.

"Christina, you are experiencing burnout. Have you ever felt this way?" she inquired.

I shared what was happening in my life, including my complete dissatisfaction and the disdain I felt about my situation. I told her that the only remedy that seemed to work when experiencing a panic attack was the stillness of isolation.

"You must address these feelings with your husband and get into psychotherapy," she said. "And for now, to support the functionality of your system, I will prescribe you Xanax, three times a day, in small doses, to restore the chemical imbalance in your brain. We start here, and today."

That was in early 2017, right during the teacher training that was intended to move me out of my mess—the prison, the cocoon from which I so desperately wanted to emerge.

Training would last almost two years, divided into long weeks between Brazil, Canada, and the United States. When I had to travel, the meds accompanied me in my purse. It gave me tremendous anxiety, worrying about the possibility of forgetting them, so I was constantly making sure my "crutches" were there. The medication was necessary—physically, mentally, and emotionally—and I accepted it as the symptoms slowly began to fade. But they were only symptoms. The root of it all still lived quietly inside me, untouched and unresolved.

Fear, frustration, irritation, mouth sores, back pain, insomnia—*what was underneath it all?* I wondered why I was manifesting these conditions to the point that I was afraid to leave the house. The only way I could find to manage the panic was to lie down in the sun by the pool or on my bed in absolute silence. I couldn't tolerate any voices.

"Please, leave Mom alone," I used to say to the girls.

Mark, in his way, was worried about me. He was losing the fun, light, and joyful woman he had met years before. And now I was in bed, isolated from the social world outside, incapable of being myself.

Where did I leave her? What did I do to myself? These were the unanswerable questions that ricocheted through my brain.

As the training segments neared completion, yoga and meditation practices became part of my daily routine. I truly believe the teacher training saved me. As I committed to practicing the lessons I'd learned in class, the body-mind system began to adjust and regulate. As a result, my medication was reduced until I went off it altogether. It took me three years to come off the medication; I had a few episodes after 2020, during the COVID-19 period. But I began to recognize when my anxiety might turn into a panic attack, at which point, I would take a pill—at that time, a form of antidepressant called Escitalopram.

I continued that regimen until one day, in preparation for another healing journey with the plant medicine Ayahuasca, I was required to have a body completely clean of any chemicals coursing through the nervous system. After a few interviews with Soltara Healing Center's facilitators, we made a plan to quit the antidepressant and see how the body-mind connection would function. I can reveal that it's still going well without the meds. However, being aware of my triggers has helped me pay attention to the moments when anxiety begins to creep back into my mindset.

Nothing changed overnight, but things got progressively better over the following months and years. Nevertheless, before everything turned brighter and more balanced, I still had to experience significant lessons that would shape the woman I was becoming. In the words of Martin Scorsese: "In life, judgment can turn into mercy." My next awakening would require the transmutation of judgment into mercy. And it was going to be a challenging lesson.

I became a certified yoga teacher in 2019. The stars aligned, and I was offered to partner, as an owner, in a yoga studio in Dallas with a group of teachers from Brazil. It would soon turn into a remarkable experience that would enhance my understanding of self, others, and business.

Being an entrepreneur is a challenge, especially when you're in charge of day-to-day operations, as I was. The other partners were in Brazil and were available for guidance only. From greeting to cleaning, teaching, opening and closing, booking and cancelling, I lived between my two houses: the family home and the studio, which I named Kasa Yoga Dallas—Kasa meaning "home" in my native language. Balancing my time between the studio and my young children, who were still too little to fully grasp that their mom now had other commitments, was a constant source of distress. Traces of anxiety and panic still lingered in my body, along with occasional bouts of insomnia. More than once, I found myself sitting in the car outside the studio, taking extra time just to gather the strength to walk in and teach, all while managing the quiet storm of anxiety rising on my way to work.

I dove into the partnership offer without any hesitation, despite advice from my attorney, my friends, and other yoga teachers who knew my new partners.

It didn't take long for me to realize that "us" really meant "me." I did everything, which is why I ultimately called off the partnership and unilaterally ended the commitment. I learned something valuable through that experience, though: Liking someone is not the same as trusting them.

The pandemic hit in 2020, just seven months after I opened my yoga studio. With only fifty-five students, just enough to cover the rent, the dream I had worked so hard to build suddenly came to a halt. On March 17, 2020, I locked the doors, unsure when or if I'd reopen them.

Back home, I sat in silence, staring at the ceiling, the weight of uncertainty pressing down on me. *What now?* I thought. *What about everything I poured into that space—my savings, my time, the training hours, the belief that this could be something real?* I was torn between two voices: one whispering, *You tried; it's okay to let go,* and the other, louder and firmer, saying, *No, not yet. You haven't even begun to show the world what you're capable of.*

Three months later, in June 2020, I reopened the doors. Slowly, the community began to return, and over the next five years, the studio grew into something beautiful and alive. Eventually, the space that had once felt vast began to feel too small, not just physically but energetically. As I deepened my healing journey and embraced a lighter, more expansive way of living, my vision for what I wanted to offer the world grew with me. It was time to evolve again: mind, heart, and hands aligned with something even greater.

Kasa, Haute Yoga is my new studio in Dallas. It's a sanctuary that provides a mature and refined way of practicing and developing self-care, self-love, and commitment to a longer life, one in which "more" represents quality of health. This is who I've become: empowered, focused on all aspects of health, and a willing voice in prioritizing one's needs. I'm proud to declare that what I have created today—my community, my brand, and my studio—all started with a $3,500 line of credit and the dream of reinventing myself.

One of the studio's signature offerings is The 10-Year Club, a program I created inspired by Robin Sharma's *The 5 AM Club*. Its focus is clear: to guide members through the next decade of their lives with purpose, discipline, and joy. Rooted in the belief that aging is not a decline but a continuation of living fully, the club champions community, consistency, and conscious living. Again, much of it was inspired by the lessons from my mom, who in her eightieth year is only now starting to show signs of mental decline but still possesses a strong body and a lovely, well-groomed appearance.

While 90 percent of people accept degeneration as inevitable, we choose another path. At Kasa, through mindful movement, joyful connection, and a deep commitment to wellness, we aim to age with strength, grace, and vitality. We all know that death is part of life, but we want to meet it with dignity, not disease. We are, quite literally, tracing the dots backward from the end, intentionally shaping the years between now and then.

I vow to live well—vibrantly, consciously, and completely—right up to my final breath, another lesson inspired by Mom.

···21···

THE LAST TIME I HELD HER

AFTER DAD DIED, Mom had about ten good years, traveling back and forth between the US and Brazil. She used to come every summer and spend six weeks with us. The days were illuminated in brightness, love, and laughter. To see her travel so freely was a sense of relief. She was no longer constrained financially, mentally, or emotionally. Traveling to see her granddaughters became her favorite annual activity. Between afternoons by the pool, backyard barbecues, evening coffee, and long, heartfelt conversations, Mom seemed transformed. Maybe this version of her had once existed, back when she first met Dad in her early twenties, but had been buried under years of sacrifice, love, and quiet devotion. Now, her days revolved around herself, her grandchildren, and her children. Holidays became moments of reunion, of gathering close to a big, affectionate family. She was living her dream, the one she had always imagined life might be.

Sadly, on one of those trips, Mom endured a mental collapse on a flight. She lost all sense of where she was and began showing signs of schizophrenia. Fabiano and I were with her during that flight, and it was challenging to make any sense of the scattered pieces of her mind.

At that moment, we lost our mom. She was unrecognizable from the methodical parent who always had our best interests at heart. The next day, she had no memory of what had happened. But we did.

A couple of years later, she collapsed again. This time, it felt different. Fernando found her in her house, disoriented and unable to put words together. Sensing the profundity of the moment, I flew to Brazil to check on her and do whatever I could to make her feel loved, comfortable, and safe.

She never came back; she was never the same woman.

We learned that she had developed Lewy body dementia, which is characterized by changes in thinking, movement, behavior, and mood. She also lost her sight due to retinitis pigmentosa, known as RP, a genetic disease her mom's side of the family carries in their chromosomes. Grandma Teresa also died blind, and it's unfortunate that Mom will, too. I hope I can change this pattern for myself with the prevention choices I'm making. I also carry the chromosomes.

Having lived her entire life in Brazil for eighty-two years, my mom, Ligia, continues to express her beauty and her sense of humor. She loves to laugh, and she's still as beautiful to me as she was when we were kids and when she was a bank teller—before her dreams were snuffed out. However, whenever I see her, I often reflect on why she's been afflicted by mental disease. Mom has always eaten healthily, has been physically active, and has been socially connected and loved by so many. These are precisely the habits that the medical and psychological fields suggest we do to prevent mental illness like dementia and Alzheimer's. Bewildered, I asked myself, *Why did her brain get affected when her habits were all so supportive of a good and healthy life?*

Perhaps the answer lies in trauma. I can only guess that the immense trauma she endured at the hands of Dad has not healed.

Despite her deep love for my father and the countless efforts she made to keep their marriage intact for the sake of her children, my mother sacrificed so much of herself. The weight of physical, emotional, and psychological abuse, the constant tension over money, and the quiet chaos of a dysfunctional household left her imprisoned within her mind. She carried unspoken pain for years, trapped with feelings she had no space or permission to express. Now, with dementia blurring the edges of her memories, I see how long she held everything in.

As I reflect on my life at fifty-two, I can still look back on my childhood and feel a sense of eternal gratitude, especially for the parents God chose for me. Dad had a chance to be a father and do the best he could despite his childhood experiences that were void of parental love. For him, I have mercy. I know he is watching over me from Heaven next to Fabio, Tets, and Grandma Teresa.

Forgiveness, I've come to understand, is not a gift we give to others. It's the liberation we grant ourselves. It doesn't change the past, but it transforms the hold the past has on us. For years, I carried anger like armor, convinced it was the only thing keeping me safe. However, in time, I learned that true safety, true peace, comes from letting go of what no longer serves me. I forgave my father not to excuse him, but to release myself from the burden of his choices. I forgave my mother, too, for the silences and the fears that shaped my early world. In doing so, I forgave myself for staying, for not knowing better, and for the years I lived out of alignment with my truth. That is the healing power of forgiveness: It clears the path back to love, to self, and to freedom.

I am determined to learn from my parents and not waste the opportunities they've provided, whether intentionally or unintentionally. The vision I have created for myself is one of movement: the flow of healing and learning as circumstances appear.

I still believe there's a sacred thread that connects every dot in our personal stories. Each experience, whether joyful, painful, or somewhere in between, adds to our evolution. Every chapter we live through becomes part of the map that guides us toward the person we're meant to become.

I believe we must cultivate alignment between our actions, words, and thoughts. If we hope to raise a healthier, more conscious generation, the most powerful way to teach our children is by living the values we want them to learn. Raising two daughters through the lens of distinct cultures has been a meaningful and enriching experience for Mark and me. What's considered a gesture of motherly love in Brazil might be seen as spoiling in the US, but blending the warmth and expressiveness of Brazilian parenting with the independence and structure often valued in American culture has helped us shape a unique foundation. The result is a balanced upbringing rooted in love, ambition, and integrity. I couldn't be prouder to say that Sophia and Helena are a beautiful evolution, an improved version of both Mark and me.

❦

"Mom?" Helena's voice brought me out of my thoughts. We were curled up on the couch again, the three of us.

"Yeah, *meu amor*?" I looked over at her, admiring the compassion in her eyes.

"Do you ever think about how far you've come, like all the things you've lived through to get here?"

Sophia leaned in, too, quiet but attentive. I smiled at them both, my two daughters, my two mirrors.

"Every day," I said. "Sometimes, it feels like I've lived a dozen lives. And each one brought me closer to this one, the one where I get to be your mom and tell these stories with an open heart."

"Mom," Sophia said, "do you think you finally let go of all the things you used to cling to?"

I smiled, turning the question over in my mind like a smooth stone. "I think I've let go of most—maybe not all."

Helena looked up. "What's left?"

I glanced through the window, a reminder of my youth, before turning back to my daughters. "Expectations, maybe, of myself and of what life was supposed to look like. I chased a lot. I clung to perfection, roles, and approval. And for a long time, I didn't know how to be free unless someone else told me I was allowed to be."

Sophia shifted in her seat. "And now?"

"Now, I don't ask," I said. "Now, I listen to what feels true. And that means not gripping so tightly—even to you two."

Helena reached for my hand, a quiet reassurance. "We're not going anywhere, Mom."

"I know," I whispered. "But part of loving you means giving you space to go, just like I needed, even when I didn't know how to ask for it. You both taught me that freedom is a kind of love, too."

Sophia's voice was soft, steady. "I think that's what you've taught us."

The silence that followed wasn't empty. It was full of recognition, a thread weaving between our lives, one that didn't cling but connected—gently, honestly, with room to breathe.

"Do you still get scared of making the wrong choices?" Sophia asked.

"Of course," I said. "But fear doesn't paralyze me anymore. Now, it reminds me to pause, to listen. I trust myself to make mistakes and still be okay. That's a kind of freedom I didn't always have."

Helena tilted her head. "Was that the biggest thing you had to learn?"

I thought for a second. "No," I said. "The biggest thing I had to learn was that my voice mattered, that I was allowed to take up space, that I didn't have to earn love by shrinking myself. Once I understood that, the rest started falling into place."

Sophia looked down at her hands for a moment. "You know I'm leaving soon, right?"

I nodded. "I know, San Antonio—a whole new chapter."

"Are you okay with it?" she asked.

"I'm more than okay," I said, tears gathering but not falling. "I'm proud. You're chasing the horizon I used to dream about. But you're doing it with your eyes open and your feet firmly on the ground."

They each leaned into me, warm and quiet.

"You always say life is about connecting the dots," Helena whispered.

"It is," I said. "And right now, this moment—it's one of the most beautiful dots of all."

···22···

A DAUGHTER AT THE GATE

"DO YOU HAVE everything you need, Sophia?" I asked, double-checking the zippers on her suitcases and a few boxes filled with pieces of her bedroom life. She was leaving for college—UTSA, the University of Texas at San Antonio—the next day. I was also heading out, boarding a plane to Italy to lead a yoga and meditation retreat in Puglia, near the Ionian Sea.

As I watched her move through the house with calm assurance, I thought back to my girlhood, to the mysteries that once stirred beyond the window of my childhood bedroom in Brazil. I couldn't have imagined that my daughter would leave home ten years earlier than I had the courage to, not in a scream for independence, like I once did, but with grace and certainty. She looked confident, strong, and joyful.

"Yes, Mom, I'm ready," she said, her eyes bright. "Go do what you do best. Your students love you, and you love teaching. Come visit me when you're back. I'll pick you up from the airport, and we'll have a girls' weekend!"

She was only eighteen, but I saw something deeper in the tilt of her chin—trust, not just in the world but in herself. She knew how to ask questions, how to make decisions, and how to come back to herself when things got hard. She had started tracing her lines, and I could already see the beautiful pattern unfolding.

I held her tightly, pressing my forehead to hers. "I love you, *filha*, more than you know. Be brave, and don't let fear stop you. Be kind to yourself and to others."

"Tiki, it's time to go," Mark called gently. Helena had just come in from school, her car keys dangling from one finger—our new driver in the house. She wrapped her arms around me, joining Sophia in a tight embrace. Their faces rested on my chest, eyes closed in that sacred, wordless expression of love.

"Mom, we'll miss you," they said in unison. "But we know how much you love what you do. Have a safe trip."

We kissed, hugged again, and Mark helped me load my bags into the car for the drive to the airport.

We were quiet for most of the ride. In that silence lived a complex beauty: two parents divided between the ache of separation and the pride of watching our daughters rise into their lives. Mark's trips often revolve around golf, mine around healing and yoga. Now, our girls had places to go, too—one leaving now, the other preparing to follow in two years. It was the bittersweet harmony of a family evolving, the dance between holding on and letting go.

"Mark," I said softly as we neared the airport.

"Yes, love?"

"No matter how much changes, no matter what we overcome, one thing has never changed for me. I can't imagine this life with anyone else. Thank you for walking with me."

He reached over, eyes steady, full of knowing. "I feel the same," he said. "You'll always be the one."

As I picture us growing older together, watching our daughters carve their paths, grounded in the love and values we've poured into them, I hold onto a simple, beautiful vision. At the end of it all, I want to be beside Mark. I want to look into his eyes the same way I did that first day on the white sands of Cancun and feel what I felt then: safe, seen, loved, and deeply desired.

Our journey as a couple is as complex as anyone else's. We persevere through the challenges and celebrate the victories. We nurse the tensions and invite relaxation. We are at times unsure and at other times resolute. I believe this is the way life in pairs is supposed to be: the constant manifestation of support, forgiveness, and mercy. In the end, we are not perfect enough to expect perfection in others, and that's where the true beauty of living together lies. However, we can always aim to raise our vibration and evolve into the best versions of ourselves.

As author Roxie Nafousi says, "Feelings of trust, assuredness, and unwavering confidence are all high vibes, and they enable you to effortlessly attract abundance into your life." This is the direction in which Mark and I are traveling—abundance of understanding, abundance of respect and care, abundance in all forms in our home.

There is no end to the dots we create in life. As long as I breathe, I will continue to trace the lines of my life from one dot to another. As I step back, the connection of those dots forms images that I can only marvel at. Some are gruesome, and some are so spectacular they rival the greatest natural wonders.

Recently, I traced the dots back to my childhood home in Brazil. I was surprised to see how small it was. Compared to the enormity of everything in Texas, my home of origin seemed small. Today, the thought of life in Curitiba conjures emotions of love, sadness, and possibility. I could sense my family there, but the truth is, I feel my family everywhere. They're all cheering from above for Dr. Spicy, the fiery force who walked through hell and came out louder, bolder, and freer. I was even able to look at Mom during one of the hardest chapters of her life and, with my hands over her heart, offer back the words she once gave to me: "Each of us has our story. I'm tracing mine now, Mom, just as you taught me. And you're still tracing yours."

The lines find me now as a woman who finally found her voice, claimed her boundaries, and chose peace, not out of escape but out of deep, unwavering self-love. Though my past is written, I'm still full of hope and excitement. The past doesn't define me; it intrigues me. I am free to make today what I choose. I am free to expand the canvas and place more dots.

This is true freedom. And we can all have this. Finally, unapologetically, I am taking up all the space I need, not clinging to anyone or anything, right here, right now—*Baixinha,* the little one at five feet tall, now the fullest version of myself.

Living in course, no longer clinging.
Living, still tracing, but on my terms.
Fully, freely, finally.

www.ingramcontent.com/pod-product-compliance
Lightning Source LLC
Chambersburg PA
CBHW021146060526
44107CB00146B/1341/J